From the Bronx to the Bosphorus

FROM THE BRONX TO THE BOSPHORUS

Klezmer and Other Displaced Musics of New York

Walter Zev Feldman

EMPIRE STATE EDITIONS

AN IMPRINT OF FORDHAM UNIVERSITY PRESS

NEW YORK   2025

Fordham University Press has no responsibility for the persistence or accuracy of URLs
for external or third-party Internet websites referred to in this publication and does not
guarantee that any content on such websites is, or will remain, accurate or appropriate.

Fordham University Press also publishes its books in a variety of electronic formats. Some
content that appears in print may not be available in electronic books.

Visit us online at www.fordhampress.com/empire-state-editions.

For EU safety / GPSR concerns: Mare Nostrum Group B.V., Mauritskade 21D, 1091 GC
Amsterdam, The Netherlands, gpsr@mare-nostrum.co.uk

Library of Congress Cataloging-in-Publication Data available online at https://catalog.loc.
gov.

Printed in the United States of America

27 26 25   5 4 3 2 1

First edition

CONTENTS

Preface   vii

Invocation: Klezmer Island Revisited   xv

Part I: In the Bronx

1. Meshilim's Legacy   3

2. The Shul and Sacred Sounds   8

Part II: Musicians and Mentors in Manhattan, Brooklyn, and Queens

3. Village Rituals of New York: Iranians and Armenians in the New World   19

4. Balkan Phonograph I: Child of the Makam   41

5. Greek Town   49

6. Journey to Byzantium in Washington Heights   56

7. Limberis: Revelation of the Greek Cimbalom   61

8. Balkan Phonograph II: The Later Days of Aydın and Nikita   68

9. Zebulon: A Survivor from the Caucasus in Brooklyn   77

Part III: Colorado Interlude

10. Yerevan in the Rockies: An Armenian Winter's Tale   97

Part IV: The Journey to Klezmer

11. Antranik Aroustamian: From Kharkiv to East Harlem   131

12. Andy Statman: From Bluegrass to Greek to Klezmer   145

13. Dave Tarras Plays Again   149

Postlude   163

Acknowledgments   169

Glossary   171

Readings   175

Discography   177

Photos follow page 76

PREFACE

This book was written over a period of more than two decades. It had its genesis rather far from New York, in Montreal, the location of my mother's Belarussian extended family, or *mishpokhe*. During her long final illness there in the mid-1990s, on snowy winter nights, I began to recall what seemed most vital in my earlier life. This usually involved music, dance, and the musicians I had known in my youth. All of them were displaced from some part of the world or were the children of such displaced people. Along with music, they also brought languages. There were the Yiddish, Russian, Romanian, and French, spoken in my early familial environment, and the Hebrew of my education. Turkish made its appearance as the lingua franca of all of the formerly Ottoman communities—Sephardim, Greeks, Armenians, Albanians, and even the outlying peoples of the Caucasus.

It is well-known that those on the periphery will look to the center, or else they will huddle in on themselves. But the experiences described in the present work suggest another principle: those on the periphery can also look to other peripheries. Then as now, the Bronx was a periphery of Manhattan. As a young art student and painter, I was fortunate in being a member of the Metropolitan Museum of Art, and a student at the Art Students League, both from age eleven. These involvements made me somewhat aware of the cultural center of New York and gave me a perspective from which to view my experience of the Bronx. Perhaps this awareness of a wider world—and one that was so close to mine geographically—rendered me more interested and relaxed in the peripheries in which I spent most of my days. For Jewish culture, of course, the Bronx was another kind of "center." The neighborhood was extremely rich in synagogues of many types. Besides English, the dominant languages were Yiddish and Ladino. Of course, there was a radical split separating the Ashkenazic and the Sephardic Jewish cultures, and much diversity within each of these large groups. Although generally far from my horizon then, the neighborhood was also home to Yiddishist and Communist Jews, who viewed life from an utterly different perspective.

Even though my rather progressive yeshiva/Talmud Torah was coed, the gender divide was strong in other areas. Yiddish lyrical song was part of a women's world that I never entered. It was only decades later that I came to know and admire the brilliant poet and songwriter Beyle Schaechter-Gottesman (1920–2013)—originally from the formerly Austrian zone of historical Moldova. She had been residing with her family in another part of the West Bronx. It was largely through her and the rich cultural environment she created that I came to appreciate the depth and beauty of Yiddish song.

In writing these stories I have also begun to discern an invisible map of New York, a palimpsest lying underneath the city of today, running from Washington Heights down to Battery Park, and from the old Armenian neighborhood in the East 30s to old Greek Town in the West 30s. As I left the NYU campus recently, walking along Waverly Place, I mused about who today can remember the sounds of Turkish and Armenian music that used to waft late at night from the Armenian nightclub formerly located at the corner of Greene Street? Many more might recall the numerous Greek nightclubs that formerly lined the area of Eighth Avenue near 30th Street. But far fewer had been familiar with the diminutive local Balkan Phonograph shop, where the Greek and Turkish immigrant or visiting musicians from these clubs sometimes congregated.

Today, the American descendants of Jewish immigrants from the late nineteenth century usually blur regional origins into such huge geographical swaths as Russia, Austria, or Poland. But for most of my local contemporaries—who were the children of immigrants, and not infrequently of Holocaust survivors—geographical origin was extremely specific. It included not only a country, and a region, but even the name of a particular city, *shtetl*, or village. My father had been a proud member of the Edinetser Society, the *landsmanshaft* organization of Jewish immigrants from an important town in the north of the Moldavian territory known as Bessarabia.

Speaking of peripheries, within Europe today nowhere could be more peripheral than Bessarabia, which has reverted to its old historical name of Moldova. This was the largest chunk of the Principality of Moldova—long subject to the Ottoman Empire—that Imperial Russia had annexed in 1812. Following the Pruth Campaign of 1711 in which Tsar Peter the Great failed in his attempt to conquer Moldova, the Turks installed Greek governors from Istanbul. In order to build up the local economy these Ottoman Greeks facilitated the immigration of merchants and skilled craftsmen from among the Greeks and from both the Sephardic and Ashkenazic Jews. Among the latter were my father's ancestors. By the end of the nineteenth century almost all of the local Sephardic Jews had come to speak Yiddish and identified themselves as Ashkenazim.

These unique social conditions in Moldova for three centuries had given rise to a musical symbiosis, linking Ashkenazic Jews, local Roma/Gypsies, Moldavians, Turks, Tatars, and Greeks. This was a large part of the klezmer music that was brought to America 140 years ago. It formed the vanguard of the klezmer revitalization that I helped to create a century later. Memories of this powerful musical fusion still survived in New York, even in the 1960s, among older Greek and Armenian musicians. The Istanbul-born Greek musician and entrepreneur Theodotos Demetriades (1897–1971)—then living in New Jersey—had issued many recordings of the outstanding klezmer clarinetist Dave Tarras (1897–1989), who was then living in Brooklyn.

Apart from the Greek nightclubs on Eighth Avenue—which I will describe in a some of the following chapters—I got to know the celebrations of the Greek society at the City College of New York, where I frequented the dances. Through this City College, Greek connection I was invited to play percussion in the Greek American Leventiko Pende band, led by George Stathos. During the summer of 1967, we played at the Acropolis Hotel in the Catskills. Evidently the fact that the *darabukka* player was a young Ashkenazi Jew quickly spread. As we entered the hotel dining room, many of the middle-aged Greek men and women stood up, looked at me and exclaimed: "Dave Tarras! We love Dave Tarras!"

What all of these different Jewish, Christian, and Muslim groups shared—apart from any specific historical connections—was a culture that emphasized prayer, lament, and worldly celebration. Very often all of these were combined, especially in the repertoires of weddings and dance. I believe now that it was largely this cultural complex that distinguished all of us from a Western cultural environment, in which these diverse ways of viewing the world are often kept more separate. I am sure this was a large part of what propelled me with relative ease from East European Ashkenazic, to Sephardic, Greek, and Armenian musical and cultural environments. After years of travel and study in Turkey, Greece, Romania, and Moldova, it even seems to me now that the cultural explorations and syntheses that occur in these pages could have been accomplished more readily in New York than in Istanbul, Thessaloniki, Bucharest, or Chişinau in those post–World War II years. Especially after the population exchanges, Stalinism, and the Holocaust, within these relatively new nation-states or Soviet republics, ethnic "minorities" felt the pressures to conform. They would be reticent about expressing cultural choices and affinities different from those of the national or regional majority. In New York, peripheral as we all were, that kind of political pressure did not exist. And even the religious and ethnic prejudices that might still persist from the Old Country played almost no role in the lives of musicians. I hope that the reader will relish the unexpected advantages of this situation, while exploring these episodes from a hidden and now largely vanished New York.

Among all of these groups, perhaps the least visible were the Ottoman Sephardic Jews from Turkey, Greece, and Macedonia. Even in 1924, the Yiddish, Romanian, and Greek-speaking journalist Konrad Bercovici, in his delightful book *Around the World in New York*, devotes only half a sentence to the "Spanish Jews," then living on the Lower East Side of Manhattan. Once they had moved to the Bronx, they remained almost totally invisible to Jew or Gentile. During the early 1970s, the entire Jewish population of that part of the West Bronx moved away. Within their new location in Forest Hills, Queens, the Sephardim are "on the map" mainly to the newer Bukharan Jews, who have sometimes joined their Turkish congregation. Even lesser-known were the tiny minority of Muslim Tatars, Karachays, and Azerbaijanis in the West Bronx, originating in Russia and the Caucasus. They had lived securely and comfortably among the Russian-speaking Ashkenazic Jewish immigrants and their children. They formed a small but remarkable Muslim-Jewish symbiosis in North America.

Shortly after my bar mitzvah I began to study percussion with Ruth Ben-Tsvi, a creative and witty Israeli darabukka player. I could never have imagined how many sounds could emerge from this ceramic drum! I got to know Shoshana Toubi, a professional female entertainer who was then living with her husband in Brooklyn, but who had been born in Sana'a, Yemen. She had been a soloist with the renowned Yemenite-Israeli folk ensemble, Inbal. Beating a large frame drum, seated in her bedroom, I accompanied Shoshana's love songs in Judeo-Arabic, while she struck the rhythm on a brass tray.

The Structure of This Book

As these New York stories multiplied I came to understand how they differed from anything I had written about my later musical experiences once I began to travel outside of North America. Their style is memoiristic—in a literary form. In most cases they portray events and personalities whom I encountered long before I had any academic training. Hence, I do not impose a strictly musicological methodology in analyzing either the musical performances or the social situations in which I found them. While by my later teen years I was doing some casual ethnomusicological research in such languages as Russian, Yiddish, and Hebrew, I kept neither diaries nor "field notes" about my nonacademic encounters with musicians—but I am quite certain about the vast majority of the names and locations mentioned. In a minority of cases I have had to reconstruct certain names mentioned in the stories, even though they are all based on actual events, people, and places.

In my later expeditions abroad to unfamiliar locales, I usually had a fair amount of specific information to guide me, and my field techniques permitted the asking of direct questions. But as a very young person confronting my elders, I could rarely ask in this way. My immigrant teachers (beginning with my own father) were always unsure about how much of their Old World environments and experiences an American-born boy would be able to assimilate. And in our culture, there was no opposition between the world of prayer and the world of dance. Most Jews davened in shul and danced at weddings. The earlier chapters of this book try to bring to life this reality as it had transferred itself to New York.

Nevertheless, a striking fact of American Jewish life in the post–World War II period was the failure of the immigrant generation to transmit their expressive culture to the next generation. These two expressive arts: the *davenen* prayer chant practiced by the entire congregation but led by the *baaltfile* precentor; and the communal dance, led and epitomized by the *tentser*, the expert Yiddish dancer, had no clear group of living successors, nor were they documented in sound or film. Something is still known about the famous cantor Mario Botoshansky, a Moldavian who had been the cantor of the Great Synagogue of Rome. In the Bronx he sang at the Conservative Adath Israel on the Grand Concourse; he was also the father of friend of mine from my yeshiva, and so I have personal memories of cantor Botoshansky. The neighborhood was home to many small Orthodox synagogues with their baaltfiles, not one of whom was documented, nor did they transmit their art. This lack has reached the point where even the

Yiddish term davenen is today often misunderstood by English-speakers as a bodily motion during prayer, rather than a highly sophisticated form of musical improvisation.

Corresponding to the baaltfile was the tentser, the artistic dancer among the Jews. My generation was not encouraged to learn this largely improvised art. Even the basic steps and figures of the common Yiddish folk dances, *freylekhs*, *sher*, and *bulgar* were only learned by a small minority of the postwar generation. While in the interwar period, the Polish-born Nathan Vizonsky (1898–1967) established a Yiddish dance troupe in Chicago, this ended in 1947 when he moved to LA. In New York, no Yiddish dancer created a comparable enterprise. Even the fine Polish Yiddish dancer Felix Febich (1917–2014)—the student and later the husband of Judith Berg (1912–1992)—who had choreographed the film version of *Der Dybbuk* in 1936—became an artistic stage dancer while utilizing some materials coming from the art of the tentser.

The situation of Sephardic sacred and secular music was no better. The illustrious pianist Murray Perahia came from our Bronx Sephardi congregation, but no American-born member of the community became known either as a Turkish-style cantor or a Ladino singer.

Of course, as an early teenager I had no way to explain this situation. Even today its full scope is not well-understood. There were forces within the Jewish community that sought to assimilate rapidly and hence to de-emphasize the ethnic distinctiveness of the Jews. Following the Holocaust there was also a widespread movement to replace any secular Jewish expressive culture (whether Ashkenazic or Sephardic) with Israeli song and dance. My own yeshiva—which I adored—was partly run and staffed by Israelis. Soon after graduation I made the acquaintance of both Israelis and American Jews of my age involved with the Leftist Zionist Ha-Shomer HaTza'ir. At the occasional meetings that I attended near our home in the Bronx I had ample opportunity to observe and participate in Israeli dances and songs. But even then, I contrasted these unfavorably with the Yiddish dances and klezmer music of my childhood. Compared to our bulgar, their "hora" was acrobatic and stiff, lacking all expressive nuance or musicality. My father would never have approved! Of course, these cultural critiques should not be misconstrued as a general criticism of Zionism or of Israel—a country which I had not yet visited.

No doubt a potent factor in this lack of cultural transmission was the more or less "official" definition of the Jews as a religious group in much public English-language discourse. As James Loeffler had noted in his book *The Most Musical Nation*: "Jews were repositioning themselves as a religious community, rather than an ethnic or national minority" (2010:

198). This treatment still dominates most English-language journalism in America. However, coming from a Yiddish-speaking home, and attending a Hebrew-language yeshiva, I was unfamiliar with the English word "Judaism" until close to my bar mitzvah. As we understood it, we were "Am Yisrael," "The Nation of Israel" who observed the precepts of the Torah. Of course, secular Yiddishists would have expressed themselves differently. Their usage of "Yidishkayt" was much closer to the original meaning of "Iudaismos"—the origin of the English term "Judaism"—(i.e., in Josephus's works). This was "the Jewish way of life," as opposed to the Greek way, which was "Hellenismos." But in my generation, there was no rationale for a "religion" to possess a unique form of ethnic dance or its accompanying music. So why would these be worth transmitting to future generations?

This glaring cultural lack led me to seek out other related immigrant communities whose means of cultural transmission were stronger. Two factors in my favor were the Bessarabian cultural background coming from my father and his landsmanshaft community, and my membership in the Turkish-Sephardi congregation (as the only Ashkenazic member). The latter gave me an early exposure to both the Ladino and the Turkish languages and music. Through a series of apparent coincidences, by age fourteen these facilitated my exposure to and participation in the living dance and musical traditions among both the Armenian and several Greek immigrant communities in New York. I benefited from the solicitous mentorship of a small number of older members of the wider Ottoman immigrant and American-born generations of musicians and music lovers. This even extended to the music of the Greek Orthodox Church.

Due to the fact that the stories presented here have been written over a space of more than twenty-five years as a series of musical memories and personal vignettes, the time span represented in one story may differ from others. It is inevitable that some of the stories may contain references to events and personalities that also appear in earlier or later chapters. During the editing process I have tried to minimize such repetitions.

The first two chapters of this book speak about my father, our synagogue environment, and his love for traditional music and dance, and is followed by my invitation to our local Turkish Sephardic synagogue—all of this taking place in the Bronx. My discovery of the related non-Jewish communities begins with "Village Rituals of New York," where I am brought to the unique nightclub of the Anatolian Armenians in Greenwich Village. Remarkably, a few minutes of footage of the dancing at this club became part of the 1964 film *Only One New York*, by the famous Dutch director Jan Yoors. I only saw this footage in 2018, at the Manhattan home of

Harout Derderian who had created this Armenian club. Regrettably, Mr. Derderian passed away just this month.

This chapter also introduces the Chicago-born, Greco-Albanian Pyrrhus J. Ruches (d. 2008). I met Pyrrhus in 1964, and he became a musical and ethnographic mentor in those early years. As a journalist and an amateur musician, Pyrrhus imparted an understanding of the complexities of ethnic formation and identification with a sophistication not surpassed even by my later graduate school studies at Columbia University. I dedicate this book to his memory!

These earlier chapters portray me as a spectator and a student, while being recommended to various older immigrant musicians. The turning point occurs in 1975, when I was invited to perform and lead at an Armenian nightclub in Colorado. I tell this story in "Yerevan in the Rockies"; the only chapter taking place outside of New York.

The succeeding chapters portray me as both a musical student and a professional accompanist. The formative episode was my accompanying the Armenian *kemanchist* Antranik Aroustamian (1918–1996), who had recently emigrated from the Soviet Union. In addition to being the greatest musician I had met up to that point, Antranik had a unique exposure to the Armenian folk and Azerbaijanian art music of the Caucasus, to the klezmer music of his native Ukraine, and to the music of the Crimean Tatars. While he rarely uttered more than a few words, his very existence as a musician personified the reality of these musics and their interconnections.

All this soon led to my joyful partnership with the virtuoso Andy Statman, in a variety of Armenian, Caucasian, and Greek musical environments, and eventually to the greatest living klezmer master, Dave Tarras. Tarras's generous teaching to both of us as musicians, and to me as a dancer, were crucial to the Klezmer Revitalization. It is perhaps a gratuitous detail that Tarras had learned some of his own musical lessons in my father's native shtetl, Edinets. As the Moldavian/Israeli composer Emil Croitor once told me in Tel-Aviv: "Edinets is your passport!" The fuller meaning of this enigmatic expression only became clearer after I began to visit Edinets, beginning in 2008 and continuing through 2015.

The episodes from my earlier life related here seem to portray the mysterious legacy of these forgotten ancestors in mid-twentieth-century New York.

Walter Zev Feldman

New York City

August 17, 2018/March 2024

INVOCATION: KLEZMER ISLAND REVISITED

Klezmer music stands across from us and apart from us. It is a little island just off the shore. On a clear day we can make out trees and pathways, half-ruined houses from the days when it had been inhabited. Sometimes ghostly music wafts our way from the island, almost too faint to hear, but at other times strident and piercing. Some free summer afternoons I think I would like to go out to the island, but there is no bridge and no ferry service. The water is unaccountably deep and turbulent—I do not dare to try to swim. I stare out at the blue, almost cloudless sky, wondering why I cannot traverse that short distance. In fact, as the weeks and months pass the island seems to move further out to sea. I can recall the days, over a decade ago, when people still managed to come to our shore from there, but nowadays the traffic has ceased. The closest we come is to listen to the tales of those who met natives of the island many years ago. We can only wonder what had gone on there. Some tales speak of hedonistic celebrations, others of ecstatic, near-mystical trances, or of sober artistic meditations. Still others tell of unspeakable vulgarity, or of bland routine days closing with a few perfunctory ditties at night.

At times klezmer music seemed to be right in the room with me. Throughout my childhood my Bessarabian father made references to it—something bright, stirring, and passionate in his hard, demanding, and disorienting life in America. After my father's death in 1970, I spent several years visiting the famous klezmer, Dave Tarras. I sat in his living room, in his kitchen, or on his balcony overlooking Coney Island. He was indeed a native of the island, and also a presence here and now, but a lapidary presence. A monumental Toltec head carved in granite, eyes expressing rich memories, full lips seemingly capable of speech, but in fact able to form new sentences only with difficulty. After a life spent in constant motion, exercising every part of his brain and his body, from his fingers to his lips, in order to convey the musical ideas forming inside him, Tarras had gradually turned into stone. He had fought ceaseless battles to express himself and at the same time to give the world what it demanded of him. He had sprinted at top speed through the torturous labyrinth of his life, had outrun and outlived all possible rivals, and at the end had been declared the winner. He never tired of pointing to the golden trophies that life had bestowed on him. But when I, his student, asked him to re-trace his steps and show me his entry point into that labyrinth, he became tired and reticent. For him, the Old World was a distant gate through which he had entered the labyrinth over sixty years ago. It was almost erased by the more numerous and exciting memories of New York in the 1920s, 1930s, and 1940s, when he was the preeminent klezmer. But Tar-ras possessed another language, far more expressive than his infrequent words. This was the language of Jewish dance, in which he was perhaps as fluent as he was in music. Tarras could reveal the meaning of every phrase of a klezmer melody through his hands, his shoulders, his head, and his feet.

All the other great local klezmorim—the clarinetist Naftule Brandwein, Tarras's early rival, the clarinetist Shloimke Beckerman, the fiddler Berish Katz, the cimbalom virtuoso Josef Moskowitz—had died or retired when I was still in high school. As I was not the son of a klezmer family there was little way I could have known them.

An encounter that took place when I was fifteen is etched into my memory. A short, stocky, and tough-looking old man entered a music store owned by a friend of mine on the Lower East Side. He picked up a Chi-nese oboe *suona* standing upside down on the glass counter, and to my amazement, proceeded to play with great facility and beauty a Romanian free-rhythm melody called *doina*. When he finished, I stood up and walked over to him. Facing me was a dark, round face that looked somehow both Jewish and Ukrainian. I asked him, "What kind of music do you play?" He replied in a thick, southern Yiddish accent, "We play Oriental music," then he turned and strode out of the store. This scene replayed itself many times in my memory. I can still hear the shrill sound of the suona, running up and down the scale, producing the exotic yet somehow familiar melody. In my mind I walk up to the old klezmer, but this time I say: "What a beautiful doina!" And now the old man replies, "You understand who I am." Together we go to Second Avenue, which he remembers from another era, and we catch the last ferry ever out to the island.

From the Bronx to the Bosphorus

PART I

IN THE BRONX

Chapter 1

⫸

Meshilim's Legacy

My Dream:
I see a crowd of men wearing Romanian broad-brimmed hats standing together on a dusty summer plain in Bessarabia. Among them is my father Meshilim or "Max." He is middle-aged, sporting round wire-rimmed glasses—as he did in his later years in America—watching a performance by a group of Jewish and Gypsy fiddlers. They are playing a bulgareasca, the wild Bessarabian dance, called the bulgarish or bulgar by the Jews. This fast chain dance, with its stamping, shouting, and nimbly aggressive slapping, expresses an unconditional freedom that pulled the line of dancers from Bessarabia to America.

AS A CHILD, I recall my father sitting at his ornately carved antique wooden desk in the foyer of our apartment in the Bronx. He was speaking over the phone in English, apparently to some kind of government bureaucrat. I overheard him say, "No, I am not an Arabian. I am Max Feldman, a Bessarabian." My childish mind thought it might not be so bad to be an Arabian—it was roughly half a century before 9/11—but this was the first I had heard of the possibility. Later that day, while my father was seated for dinner in the kitchen, breaking and sucking his beef bones, I asked, "What is Bessarabia?" "First it was Turkey," was his answer. "Then Russia, then Romania, then Russia again." The town he had come from was called Edinets (Edinet), also spelled Yedinetz. Well, we were evidently not Arabians, and the American government did not recognize Bessarabia. But our country had once been part of Turkey. Later K. S. Byatt would create a

3

"Queen of Bessarabia" in one of her delightful fables—evidently, she liked the name.

My father was born in 1899 as Meshilim ben Zev. In America he became Max Feldman. He was from a family of furriers. He immigrated to America at the age of twenty-two and ended up as a small merchant. I was born in 1949 and named Velvel Rakhmiel, answering usually to Velvele. In yeshiva I became Zev, and gradually I also came to conform to the name on my birth certificate, Walter Robert Feldman.

Among the things I inherited from my father is his passport with which he entered the United States. It was issued in August 1920 on behalf of the Kingdom of Romania. It states that Meshilim Feldman was born in 1899 in the town Edinti (now written Edinet) in the Hotin region of Bessarabia. It describes him as a merchant (comerciant/comerçant) and states that his destination is America. This is confirmed by a visa granted in October 1920 by the US consul in Bucharest. There are further visas from the Kingdom of Yugoslavia, Italy, and France. There is also a letter from the rabbi of Edinets testifying to Meshilim's good character. The visa contains a photograph where Meshilim Feldman, with short, curly dark hair, and a round face, stares out at the world. In the years in which I knew him I cannot recall ever seeing such a determined look on his face. According to the dates on the visas, Meshilim must have entered the United States in late 1920, or perhaps the winter of 1921. Might he have wandered around Europe even longer? I have a postcard of the Eiffel Tower—evidently never sent—testifying to a short stay in Paris.

My father's *kheyder* education ended at the elementary level, while I went through seven years of Talmud Torah, which we Americans magnify with the name yeshiva, and continued through art school and further. His scanty Jewish education did not enable him to share in my biblical or Talmudic studies. Nevertheless, whenever a question occurred to me about life in the Old Country, his answers were clear and full of interesting details. Edinets was a *shtetl*, but hardly a "ghetto," as the Jews made up the large majority of the town. Unlike those Jewish immigrants who had gruesome tales of pogroms, or at least poverty and humiliations in Europe, my father looked back to life in Bessarabia quite fondly. As the son of local bourgeois furriers, his shtetl life had been rather idyllic, and America had not lived up to its great promise. Many of my father's memories concerned his family and their profession. He described for me the details of what every "nationality" wore in Edinets, such as the fur coats with the fur on the outside worn by the "Volokh" Moldavians.

When I was about ten years old, he even intervened when he judged

that my yeshiva or perhaps others had been portraying an overly sche-
matic view of history. He sat me down in the living room and explained.
It was true that during the Holocaust his family had been murdered by
the fascist Romanian army, but that did not mean that pogroms or any
kind of violence had been frequent in his time. He insisted that, on the
whole, our non-Jewish neighbors had been good people. My grandfather
Reb Zev was evidently well-liked by them, and they put him up for weeks
while he traveled throughout the Moldavian villages doing custom work.
Communication was facilitated by his fluent Romanian, yet he was strictly
kosher, so his trips must have required a certain ingenuity on the part of
both of both him and his hosts.

What had distinguished my father's homeland was a peculiar form of
"multiculturalism." As he explained it, in his region lived many nationalities—the Volokhs (or Moldavians), the Khokhols (or Ukrainians), the
Katsaps (or Great Russians), and the Jews. There were also some Turks
and some Gypsies. At one point he mentioned buying bread from the
Turkish bakery, which was the best in town. Only decades later, when I
discovered the remarkable 1943 Yiddish memoir *Mayn Shtetl Edinets*,
published in Argentina by the writer Golde Gutman-Krimer, I understood
what an interesting institution this bakery had been. Her father had been
one of the Jewish bakers for Mehmet the owner, who "could speak Yiddish
like a Jew." Around the same time, in New York, I met with a couple of
non-Jewish Edinetsers, visiting their son in America. They also were told
by their parents about this famous prewar Turkish bakery, which none of
us had ever seen.

Shortly later in Berlin, I could connect these remarks with this statement volunteered to me by the owner of a carpet shop selling Bessarabian
flat-woven *kilims*:

> My mother's family were Bessarabian Germans. We had been settled
> there for two hundred years. Many nations lived there—Moldavians,
> Ukrainians, Russians, Jews, Greeks, Armenians, even Gagauz—
> Turkish Christians. I was told that they all had lived in peace, with no
> serious friction.

According to my father, Jews and Gentiles appeared on the streets together, did business together, even drank and danced together. But he
explained when the Romanian army had first come into the town in 1917,
they had murdered a number of Jews in cold blood. Before the First
World War, when the Russians were still in charge, there had been rumors
that pogromchiks were heading for the town. Evidently there were no

preparations for a pogrom within the town itself, so that outside agitators were needed. Some young Jews had gotten their rifles and patrolled the outskirts of town. The pogrom never materialized. But Kishinev (nowadays Chişinau) had been another matter. My governess Fenye was never to get over the trauma of the 1903 pogrom there, in which they murdered her beloved teacher. Of course, Kishinev was a Tsarist governmental center, and the massacre had been well-organized.

In 1934—in the depths of the worldwide depression—Meshilim's economic situation allowed him to visit his homeland. This journey back to Edinets is documented by several photographs—of his parents, his sister and brother, and one group photo with four of his friends. All are standing on the balcony of a substantial bourgeois home with wooden pillars and large glass windows. This was the only photo that was not posed in a studio. Judging by the houses I saw in the old Jewish district of Edinets when I visited it in 2008 and then several times while doing musicological fieldwork between 2011 and 2015, it had been one of the more substantial among the middle-class dwellings. While now only a few Jews still made their homes in Edinets, physically the town had not changed much. As I came to know our shtetl, it was still as beautiful as my father had remembered it. I became the heir to so many of my father's memories. Perhaps they determined much of my life?

Music also figured in these memories. My father recalled the beautiful slow melodies played by the shepherds on their flutes when his father took him up into the hills to purchase cheese. Edinets was home to a band of klezmorim, who were led by both a Gypsy and a Jew. The Gypsy played the violin while the Jew played clarinet. My father had loved their music and wished that he could have studied with the fiddler. Only much later, when I was able to travel to Edinets, did I discover what a famous musician the Gypsy *lautar* violinist Ioan Stingaciu had been. In 2013, near Montreal, I was even able to interview Boris Stambulsky/Sela, who had studied violin with him after the War. These lessons had been conducted in Yiddish. Like all the lautar professional musicians in our area, Stingaciu was a fluent Yiddish speaker.

I recall one winter sunset, my father reclining on my bed as we listened to mournful clarinet laments from Epirus in Northern Greece. His tall, portly form relaxed, and a misty expression in his eyes. I knew that the sorrow that this music reached within him must have been much deeper than anything within my heart at that young age, and yet he trusted me with this sorrow. Over the past couple of years he had been slow to believe that I, an American-born newcomer, would willingly accept the burden imposed by this music. Over these same years I had grown increasingly impatient with the popular music churned out for mainstream American Jews. I remember looking at my father, silently asking the question, why do you let them feed us these stones? We are your children; we need food, music that will nourish us. Despite all the hardness of your life, the loneliness of emigration, you know what music is. Stop hiding it deep in your heart. Trust me with it!

Chapter 2

The Shul and Sacred Sounds

THE GRAND CONCOURSE is one of those sweeping gestures of horizontality that remind the inhabitants that they do not merely dwell in a neighborhood but are citizens of a large and complex metropolis. We lived on Townsend Avenue, in the valley formed by the hilly West Bronx and the plateau of the Grand Concourse. Leaving the coziness of our little street, I would venture up to the slightly commercialized Mt. Eden Avenue, and traveling two blocks eastward, I would be dazzled by the broad expanse of sky, bright sunlight—it always seemed to be sunny on the Grand Concourse—and trees waving their branches in the breeze. Traffic was heavy enough to seem respectable for such a boulevard but never menacing. While I might have other reasons to make this small journey, on holidays I invariably made it in the company of my father, as we crossed the Grand Concourse in the direction of our little synagogue, or *shul*, as we called it. Several blocks farther down the slope there stood an imposing Conservative synagogue built of stone. The rabbi was rather famous for his English-language sermons, and I suspect that my mother would rather have attended services there. But my father preferred the two-story brick residence that had been turned into an Orthodox *shtibl*.

The Holy Street

The Bronx, too, once had its holy places. I was fortunate to grow up near one of them—169th Street, the Street of Synagogues (the Holy Street).

One block south of the worldly attractions of bustling, commercial 170th Street, one descended the westward slope and entered a quiet, timeless zone. It is not known according to whose plan it was decreed that this street would shelter no fewer than three synagogues, each one representing a distinct Judaism. In my childhood there was no overt hostility between these denominations, and I felt I could explore them all. One of them offered me a glimpse of a distant and exotic world whose passionate and ethereal music determined much of the course of my life.

On the corner of the Grand Concourse, the world claimed its due in the form of a monumental, Pantheon-like Conservative synagogue, whose pseudo-Protestant service brought it rather closer to the Reform. To me, raised in an Orthodox shtibl, this was a depraved institution which I thought never to enter. But once I became friendly with the son of the Conservative cantor—who was my classmate in yeshiva—I had to break this unspoken vow. I was thoroughly charmed by his Francophone father, born in the old Moldavian capital, Iași. But this charm did not extend to the music of his service—complete with an organ—which I regarded as the precursor of the Muzak piped into elevators and restrooms.

In all the years I had attended my father's synagogue, I came to understand that one great virtue of this institution was its separateness from the world. We stood face-to-face with the stern and grand ancient words, written with the certainty of a high priest who had seen the holy of holies. And the music linked all of us in its timeless flow, floating in the air, occasionally brought back to earth by a rhythmic tune, melodies changing their tempos and dynamics, sometimes slow and luxurious, sometimes rushed and almost whispered.

But the next synagogue down the Holy Street was another extreme— it exuded a militant otherworldliness, almost assaulting the passersby. I was unable to penetrate this emanating force, and I rarely ventured inside. Whenever I did so during a service, my ears were met by a low, dark droning—a grim, threatening hum. It was like my father's shtibl, and yet it was not. Somehow our rather cheerful heterophony here became a dull growl, threatening all those who may not have kept up the standards of purity preferred by this congregation. Whenever I entered, some elderly bearded figure would thrust a prayer book into my hands. I listened carefully to the grumbled words because anyone who did not know the sequence of prayers more or less by heart, did not belong in this shul. However, when I looked up, I found myself cheered, even amused by the vision before my eyes. On the eastern wall a folkloric hand had painted the ideal Jerusalem with the ancient temple, the Beis Ha-Mikdash in the center. The painter must have come from somewhere in Eastern Europe where he had certainly seen some of the venerable paintings on the ancient wooden synagogues, all of them gone up in smoke a few years before I was born. In Eastern Europe there had been guilds of synagogue painters; perhaps this artist in the Bronx had stemmed from one of these?

My father's shtibl was located not on this Holy Street of synagogues, but on little Mt. Eden Avenue. There, the land sloped downward and turned into a small park lined with benches on either side. One walked up several steps to enter this structure of which I cannot speak of any architectural features—it was a simple square house. The tall windows, sporting neither stained glass nor curtains, admitted abundant sunlight. The interior walls of the ground floor had been removed to create a single space, divided only by a *mekhitsa*—a screen and a curtain. The first rows as one entered— behind the mekhitsa—were reserved for the women. In the middle of the floor stood a table covered with a gold-fringed velvet cloth and a lectern. The *baaltfile* or precentor sang from there with his back to part of the congregation while he faced the ark with its Torah scrolls. In front of the ark stood a raised, carpet-covered platform, with a carved wooden balustrade, to whose corners electric lamps in the shape of leafy flowers were attached with nails. The rabbi occasionally spoke from this bounded platform. He and his family lived in an apartment on the second floor.

Our rabbi was a colorless product of the more Old World wing of American Orthodoxy. Perhaps in his thirties, he seemed to have been brought here after the War as a child survivor. Judging by his Yiddish he must have been a Litvak, a Lithuanian Jew. His emaciated figure, and weak, bespectacled eyes bespoke earnestness and kindness, but his limited verbal expressiveness either in Yiddish or English imparted a desperate twang to his voice. He was in no way charismatic or imposing. Perhaps for that very reason my father took to him well.

This unassuming space with its equally unimpressive spiritual leader acquired an importance for me utterly disproportionate to its visible qualities. This little house was the primary locus for two significant phenomena in my childhood—music and God. All He needed was a little bit of space and silence and then He would appear. The space within our shtibl was small, and only occasionally silent, but it was entirely dedicated to Him.

Davenen

The counterpoint to silence was the form of music we heard and created in the shtibl. Except for a few early exposures to klezmer dance music at my father's *landsmanshaft*, and the rare Yiddish and Russian folk singing of my grandfather's second wife in Montreal, this little shul was my principal source of music.

It is difficult for me now to distinguish the many services I had heard there since my early childhood. There was a gradual development in my understanding of the music. As a small child I recall tunes with a fixed, dance-like rhythm, usually sung by the entire male congregation. Perhaps the most striking of these was the tune for the hymn "Anu amekho," "We are Your people," sung during Yom Kippur. This slow, dance-like tune in minor, with its repetitive rhythm guiding the entire melody, united all the men, seated as they were in their prayer shawls. But I had to wait a very long time, sometimes almost an hour, to hear such melodies. After some years I became aware of another kind of music. These were slow, drawn out tunes sung by the baaltfile, especially on Sabbaths and certain holidays. Year over year I came to appreciate their grandeur, unhurried yet without self-indulgence. The last kind of music to enter my consciousness were the melodies that each member of the congregation created for his own prayer; what they described with the untranslatable Yiddish word *davenen*. My father was not particularly skilled at this—he simply mumbled his prayers in a low voice. But here and there I could make out musical phrases, snatches of melisma, occasionally a delicate filigree, from this or that old man, often seated somewhere toward the back. Little could I have known that some twenty years later, in Budapest, my future wife Judit Frigyesi Niran would be documenting and recording exactly the same kind of davenen. In all of Communist Eastern Europe she was the only person to have done so.

As I grew closer to my bar mitzvah, I came to enjoy following the different sections of the congregation. I also came to understand that these melodies of davenen, unlike the precentor's festive hymns, or the group songs, had neither beginning nor end. They could be rushed through hurriedly or lingered upon at leisure. They seemed to correspond to our thinking, where thought joins thought in a seamless progression, whose ultimate goal is never clear beforehand. Sometimes one thinks rather dryly, at other times under the impress of deep emotion. And so it was with our congregation—forty men thinking and feeling aloud for hours on end. And it was only decades later that I came to understand the connection of these "gestures of the soul" with the improvised movements performed by the best sort of Yiddish dancer, the *tentser*.

For me, the two grand holidays—polar opposites—were Yom Kippur, the Day of Atonement and Simkhes Toyre, the Rejoicing in the Law.

While the preceding Rosh Hashanah, the New Year, was something of a fashion show for the women of the community, where jewels, new hats, and other items might be exhibited, Yom Kippur was deadly serious. I can only describe it as a communal catharsis. Each year the precentor/baaltfile brought out the same ponderous melodies and was met by the same sighs and even tears from the congregation. I recall the famous prayer where God is compared to a shepherd numbering his sheep which our baaltfile sang in slow, broken phrases, choked with emotion. His sense of balance was always expressed by his slow deliberate tempos. He never exhibited his emotions, so the slight suggestions of real sadness and fear in his voice never failed to move me. I could see normally rather cheerful men shed tears, and my reticent and melancholy father never failed to weep while enumerating his sins. I was not aware of sins nor was I particularly afraid, but I responded to the sadness and tension surrounding me.

Simkhes Toyre was a carnival, a total contrast with Yom Kippur. With its procession of children bearing aloft little flags topped with apples, this was our special holiday. While the presence of Torah scrolls added a certain dignity to the proceedings, by the evening inhibitions were loosened. The wooden seats were cleared from the carpeted floor, and the whole synagogue became a dancing space. Amounts of whisky, brandy, and vodka were consumed. The men sang sprightly, joyous melodies, utterly unlike the mood of most of the rest of the year. I can recall two older men, one of them wearing an old-fashioned Russian fur hat with a bejeweled Tsarist eagle brooch, holding one another's shoulders, leaping and squatting together.

Hasidim

I was soon to experience a very different kind of service, and rather far from the Bronx. Shortly after my bar mitzvah, my father took me to a Friday night service among Hasidim in the Catskills, where we rented a bungalow every summer. The wife of the local Hasidic rabbi was from northern Bessarabia, and somehow she had invited my father to attend their Shabbos prayers. This was an unusual event for me because my father was a *misnagid*, an opponent of Hasidism, as were most long-established Bessarabians. Later I understood that it was mainly descendants of the relatively recent Jewish immigrants from Galicia and Ukraine who maintained their ties with their Hasidic *rebbes*. When our ancestors entered Ottoman Bessarabia in the eighteenth century, Hasidism was only beginning its development. This was also a fundamental difference between the Jews in our Hotin province and the neighboring Austrian Bukovina, where the rebbes of Sadegora and Vizhnitz were so widely revered. This Hasidic community in the Catskills seemed to have originated in Bukovina. While my father said nothing at the time, later I understood that most of them had been liberated from Romanian concentration camps less than fifteen years earlier.

Now the two of us went alone, walking along darkened country roads from our little bungalow colony to theirs. It must have been the end of the summer, for the air was rather cool. We entered a mid-sized bungalow whose door remained open. Outside, the women and girls stood to listen to the service. A wooden table and a few chairs stood in the middle of the room. An elderly rabbi stood behind the table, while a couple of dozen Hasidim stood near the chairs. My father and I were shown to chairs on the rabbi's right-hand. I was struck by the rabbi's age and frailty and by the beauty of his garments. He was clothed in blue and white silk, in the Polish Jewish style of the eighteenth century; on his head sat a large, flat, fur *shtreimel*. The Hasidim were likewise dressed in blue or white. Most of them wore shtreimels or fur *spodiks* on their heads. There did not seem to be any *baaltfile*, but the rabbi read the prayers in a quiet voice while the Hasidim responded thunderously. Toward the end, all of them stood up and sang a number of rhythmic hymns, *zmires*. Neither I nor my father was familiar with any of these hymns, and their beauty and the ecstatic musicality was like nothing I had ever heard. Across from me a young, tall, and handsome Hasid dressed in blue silk flashed our way an occasional proud but not unfriendly smile as he loudly sang the hymns. To use the phrase with which V. S. Naipaul characterized the Sikhs, these were "whole men," and their music was wholesome.

From Ashkenaz to Sepharad

Returning to the Holy Street, the most exotic was the last synagogue on 169th Street in the Bronx, closer to Jerome Avenue; its square brick facade was graced by a peculiar stone arch that, after several trips to the Met Cloisters in Fort Tryon Park, I recognized as Romanesque. I had not given much thought to the identity of this structure until my last year at yeshiva, when I came to know a new boy at the school. Although slight of build, he was very handsome, with curly dark hair and open blue eyes. Robert glided through his classes with the smooth confidence and cheerful humility I felt were the products of a serene and loving home. His last name, Murciano, was Spanish, and Robert was apparently the only Sephardic student in our Ashkenazic yeshiva. I learned that Robert's father was a rabbi from

Tangiers in Morocco, who headed a congregation in my neighborhood. One day Robert suggested that I come to his father's Sabbath service. This proposal interested me.

Our yeshiva did have one Sephardic teacher. Rabbi Avraham Portal—apparently from Casablanca in Morocco—was thin, and delicate-boned, almost ornithic. The skin on his long head was an odd, pasty white, almost a grey hue that I had never seen on anyone else. The following Saturday I learned the identity of the third synagogue on 169th Street, with its Romanesque arch. As I entered the building, Robert pointed out the English inscription in the stone—"Sephardic Jewish Center of the Bronx." Near it was a smaller inscription—"Jewish Brotherhood of Monastir," named for a town in Macedonia. A black sign announcing the times for services, displayed the name of Rabbi M. Asher Murciano and other synagogue functionaries. The interior of the building was distinguished both by its lack of ostentation and by the quantity of light streaming in through the tall stained glass windows. The women were seated separately on the left, but without a curtain or screen, that we called a mekhitsa. Robert seated me close to the front from where I could make out the dark, rounded features of his father behind his thick horn-rimmed glasses. A much older man with lighter skin and white hair stood beside him. On the right, off the podium, a boys' choir was led by an elderly, thin, and elegantly sinister-looking figure wearing a silver-embroidered skullcap. When the rabbi pulled down his prayer shawl, I saw that he was balding, but almost everyone else sported a full head of white, black, or red hair. I could not account for this strange vitality exhibited by the men of all ages.

As I rummaged through the prayer book, I noticed several loose pages pasted to the inside cover. These were printed in Latin characters, and the language looked like a kind of Spanish—I caught phrases about "Tu pueblo Israel." It was easy for me to follow the sequence of prayers because of the clear diction, especially that of the rabbi. In my yeshiva I had learned the Sephardic pronunciation of Hebrew both from the Israeli teachers and from our Sephardic teacher, Rabbi Avraham, whose Moroccan accent clearly distinguished the Hebrew phonemes. On the Sukkoth holiday of the following year, Avraham visited the Bronx Sephardi synagogue. After the service, he took me up to the *bima* and introduced me to Rabbi Asher Murciano (1924–2020). To my great surprise the two of them revealed themselves to be old friends! They began to joke in a mixture of English and French, and Rabbi Murciano held Avraham by the waist, announcing that they had both come to America on "the Moroccan Mayflower." It was only years later that I came to know something of what an extraordinary human being Rabbi Asher Murciano had been.

But the melodies of this synagogue were utterly strange to me. Many chants seemed to hang somewhere in space, never returning to what I could hear as a final tone. The old cantor from Istanbul seemed particularly fond of this kind of tune, as was the choir leader, whose voice guided the melody through meandering paths, shaking or trembling in this or that direction. I noted though, that the choirboys were firmly rooted in the American aesthetic of the 1950s—all of them tried to sound like the Syrian Canadian Paul Anka. At any rate, none of these youngsters tried to imitate the vocal style of the choir director, who was also from Istanbul. The congregation had no lack of good voices in the older generation, and from all around me in the pews I heard white-haired men responding with gusto.

This Sabbath service afforded me several hours to accustom myself to the exotic musical surroundings. I sensed something bright and optimistic—the gratitude and dignity of strong and satisfied people giving thanks to a power that governed their lives and helped them to thrive. I knew I would return to this place. I was able to negotiate a schedule with my father, whereby I divided the Jewish holidays between his Ashkenazic *shtibl* and the Sephardi synagogue.

One Sukkoth weekday, I stood outside this synagogue on 169th Street, listening to the modal chant of the *hazzan*. I felt bright Mediterranean sunlight flowing over me, and I knew that one day I must see those countries from which our Turkish, Greek, and Macedonian community had emigrated. But some years before I would be able to accomplish such journeys, my own city allowed me to experience a variety of performances originating with the natives of those countries or with their American-born children. It is to these varied performances in New York that I will now turn.

PART II

***

MUSICIANS AND MENTORS IN MANHATTAN, BROOKLYN, AND QUEENS

Chapter 3

▮▮▮

Village Rituals of New York

Iranians and Armenians in the New World

ON A SPRING night in 1963, four Zionist youths from the Bronx, aged
around fourteen, wandered after 9 p.m. along Alphabetville in the East
Village of Manhattan. Their destination—a nightclub, the Club Khayyam.

These leftist Zionists, whom I discovered after graduating from yeshiva
and entering the High School of Music and Art, formed a much-needed
bridge between my old religious identity and my new identity as an artist.
Tall Maxie—a wrestler imitating a clown. Lee—serious to the point of ped-
antry, an excellent math student; he wore round eyeglasses and parted his
hair down the middle. Lee's parents had emigrated from Poland, and he
spoke Yiddish in addition to Hebrew and some Russian. I felt close to him,
except for that almost morbid softness that I expected from the fathers of
my schoolmates from Poland, but not in anyone born in this country. And
there was Moshe, a handsome blue-eyed Israeli with black curls who had
told us about Club Khayyam.

Leaving the noise and lurking dangers of 1st Street we opened a door to
a small restaurant (or club) located on the ground level. The interior was
dark except for a small stage that sent out waves of amplified music. Tables
swam like little islands in a dark sea. Most were vacant while a few held a
solitary customer. Beyond the stage we could dimly see a partially raised
area enclosed by walls holding a few more tables. I had never seen a group
of people so disparate. Back in the Bronx, or in Jewish Montreal, people
came in groups, blocks of similarity, family and cultural resemblances. One

recognized the question in the eye of the other, and prepared to respond with humor or anger, interest or indifference. Here each human being seemed absorbed in his own time, in his own gaze.

The four of us easily found a table near the stage and from that point, for the rest of the evening, my friends faded into obscurity. Like the other customers I had entered my own time. The two figures on stage were among the strangest I had ever seen. A tall, dark man with a wrestler's build, a smiling Assyrian lion, cradled a large lute *oud* while he sang in Arabic or Hebrew. He looked rooted, dull-witted, and utterly sure of himself. Next to him sat a man who was his opposite in every way. This player of the hourglass drum, the *darabukka*, was blond and blue-eyed, perhaps ten years younger than the thirty-five year old singer. His handsome face sported a neatly trimmed blond beard and moustache, on his back a collegiate tweed sports jacket. While the singer leaned back, mouthing histrionic gestures, the drummer sat straight up, placing his hands evenly over the face of the drum that he held in his lap. His blue eyes were vacant as he leaned forward to hear every nuance played on the oud so that he could imitate or respond to it. I had seen this drum played before and had begun to study it with an excellent Israeli teacher, but I had never seen such intensity. His fingers rolled in long and even strokes, obliterating sections of the rhythmic cycle in even brushes of sound, punctuated by sharp pops and snaps along the drum's rim, and occasional dark thumps toward the inner part of the face. The playing was so beautiful that I continued to gaze at the crisp drumskin stretched neatly over the metal tuners on the ornamented, nickel-plated brass body.

I was hooked by something in the drumming and a couple of weeks later I returned on my own. I sat myself at a table near the stage, where the same caricature of an oudist was once again accompanied by the extraordinary percussionist. During their break, the drummer walked toward the raised seating area in the back where he seemed to know some people. Two choices presented themselves to me—to remain seated at my table as part of the audience, or to establish direct contact with the music in the person of the mysterious drummer. Immediately I got up and followed the drummer to the back where a festive atmosphere prevailed.

Two men somewhat older than him were seated at a table; one wore a red fez, while the features of the other were obscured by a false, hooked nose and dark glasses. At the same table sat a younger man whose stringy black hair gave him a wolfish appearance. As the drummer was about to join them, I passed before him and blurted out how much I admired his playing style. I fumbled on about how I had been studying the darabukka over the last year with an Israeli teacher. His distant, perhaps myopic, blue eyes sized me up incredulously. He was muttering some kind of acknowledgment when the face behind the false nose lit up in a smile and asked me how long I had been learning the darabukka? When he heard my answer, he smiled again and asked me to pull up a chair. When I sat down the young man with stringy hair picked up an oud lying on a nearby table and began to play a slow repetitive tune with a descending melodic line. He played with a sure stroke but little ornamentation. False nose sat with his hands folded over his stomach, exuding an aura of contentment. When it was over he said merely, "Nice. Sounds like something from the east of Asia Minor," to which the oudist replied, "Yes, I learned it last week from my teacher, the Armenian." The drummer nodded. Soon he rose to return to the stage, and when he had left, false nose proceeded to give me some information about the oud and the songs being sung tonight. Apart from the drummer, he concluded, the music was nothing special. But next week there would be a real treat, a *santur* player from Iran by the name of Nasser. I did not know what a santur was, and I had never heard Iranian music, but I said I would try to come back next Friday.

When I arrived at Khayyam's the following week there was no one on stage, but next to one wall a short man with a thick, dark moustache, wearing a sports jacket and no tie, leaned over a trapezoidal box covered with little chess pawns, supporting a great many metallic strings. The sides of the box, set upon a special stand, shone with polished woods of different shades of brown, forming angular, geometric shapes. Gradually he began to test the pitches of the strings with a slightly curved wooden hammer. The sound that emerged was quite loud, although amplified by no sound system. From where I was seated the hammer that he used was so thin and light as to be almost invisible. Finally satisfied with his tuning, he held two little sticks, and leaning forward he began to strike the strings in a motion so even his hands hardly seemed to move. The tiny mallets became a blur of feathers, as wings of sound arose from the many strings. It seemed to me that more than two hands were striking the strings as they traversed the scale like a polo field; two other sticks, held by two other hands, must be keeping an even triple pulse. The sounds of the many strings were dry, metallic, nasal, insistent, and pleading in the treble, thunderous and commanding in the bass. But all this was a kind of introduction. Now his hands paused, and I could see that there were only two of them. The musician never took his head from the strings. He began to strike them in the same mode, but without a clear tempo or rhythm. A melody was emerging, its shape changing at every turn. Frequently he closed his phrases with repeated trills ornamenting adjacent notes, and the whole instrument re-sounded in sympathy. So, this marvel was the santur!

Eventually the musician stopped. Looking up he sent his glance toward a table on his right, where a dark-complexioned couple was seated. The man, who looked perhaps thirty and was dressed in a jacket, white shirt, and tie, arose and walked up to the santur. Reaching behind the musician's chair, he came up with a wooden object that looked like a relative of the hourglass drums which I had seen only in clay or metal, called by names such as darabukka, *durbekki*, or *dumbek*. He seated himself on the right of the santur and cradled the drum on his left thigh. The mallets went into ac-tion again, but this time their deep, insistent pulse was echoed by a rainfall of rolls, brushes, and snaps, whose dull wooden sound blended with the deep bass of the santur. This music was not a series of short, simple songs like those I had heard here on previous weekends. These two instruments were opening up many paths for my mind to wander. The music seemed to draw to a close as the drummer changed the position of his drum and sang a song in a slow, measured tempo while the santur followed softly be-hind him. The words were in a language I had never heard before, whose sounds were few and whose vowels were clear and simple.

As the lights grew brighter and the two Iranian musicians walked over to the table on their right, I caught sight of my acquaintances from last week, seated in the distance, but without the fez, false nose, and dark glasses. The drummer was there too, but with my mind still wandering in a maze of music, I was not capable of gesturing to them.

I had been nibbling at some sort of Middle Eastern salad, tasting of olive oil and lemon juice, for over half an hour when Nasser, the santur player, returned along with the blond drummer. The lights dimmed again and the two played a somewhat simpler rhythmic melody, whose triple meter repeated itself under the hundred disguises heaped up by the drummer. Then the dark couple, the Iranian drummer and his wife, as I thought, took the floor in front of the instruments. Stretching out their lower arms, they faced each other in what seemed to be a rhythmic pre-sentation of martial arts. Their heads bobbed as their shoulders and arms jutted out in time to the music. Then, having established the basic pattern, they began to roll their arms before them in a continual circular motion. The man and woman smiled at one another like children and the woman's earrings, rings, and necklace shone in the spotlight. The dance did not last long and immediately the woman returned to her table. Her husband sat down next to the drummer, who rose and gave his drum to the Persian. There was now a brushing and snapping on the wooden drum as he bared his numerous finger rings that I had not noticed before. Deftly he drew those rings over the striated carvings on the side of the drum, producing a sharp rippling sound. He played more boisterously than before, displaying some of the humor of his dancing, and as the music drew to a close the two Persians seemed to laugh through their instruments.

When the lights went on again, I rose and walked to the enclosed area where I was awaited by a calm smile under the real nose and moustache, its ends curling gently upward. Without their dark shades the gray eyes looked dreamy.

"I can see that you enjoyed it. Please have a seat," he said.

I pulled up a chair, although I wasn't accustomed to sitting with adults.

"My name is Pyrrhus Ruches and this is my younger brother, Phillip."

He pointed to a potato-like form seated next to him, now looking diminished minus his fez.

"Let me introduce you properly to the drummer you've been admiring. His name is Laszlo."

The blond smiled shyly.

"We didn't get your name last week."

"It's Zev," I answered.

"Tzvi?" Pyrrhus asked.

"No, Zev, actually Ze'ev. In Hebrew it means 'wolf.'"

He said that he had never heard the name before, but that I might have heard his name in history class.

"Pyrrhus, King of Epirus," he explained.

I had not.

"Are you Greek?" I asked.

"Well, yes and no. We go to the Greek church, but at home we speak Albanian. In Boston our priests say we are Albanians, but in New York they tell us we are Greeks. Our father came here from Albania. Was your father born here?"

"No, he is from Bessarabia. It used to be Romania, but I don't think it is any more."

It seemed to me that in these Balkan countries every place had been something else not so long before and was probably called by two or more names.

"Ah yes, Bessarabia, that's also called Moldavia. There are, or rather there were many Greeks and Albanians living there. I've always liked the Jewish music from Bessarabia, it's at the same time Jewish, Moldavian, and Greek. I used to hear it a lot in New York, but lately there is more of this Israeli music."

Pyrrhus turned to the blond drummer.

"Laszlo, is anyone playing *freylekhs* at the clubs these days?"

"Jewish music. Sometimes I see an old man with a clarinet. It's nice music, something like Greek *hassapiko*. Not much for a drummer, but nice melodies. But nobody young seems to be playing it, everyone is sixty or over."

Pyrrhus went on, "Zev, if you'd like to hear some of the music we are talking about why don't you come out to visit us in Queens. Have you ever been to Queens?"

I said that I had not, but I was sure I could find the way. Pyrrhus wrote down some directions and we agreed I would come by next Sunday. Before returning to the front, Laszlo also wrote down his address and phone number.

"I'm in Brooklyn. Give me a call sometime."

For all his moustache and Greek name, Pyrrhus sounded like an educated urban American, but the drummer spoke in a rural-sounding regional accent I had never heard before. His handsome face reminded me of a Yankee officer in a Civil War painting; I could see him in a gold-buttoned jacket and navy blue cap.

The Balkans in Astoria

That Sunday I explained to my parents I was visiting a friend in Queens and embarked on the long trip from the Bronx to Columbus Circle, and from there to Astoria, the first neighborhood east of Manhattan. The brick houses that awaited me there were even less attractive than those of my native Bronx, and the overall flatness oppressed me. I could see no park or any substantial greenery. I walked for perhaps half a mile before reaching the six-story apartment building where Pyrrhus, his brother Phillip, and their parents all lived. Walking up to the fourth floor I reached a dark hallway, rang the doorbell, and was greeted by Pyrrhus, wearing a Chinese-style indoor costume—slippers, white pants, and a black coolie jacket with white cuffs. On his head he sported a black silk Manchurian skullcap. He explained that Phillip had gone out, and that their parents occupied an apartment two floors below. Asking me to remove my shoes, he gave me a pair of Chinese slippers. In any case, there was little space to walk in these two small rooms, filled with spacious divans and spread-covered mattresses. Bright sunlight flooded in from the open expanse beyond the windows, caressing the spines of numerous hardcover books lining the walls.

Seating me on a divan, Pyrrhus executed what were apparently practiced gestures of hospitality. Quickly he emerged from the narrow kitchen bearing a kind of sherbet; when I tasted it my tongue registered a novel flavor and aroma—rose water, as I learned from my host.

Sipping my sherbet, I asked Pyrrhus a few questions about the origins of his family. He seated himself on a round, stuffed object, something between a pillow and a chair, and began a discourse that was the most astounding piece of connected information I had ever heard. Until that point, family origins had been hinted at in elliptical phrases and obscure references to places floating in time and space—Bessarabia, Belorussia, Edinets, Mogilev, the First World War. But now I was face-to-face with someone who could, and did, explain all of these factors in their precise geographical, historical, and sociological detail. Lacking the historical background to make much sense of what he was saying, I tried a few more questions. Pyrrhus's gray eyes met mine briefly from behind his thick glasses. He smiled and lit himself a cigarette. He would begin again at the beginning.

A peninsula appeared before my eyes, crossed by mountains and rivers. Every territory had its own function, its population composed of two sects of Christians, of Muslims, and of Jews. What my Bessarabian father knew instinctively or from anecdotes and hearsay, Pyrrhus could explain on sound historical foundations and in meticulous detail. It was not merely a question of who lived where, but of who they thought they were in different historical eras. I had thought, surely Greeks had always been Greeks and Jews had always been Jews? But Pyrrhus's talk was beginning to cast doubt even on that idea. I recalled the biblical verse "a wandering Aramean was my father," and wondered at what point did we start to think of ourselves no longer as Arameans but as Hebrews, the people from across the river? Pyrrhus had caught my imagination.

We returned to the Balkans where, between the Pindus Mountains and the Adriatic Sea, lived a people of unknown origin speaking an Indo-European language of obscure affiliations. They called themselves by the name "Shqiptar," but their neighbors knew them as "Albanians," in Turkish "Arnaut." Slowly and very late they became Christians. Those in the north accepted the authority of the Roman pope, while the southerners gravitated toward the church of the Byzantine emperor. Enter the Turks, and in time the majority of both groups accepted Islam. Scattered among the Christians and Muslims of the south there wandered seminomadic tribes of native origin who had long ago exchanged their language for Latin, which they turned into a Balkanic tongue, vaguely related to the Romanian spoken by my father. The Greeks called them "Vlakhs." In the cities of the south there had lived Jews who continued to speak the Greek language of Byzantine times. In the extreme north some of the Albanian tribes accepted the faith of Byzantium under the leadership of a priestly, petty monarch ruling from an inaccessible mountain, bordering on Serbia. Gradually they accepted the Serbian language and became known as Montenegrins.

Finally answering my question, Pyrrhus concluded: "So you see, of course we are Albanians, but we don't think of ourselves as Albanians. We think of ourselves as Greeks."

Although Pyrrhus had tried to tell this tale without heroes and villains, it became clear that he resented the Muslim majority of Albanians for, in the past, trying to coerce his own people into Islam, and in the present for trying to force them to abandon a Greek cultural identity. While not anti-Muslim, he considered Christian Greece a higher civilization which Albania could not attain on her own. In any case, he and his brother were only half Albanian—their mother was a pure Greek from Constantinople.

But then we left ethnicity and religion behind. Pyrrhus went off into a back room and returned with an oud. Until then I had not gotten a chance to see the instrument up close. I admired the gentle shades of brown striping and its round body. Pyrrhus apologized for his poor playing, saying he was only an amateur. He knew only a few Turkish modes, or *makams*, which were the basis for many Greek dance tunes, he thought. Keeping a rather shaky rhythm, his eagle feather thumped out dances he called *syrto*, and *kalamatiano*. Then he announced he was playing a Jewish song, a *romanca*. I recognized this tune—the Sephardim in the Bronx sometimes sang it in Hebrew after holiday meals. Pyrrhus's shaky voice sang words to it in Spanish, or rather the Ladino language that the Sephardim spoke; "La rosa enflorese en el mes de Mayo."

"I learned this from my oud teacher, Mr. Malkho," he informed me.

"Do you speak this Spanish?" I asked.

"Yes. I learned to speak and to read it in Hebrew letters."

Smiling shyly, Pyrrhus put down his oud and began to describe his music collection for me. Turkish music seemed to be at the center, but all the Balkan musics were represented. As for Jewish dance music, he explained that he grew up hearing it in Chicago and then it was so common that he never bothered to collect it. He told me that many Greek clarinetists in New York used to listen to it too, and some of them, such as the Macedonian Costa Gadinis (1890–1987) had even partly modeled their style after certain Jewish musicians, especially Dave Tarras. There was some old connection between these musics that he did not fully understand.

Perhaps as the Ashkenazic Jews settled in or near the Ottoman Empire, in Bessarabia and South Ukraine, they had developed a kind of musical Zionism, he opined.

By now the sun was setting. He would soon be going downstairs to eat supper with his parents, but I was welcome to return another time. I thanked him and walked out toward the subway.

Brooklyn

The trip to Queens had brought me so much unexpected knowledge that I could not wait to telephone Laszlo, the drummer. When it came to it, though, I hesitated. A few days later, I gathered the courage and called. I gave my name and proceeded to stumble over self-explanations and self-invitations. At the other end, silence. Finally, "Sure. Come over this Saturday afternoon, then we'll go together to the Club Khayyam. You know the D train, don't you? Keep on going down to Clinton Street."

The next Saturday at noon I took the long trip south. I followed Laszlo's directions until I reached the brick apartment building. The building was a walk-up, and as I approached Laszlo's place, I heard the faint sound of singing, possibly in Arabic, accompanied by violins, flutes, oud, and darabukka. Laszlo opened the door with a distracted smile, and as I entered, the apartment overwhelmed me with its order and harmony. I removed my shoes and sat across from Laszlo at a large, round, legless, wooden table, placed directly on a rug. Around the corners of the room several hourglass drums stood, made of brass or clay. One corner was occupied by a low table piled high with what seemed to be round animal skins, and a few small tools. There were no chairs anywhere, only a large mattress covered with an Indian bedspread.

Laszlo wore a kind of collarless shirt that I had never seen before, fairly loose and made of a natural material that caused it to fold and wrinkle. No doubt cotton, a rare commodity in the Bronx of those days. The two of us sat wordlessly at the table while he listened to the conclusion of a long, flowing song in Arabic.

"Have you ever heard Abd al-Wahhab?"

When I answered that I had not, he explained that we had been listening to this great Egyptian singer and composer. That had been an LP, but he pointed to the 78 RPM records stacked neatly against one wall.

"I don't have much Turkish music, Pyrrhus has more." He shuffled over to his stack of Greek records and chose one.

"Karakosta. A Greek clarinetist. No one had a heart bigger than his."

Bending over his phonograph he switched the needle and dropped it carefully at the edge of the little black record. As it circled swiftly, I heard the bell-like sound of a clarinet and, far in the background, a tinkling, shimmering tone, reminding me of a piano and of the Persian santur. They were playing a triple meter at a stately pace. The clarinet alternated between colorful flourishes and long-held notes. Its melody was tightly controlled, expressing both great power and deep contentment. There was sunshine in this music.

Laszlo said the word *tsamiko*. Then he flipped the disc over. Now the clarinet played more quickly, phrase crashing into phrase, a kalamatiano. Laszlo explained:

"The old Greek musicians never used drums, all the rhythm is in the *santouri* or the *lauto*. But in this country, we play the dumbek with the tsamiko or the kalamatiano. Can you follow them?"

My host walked to the corner and returned with a small ceramic drum. We became immersed in the seven beats of the kalamatiano. Once he felt that I understood the rhythm he scrutinized my hands, correcting any tightness. Gradually he showed me how to vary the rhythmic phrasing with rolls, gently brushing the rim or the center of the drum. He asked me where I had learned to play, and I mentioned the name of my Israeli teacher, Ruth Ben Tsvi. He had heard of her, although she rarely played in nightclubs. Finally, I asked him how he had learned.

I discovered that Laszlo had studied with a Greek *darabukka* player named Steve, who played up in Boston. Laszlo had been born in a fishing village called Gloucester, but the only drumming he had heard there was the military drum in Portuguese religious processions. When he was my age he and his friends had gone to Boston on weekends and sometimes turned up at nightclubs where girls performed "Oriental dance," or belly dance, which I had never seen. He went on: "When I first heard Greek music there was nothing like it. I forgot everything and I had to hear more, and I had to play it. Later on, I went to art school in Boston, but I continued learning the dumbek from Steve."

Meeting with Nasser and the Santur

In another hour or so he began to dress for the club, changing his collarless shirt for a jacket and tie. As we walked together to the subway, he told me that Isaq the oudist played at Khayyam's on Wednesdays and Fridays and Nasser the Iranian santur player was there on Saturdays. He would introduce me to him. He went on:

"But you know Persians are another thing. The Greeks, the Turks, the Armenians, the Syrians, the Sephardim all listen to each other's music. But the Persians like only Persian music and never play with other musicians. So be careful when you talk to Nasser."

We were soon engulfed by the subway. The trip from Clinton Street to the club was much shorter than my way from the Bronx and in a mercifully short time we were deposited in Alphabetville. Entering the club, we walked to the raised enclosed area in the back. I recognized Nasser sitting like a caged bird, staring down at a tiny glass of tea. His large, hooked nose, drooping moustache, and receding chin gave him an ornithic profile. He stood up to greet Laszlo, who introduced me. Nasser bowed slightly and smiled from very far away. This distant, reserved friendliness was familiar—it was like the demeanor of Avraham, the Moroccan rabbi from my yeshiva.

Although tonight we were without the beringed fingers of the Persian drummer and his arm-weaving dances, the sounds of the santur occupied my total attention. Laszlo stimulated Nasser to create ever more cuttingly precise rhythmic patterns. On the santur no sound simply ended, with every stroke the entire face of the instrument continued to vibrate; and with no damping system the grating and moaning of metal strings penetrated my ears. Then the rhythm and drumming stopped. The feather-sticks floated in the air only to come crashing down in a slow, uneven, angular melody. The pulse ended while the rhythm flowed languidly from octave to octave. Nasser looked up, parted his lips, and uttered euphonious Persian syllables to a poetry-driven beat. He repeated the lines, slowly, syllable by syllable, adding elaborate cadences and trills. After the third repetition he echoed his phrases with the mallets. Then, stopping abruptly, he threw back his head and uttered a howling cry. This rapid fire succession of notes, shuttling between glottis and palate, held more sadness and passion than I had been aware of until then. A flame burned away years of my childhood.

Later in the evening Nasser stood facing me. He came up close and straightened the collar of my shirt, exactly the way my teacher Avraham had done. Nasser smiled under his moustache.

"Ze'ev, you like Persian music very much."

"I only heard it for the first time last week."

Nasser spoke with a thick Persian accent, but his grammar was clear. He invited me to visit him in his hotel room a few blocks away, where he could play me some Persian recordings.

"Come by next Friday around 6:00 p.m. We can listen together and then I will take you to the Armenian club where I play."

I asked Laszlo about the Armenian club. He answered matter-of-factly: "Harout's. It's just across town from here. They have music only on Fridays—clarinet, oud, singing, and dumbek. Nasser plays early on, before the dancing. It's fun, you'll see, but those Armenians don't understand much of Nasser's music."

The next Friday the sun was close to setting as I walked toward the hotel on Second Avenue. Some reddish light penetrated the hallways of the upper floor where his room was located, but once Nasser opened his door, I was in a space from which any sign of the outside world had been expunged. No natural light entered. Nasser's eyes looked sleepy. He motioned me to remove my shoes, but the only carpeting on the floor was a small, intricately woven rug in yellows and blues next to his bed. I sat in the single chair while he boiled water. On the stove a small teapot sat astride a larger kettle, forming a novel, sculptured entity. As he prepared the tea Nasser switched on a reel-to-reel tape recorder. Suddenly the room vanished. My attention was drawn to a small, thin, very nasal-sounding stringed instrument. The melody emerged very quickly, abounding in tremolos but refused to stay in a fixed rhythm. When Nasser returned, carrying a very small glass full of dark tea, he seemed to notice the attentive look in my eyes.

"The voice of *tar*," he explained.

"What does a tar look like?" I asked.

Nasser beckoned me toward a colorful, slim book whose cover bore large Arabic letters fluttering like banners in the wind. As I approached him, I stepped on the small yellow carpet. His face looked pained.

"Please, do not step on the carpet," he beseeched me.

My face expressed bewilderment.

"I perform my prayers there," he added.

I stepped around the carpet and came closer to the book. He opened it to a photograph of a man with a drooping moustache leaning over a long-necked instrument whose face resembled a number "8."

"In Iran many people play tar, but here I have not found any yet. I am only here one year."

These were many "firsts" for me. The first time I had heard even a recording of a tar; the first time I had met a Muslim who said his prayers on a carpet; and the first time I had visited a professional musician in his hotel room.

After Nasser changed into his jacket and tie, the two of us rode the elevator down to the darkened street. We would walk across town. Our route took us westward and down toward 8th Street. I recognized these blocks, the site of my first date, when Jessica, my classmate in Music and Art had asked me out one Saturday night. She was the daughter of Jewish people who lived in that West Village neighborhood. I knew they were artists or intellectuals because of the quantity of dust covering all the windows. Jewish women in the Bronx would never have tolerated so much dirt. How I envied Jessica's freedom to live behind such grimy windows!

Harout's

Now Nasser and I approached 8th Street. The streets of the Village teamed with all sorts of people, but I paid scant attention as I followed this silent Iranian with his long, brown instrument case. We crossed Astor Place and went on to Waverly Place where most of the pedestrians seemed to be college students, evidently from NYU. We opened a door surrounded by large glass windows, suggesting a bar or restaurant. The interior of Harout's was as dark as the Club Khayyam but, instead of spotlights, the lighting here consisted of large, covered lamps suspended from the ceiling, creating sharp contrasts between wide swaths of illumination and shrouded corners. The space was larger but also much simpler than the Khayyam. The entire area was one large room, with a stage on the far wall, and a counter on the left. The center of the room was empty, illuminated by several ceiling lamps. The wooden floor was covered in sawdust, and tables seating four or two people were scattered around the room.

Nasser sat me at a table while he went up to the stage and set about moving the tables and chairs he needed to perform. People milled about the counter, while others sat at the tables. As my eyes grew accustomed to the semidarkness, I saw many differences between the people here and those at the Khayyam. The people here were younger, the mean age might have been eighteen or twenty, although there were a few middle-aged men and women. More people seemed to be arriving every few minutes. They acted as though they knew exactly why they were here, and what they were going to find. They also shared a certain look; lots of figures of the same height, skin, and hair color. But for their darker skins they reminded me somewhat of the community at my Sephardic synagogue in the Bronx. Others looked like some of my friends, such as the Levinsons, with their olive skin, thin bodies, straight black hair, and hooked, "Semitic" features. But the other sort of Jewish type, the broad, fleshy Polish faces like that of my friend Maxie, were completely absent here.

The group here was animated, loud and cheerful, another big difference from the dreamy and alienated patrons of the Khayyam. I heard many conversations, mostly in English, but occasionally I made out a language full of strange sounds, utterly different from the Levantine languages—Hebrew, Arabic, Turkish, Greek, or Ladino—that I heard more frequently. The atmosphere was less that of a restaurant than a bar mitzvah or a wedding—everyone seemed to know everyone else.

Nasser reappeared next to a youngish looking man, with darkish skin and handsome, regular features. He introduced him as "Robert," and he was the singer of the regular group here. Robert Afarian was born in Syria in 1931, but he spoke English well. When he heard my name, he asked whether I was from Israel. I answered that I was not, but that I was studying the dumbek with an Israeli teacher. I also knew Laszlo, I said.

When Robert left, Nasser prepared to begin his set. The room was still half empty while he played his santur. His playing here was somewhat simpler than it had been at the Khayyam, mostly dance tunes and rhythmic improvisations. He played alone, without a drummer. On the left I could see a table where Robert and a few other men sat, listening intently to the music, but for the most part the animated conversations in English and what must have been Armenian continued at their previous volume. I was a little disappointed to see Nasser's music somehow diminished, but I was also curious to find out what this club was like on its own terms.

After about half an hour Nasser packed up his santur and sat down at our table. I said something about how noisy everyone was, and he replied stoically that most of the people had come to dance, not to listen to Persian music. A waiter brought a plate of shish kebabs to our table. While not observing the Sabbath, I was still fairly observant of the rules of *kashrut*, so I ordered a salad and white cheese. Amplified noise came from the stage and the two of us turned to look as the four-man band walked on and began to set themselves up. Robert sat in the center. At his left, a middle-aged man with rich curly hair adjusted his clarinet. On his right, an overweight, balding man wearing eyeglasses held his oud up to the microphone. Soon I learned that these were the famous clarinetist Steven Bogosian and the equally well-known oudist George Mgrdichian (1936–2006). Far to the right, a younger man sat, holding a metal dumbek between his knees.

When all the microphones were at their proper height, the drummer began by laying out a slow, even roll. The clarinet shot out a high, piercing melody, at times becoming a wail in a slow, flowing rhythm. Of the musicians, only Robert had been born in the Middle East, and the audience was mainly American-born as well. So, whatever music they played was to some extent mediated by the culture that surrounded us. But when Robert entered, the sweet and nasal intonation of his voice erased any impression of this New World. He sang with the same Turkish pathos I knew from the Sephardic synagogue and from the old recordings I had heard with Pyrrhus and Laszlo. The sounds issuing from Robert's throat flowed with the umlauted vowels, a kind of vocalic harmony I associated with the Turkish language. After a few lines, the melody returned to its starting point; it was less improvisatory than Nasser's Persian sung poetry.

Suddenly the drummer ceased his tremolo and thwacked his dumbek, once, twice. The band repeated a short phrase and then they were rolling together in a moderately fast dance song, whose words no longer had that undulating, umlauted quality; they clashed and clanged against one another, dragging a freight train of consonant clusters—*inch, -ank, genega*. Armenian, I thought. The empty space in front of the stage filled with bobbing figures, mainly couples, although here and there a man circled alone, arms raised, fingers snapping. The company was bewitched, as though for the last hour or so they had all awaited this moment. After the singer had repeated his song several times, the clarinet strung together notes taken from the song, holding some, ornamenting others. The dancers became more exhilarated. The oud entered, repeating and varying short, syncopated phrases. Eventually the singer returned, repeating the song and bringing it to a close. Now the oud played a few notes, a very short improvisation, before laying out a strange, broken rhythm. Over this rhythm Robert sang another song, slower, in a more melancholy mode. The dancers, still on the floor, led by a pretty, slim, blonde woman, linked hands by their pinkies, while others continued as couples in the midst of the circle formed by the blonde and her dancers. As for me, the smile never left my face—this was a play where every actor knew his or her part with precision and harmony.

The music and dancing continued for almost an hour. In the interval, Nasser had strolled up to the counter. Now he made his way to our table. "Zev, I will go home now. Let me walk you to the subway; you can come back another time." I got up immediately and soon we reached the Astor Place station. I thanked Nasser and he disappeared toward the East Village.

That week I telephoned Lee, and on Friday the two of us greeted Nasser as he climbed onto the stage at Harout's. This time Lee and I sat at a separate table toward the back, where we could see the stage and the dance floor. Nasser's playing and the opening songs and dancing repeated themselves, much as the previous week. Now I could look more closely at the steps and postures of the dances. The line dances seemed fairly simple, but the shifting of weight demanded skill. The couple dances were utterly unfamiliar, bearing only a distant relation to the Persian dancing I had witnessed at the Khayyam, where the man and woman had performed almost identical arm-rolling motions, whose aim seemed to be the creation of the most graceful patterns, allowing for no overt eroticism expressed through the hips or shoulders. Here, each man and woman could act out his or her sexual character through these motions of the arms, shoulders, hips, and legs. Most moved with grace and delicacy, although a few were clumsy, repeating the same motions with stiff, inflexible bodies.

Lee and I stayed for two sets. At the end of the second one, a dark-haired, chubby woman stood erect, then leaned backward, a kerchief in her right hand as she held the hand of her neighbor with her left pinkie. As the band played a melody with a strange, broken rhythm, the dancers hopped forward, stamping their right feet in time to the last three beats of the tune. Then the line moved slowly backward, shifting weight as each leg was raised slightly. The steps repeated themselves with increasingly subtle variations, larger or smaller, while the tempo allowed for no change. This seemed as much ritual as dance. Later I learned that this dance was the *tamzara*.

I could not find a real model for what I had seen. The Israeli parties I had attended occasionally had something of this communal quality but lacked the almost ritualistic subtlety. I reached back into my earliest memories of circle dances that my father and the older East European men had danced at weddings—the furious *bulgar*, the slow, graceful *zhok*, or the stately, almost static freylekhs. But now his regional society was virtually disbanded, his legs ached with arthritis, and the clarinets of the old Jewish musicians—*klezmorim*—had been mainly replaced by brash Israeli accordions. I discussed this with Lee on the long subway ride to the Bronx. From behind his glasses Lee's intelligent eyes seemed to be fitting what he had seen into some broad historical plan. He had liked Harout's, but I did not think he felt as though he had embarked on anything. Perhaps his gentle, religious Polish father had not conveyed the excitement of the dance to him, or perhaps Lee was thinking only of what would be danced in Israel.

That weekend I asked my father what he knew about Armenians. It was not much. There were none in his hometown, Edinets, but he may have seen some in the market at the provincial capital, Hotin. They looked something like Jews, but they were Christians, and he had no idea from where they had come. Interesting, but there must be more. Where to turn but to Pyrrhus, that walking encyclopedia of the Balkans?

The following Sunday I made the trip to Queens, where Pyrrhus once again greeted me in his Chinese jacket and slippers. About Armenians he was prepared to speak at great length. Out came a pile of hardcover books in English, French, and Greek, some containing maps of ancient Armenia, the medieval Armenian kingdoms, Armenian territories in the Seljuk Kingdom, in the Ottoman Empire, in World War I, the Soviet Union, and various diasporas in the Middle East and Eastern Europe. I learned that the Armenians were an ancient people and nation, although not quite as ancient as the Jews or the Greeks. Their language, which did not sound at all like Greek, was related to it only in the most distant degree, and the scripts were distinct. They belonged to a separate Christian denomination, different from the Orthodox. But the overwhelming fact about the Armenians was what they had suffered during this century, when they had almost disappeared entirely. Pyrrhus normally tried to present the rule of the Ottoman Turks fairly, even mentioning how nostalgic his father was for their tolerant rule in Albania—far better than King Zog, the Fascist Italian occupation, or the Communist dictatorship which had succeeded them. But he had to admit something had gone terribly wrong in the case of the Armenians. The Turks had transgressed even their own heavy-handed rules about how to govern an empire.

As he explained it to me, Armenia was not simply a territory of the Ottoman Empire like Albania or Greece—in Armenia the Turks, Kurds, Assyrians, and Armenians had lived on the same land. For many centuries, the political control had belonged only to the Turks, sometimes shared informally with aggressive Kurdish tribes, but never with the Armenians. At the beginning of this century, the Turks had lost many Balkan territories when the Christians had revolted. During the First World War they were afraid the Armenians would revolt too, and then where would the Turks go? Had the Armenians revolted? I asked. Not really, only very few, and these few usually from Russia. But then three cruel generals ruled Turkey and they wanted an excuse to rid the country of all Armenians, wherever they lived. The books and their horrendous photographs explained the rest. In those days we did not use the word "Holocaust," but I knew something about what had happened to my father's family, and to the families of most of my schoolmates at yeshiva and in my neighborhood. So, something almost as tremendous and horrible had befallen the Armenians, too. Of course, I could sense nothing of this at Harout's, where I could see only life, and no thought of the extinction of a people.

The following week when I visited Laszlo, he explained the history of Harout's. It was not an old place but had opened about a year earlier when a young Armenian American architect named Harout Derderian began to rent out an NYU college students' bar on Friday nights so that young

Armenians could get together and dance outside of the church-sponsored dances and weddings which were their usual venues—and away from the Greek-owned clubs where belly dancers performed, as most Armenian parents did not want their children to frequent such places. Harout's was a place for young Armenians, so the music played there was somewhat newer in style. The songs were in Armenian and Turkish, but some had been composed in this country. They even had a song about their resorts in the Catskills. The dance tunes were probably older, he thought. Laszlo motioned me over to one of the stacks of old recordings and took out several black discs. On the label of each one a lighthouse sent out its beams over a black background—the company was named "Pharos," after the lighthouse in ancient Alexandria. Underneath the names of the performers appeared in Latin letters—"Stefan and Haigiz." He told me that long before he was born, these two had been the most popular Armenian musicians in New England. Many Armenian families there still owned some old discs, dating back to the First World War era, when most of the Armenians had settled in Boston. They had played the violin and the santur, and he thought that Haigiz's son might still live in Boston, although neither he nor any other Armenian could play the santur. Indeed, not more than a decade later an elderly Armenian gentleman had been among the audience as I performed my santur with a friend on a summer evening in Harvard Square. Coming up to me, smiling, he introduced himself as the son of Santuri Haigiz!

But now the label of the 78 RPM recording said "Zaza Makame," and Laszlo thought he recognized the names of a Kurdish tribe plus the word makam, for musical mode. As the little black disc spun around swiftly, amid the scratches and pops a ribbon-like melody repeated itself. The violin varied the melody with tiny inflections, bending the notes ever so slightly, especially at one point in the endlessly repeated melody. I saw a caravan stepping swiftly and evenly through the Anatolian desert. The melody was supported by the percussive hammering of the santur, striking one course of strings and its octave, occasionally one tone below, in a hypnotic, trance-inducing pulse. This was the grandfather of some of the tunes I had heard at Harout's, but somehow simpler, more intense and introverted. On another disc, one of the two musicians sang a short melody in Armenian, to the strange, broken rhythm to which they had danced the other night. Laszlo told me this was the sauciest Armenian rhythm. In Turkish it was called *jurjuna*, and it had a naughty lilt. He said the older Armenians knew an endless repertoire of songs in both Armenian and Turkish using this ten-beat rhythm. On some nights he had to expend all his powers of invention to vary and embellish it, as the Armenians danced to one song after another.

Laszlo suggested I go to Harout's the next time he played there, in about a month. I should stay on until the end of the music and dancing, which would be around 4:00 a.m. That would be late for me, so he suggested I warn my parents in advance.

Later that week my plans provoked a minor crisis at home. Although my father *davened* every morning and kept kosher, Shabbos had become negotiable, as he was often obliged to work on Saturdays. There might be a Sabbath meal on Friday, but usually no synagogue on Saturday. As a result, I felt Saturday to be my own time. In the past, I had spent it at the Metropolitan Museum of Art and later at a painting class at the Art Students League near Carnegie Hall. But to disappear on Friday night and not return until the early hours of the morning was stretching the family rules. I explained that I would be with a friend who was much older than I, an adult. My father exclaimed in Yiddish that he had not come to America so that his son could spend Shabbos eve dancing with *goyim* until sunrise! But my mother countered by saying that I had been to yeshiva and I understood what the Sabbath was; I knew how to keep it properly whenever I might want to. And in this country I must learn to live with all kinds of people. Still muttering, my father finally gave in.

When I arrived at Harout's that Friday evening Laszlo was already seated with the Armenian band and Nasser was nowhere in sight. Light sometimes shone through the translucent fish-skin head on Laszlo's drum. After the opening piece in the meterless, flowing rhythm, the beat emerged from the darabukka with greater clarity, adding brightness and precision. As Robert sang a simple tune in Armenian, the floor filled with dancers. The word "Catskill" repeated itself in the opening line of his song. As the music turned more sensual and erotic, couples broke off, facing each other.

Unlike the playful and graceful Persian dancing, here the role of the male and the female were more clearly defined. The woman had to appear serene, only occasionally flaunting her sexual power through the movement of her hips, shoulders, or even the muscles of her stomach. The man expressed an inner pain as well as a willingness to serve her by looking downward, spreading his arms wide. At this time, I could not associate these graceful and expressive motions with sexual desire. My earliest memories of this erotic dance of the Middle East, the *chifte-telli*, are strangely chaste—I cannot recall a feeling of desire or attraction to any of these often quite shapely Armenian girls. I was the youngest person at Harout's, and apart from Laszlo and Nasser, the only non-Armenian; in native terms, an *otar*, a goy. This non-Armenian identity made me feel somehow apart, almost invisible. At Harout's, these dozens of young Armenians enacted their erotic rites unhindered by the prying eyes of foreign voyeurs.

In the future, as the weeks and months wore on, I formed no personal relationships with anyone and established some rapport only with the musicians. In the next couple of years, I discovered one Armenian girl in high school with me. At one of our many youthful parties, Kathy danced the chifte-telli to a new Armenian recording she had brought, while I added a live percussion accompaniment. Later I danced with her, and whenever we came across one another in school we laughed conspiratorially. Yet we both understood that we occupied different worlds. I was a young artist-intellectual headed on a trajectory away from my ethnic community, while she was much more firmly bound to the values of other Armenians of her age. She reminded me of an Orthodox Jewish girl who had somehow been permitted to attend secular school; and her ethnic tradition included openly erotic dance, as ours did not.

Now the second set opened with a cameo appearance by the eponymous owner of Harout's. As the band played a lively jurjuna, a tall man with a handsome, but almost brutal, boxer's face took the floor, dancing with threatening physical strength and pride. He seemed on a larger scale than the other Armenians, and he came to symbolize for me much of the spirit I sensed in Armenian social events—sensuous, hedonistic, and proud to the point of aggression.

As the night wore on, there was a progression from couple to group dances; around midnight another woman led a line of the slow, hopping tamzara, while Harout linked arms with another man, performing the same steps in a whirling circular movement. Later on, Harout led the *sepastia bar*, which began as a simple chain dance and turned into an ecstatic and demanding series of hops and claps. Laszlo told me that sepastia bar separated the men from the boys, but that the real dancing took place after 2:00 a.m. It was called the *halay*.

Alcohol was not allowed at Harout's, but by 2:00 a.m. most of the young men were in a euphoric state brought on by the music and dancing. As the clarinet wailed a lugubrious *maya*, a rubato melody, the younger men assembled under the lights in the middle of the dance floor. I was surprised to see that Harout was not among them. But this was not his age group, and in this society, age seemed to matter a great deal. The leader was a tall, handsome youth of perhaps twenty, clean-shaven and athletic. At his left, seven or eight young men linked arms and huddled close together. Laszlo struck his drum. The oud entered with a slow rhythmic tune and a spasm went through the young men's bodies. The whole group leaned backward, then slightly forward, finally closing with a small step to the right. The leader threw back his head, guiding the line with a kerchief he held in his right hand, while with the other he grasped his neighbor's arm. Between each dancer and the next, one could not insert so much as a knife blade, each was that glued to his fellow. As the tempo gradually increased the steps became slightly larger, the shifts of weight more pronounced.

Another line had formed behind them. The same slender blonde, her features delicately aquiline, led the smaller line of women. Their movements were much less aggressive than those of the men, but at the second beat of each cycle their spines swayed backward, then forward, before crossing to the right. They accomplished these movements by such slight stages that I could see a line of poplars swaying in the breeze.

The clarinet melody discovered new twists and corners, always remaining within the same tune. After many minutes, the tempo increased slightly, and the oud thrust itself in with endless, repetitive rhythmic variations, no longer the tune proper, but archetypal phrases, the matrix out of which that tune had been born. The violence of the men's movements increased as the whole line swayed back and forth, up and down, arms ending in tightly clenched fists shot upward, outward, then down again. For a time, the leader bent forward, kerchief behind his head, while the line hovered over the floor, about to collapse like a broken wall. He shouted something in Armenian and immediately the steps became miniscule. With a flash, the white kerchief fluttered in the air as the entire line leaped and hopped, all the while shifting the weight on their spines inexplicably, irrationally, exploding through the swinging arms and buckling knees. The entire attention of each man focused on starting to ripple his spine backward and forward at just the right moment so that he could finish the movement at the same instant as his neighbors, when, pulling their arms forward together with clenched fists, they threw all their weight onto their left feet. There seemed no end to this but death. Closure came in stages; the band began the next measure at a somewhat slower tempo, spines leaned backward and the halay line stretched itself like a long cat before ending with a self-satisfied purr. Sweat poured off the dancers' brows; linking their arms around each other's shoulders they moved off like a football team.

From the stage, Laszlo flashed a brief smile my way then began to pack up his fish skin-topped darabukka. We heard laughter all around us as we made our way into the nearly silent, dark street. He apologized for not being able to take me home, and we walked together toward Sixth Avenue where he traveled to Brooklyn and I to the Bronx.

My mind was alert on the long ride. I walked homeward along Townsend Avenue at an hour later than I had ever seen it, the moon obliquely visible above, while at every side I heard the throbbing of the clarinet, the snapping and thumping of the darabukka. My eyes followed the halay, stretching endlessly before me.

Entering our second-story apartment with my key, I found my father at the kitchen table, reading *Der Tog*. He raised his eyebrows as our eyes met, but he was silent. I smiled sheepishly and strode into my room. I knew I would follow that halay wherever it led.

Chapter 4

▝▝▝

Balkan Phonograph I

Child of the Makam

"The makam is our mother and we are her children."

—Uyghur proverb

AN AFTERNOON IN spring, 1964. Along both sides of Eighth Avenue in Manhattan brightly painted signs and neon lights announce the nightclubs of the Levant—"The Egyptian Gardens," "Club Istanbul," and others. During these weekday afternoons the overweight club owners wear distracted looks, drinking coffee and smoking cigarettes while they await the first real customers of the evening.

The din of the traffic along Eighth Avenue barely penetrates the sleepy seclusion of 29th Street. Among the low buildings, one of the many narrow shop entrances bears the sign "Balkan Phonograph Company: Turkish, Greek, Armenian, Albanian, Romanian and Spanish-Oriental Recordings." Upon entering the long, narrow shop, one is fixed by the gaze of the Caterpillar from *Alice's Adventures in Wonderland*. But he is not seated on a tall mushroom, nor does he put forth direct questions like "Who are you?" He stands behind the counter, without a hookah. He has a huge bald head, whose rotundity seems to become rather broader toward the top. He is tall and his overall shape of a somewhat elongated egg is clothed in a dark, three-piece suit, faded and passably clean, but he wears no tie. It is impossible to estimate his age; he might be somewhere near seventy.

What he says to you will depend upon what language you speak. He himself is fluent in all the languages mentioned on his sign plus Bulgarian and

Serbian. However, English, a language that he first encountered forty years ago when he immigrated to America, still lies rather heavy on his tongue.

A long wooden bench, almost a church pew runs the length of the wall. I notice that sitting there is a white-haired figure wearing a gray suit. He is slumped over, his hands clasped together. When he looks up, his eyes seem clouded behind his thick glasses, yet they look kind and welcoming.

So many years have passed since I first entered that shop. I cannot recall the first words that were spoken to me there. But after that first encounter, and throughout my teenage years, my way through Manhattan frequently drew me toward 29th Street where I would settle into a corner of the shop and browse. I made occasional purchases, mainly of the oldest 78 RPM recordings, but it soon emerged that my true function was less as a customer than as a student. Topics were not difficult to find, but language did present some problems. The old man on the bench was more comfortable with English than was the owner. I discovered him to be a fiddler from one of the Greek Islands. He spoke fewer languages than the owner, but perhaps for that reason was able to focus somewhat more on English.

Our host the Caterpillar bore the Turkish name Aydın Aslan, but his exotic surname, Leskoviku, revealed him to be an Albanian. He himself had been born into a family of professional musicians in Istanbul. He was a modest performer on the Turkish lute *oud*, but his relatives had been formidable musicians in the style of Southern Albania. The First World War had sent Aydın into service in the northern Balkans, and at the end of the war he had found himself in my father's homeland, Bessarabia, or as it is called now, Moldova. Rather than return home he had moved to the Romanian capital Bucharest and settled down on Strada Armeneasca, the Armenian Street, which was then home to many musicians from Greece and Albania. After several years in Romania, he decided to transplant himself even further and immigrated to New York. There he became an entrepreneur, arranging performances and recordings for his own company, Balkan Phonograph. He cornered the market for south Balkan and Anatolian music, which was not inconsiderable at that time. Although this was the 1960s, he still dealt almost exclusively in 78 RPM recordings and LP reissues of the same. Sound fidelity was of little interest to him, and his reissues often emitted loud hissing noises. Among his most popular (and best recorded) reissues was an LP of older recordings of the renowned Sephardic female singer Roza Eskenazi (1895–1980) who had left Istanbul with her family for Greece, traveled widely including in America, before finally returning to Greece for most of her life. On the cover of the record, one could see a marvelously cluttered middle-class Turkish living room with musicians playing Turkish instruments like the oud, *kanun*, and *kemençe* as well as clarinet and violin. Many years later I came to recognize the faces of the Roma clarinetist Şükrü Tunar (1907–1962) and the Greek kemençe virtuoso, Lambros, but at that time I could only remark on the instruments. A bright-eyed woman wearing a kerchief played the percussive wooden spoons. In the center stood a plump, late-middle-aged woman with tightly curled black hair—Roza Eskenazi—and near her, a microphone stand. At her side stood the producer, Aydın Aslan.

The Albanian ensemble of Aydın's uncle Selim emitted far stranger sounds. On first hearing them I thought that Aydın had found a way to record music backward. Selim's phrases on the clarinet (whose mouthpiece seemed to be somewhere in his throat) made sense only when listened to in reverse. When the singers entered, my confusion increased. The accompanying voices seemed to be trying to divert the melody from its direction by flinging unforeseen obstacles at the lead singer. I did not share these observations with Aydın but waited for time to enlighten me. It did. I had fewer problems with the single-voiced songs. Aydın would patiently explain the rhythms to me, using a code for long and short beats based on striking the fingers and heel of his fist on the counter or table.

One day the fiddler introduced himself. His given name was Nikita, "like Nikita Khrushchev," he quipped. Evidently this was a Cold War witticism used by Eastern Orthodox immigrants in the post-McCarthy era. He wrote his surname Tsompanides, but on the Greek island where he was born under Turkish rule, he had written it Chobanoghlu. He had learned to read Turkish in the old Arabic script and he was able to guide me through the labels of some of the oldest recordings in the shop. In the back room of the store, Aydın kept an old phonograph on which he could play 78 RPM discs. Nikita would beckon me into the dark, windowless back room, carefully holding a brittle old record. As we listened to the sounds of voices and exotic instruments, he would explain the musical system underlying these sounds. This system was called *makam*, he explained. I could understand that it was literally the Arabic equivalent of our Hebrew word for place, which was *maqom*. All music used makams, but only musicians who had been educated in the system were aware of it. Sometimes he put on old recordings of Greek folk music, and he explained which makams the musicians were using. At times we listened to very rural sounding pieces, and he said: "This is a makam without a name. In the country musicians play it, but they have no name for it."

Sometimes Nikita put on recordings of dance music. Several of these were called *zeybek*, and he related that these were dances of the Turkish and Greek people who had lived near the coast of Asia Minor, across from the island of his birth. He would raise his arms and execute a slow, intricate pattern of steps that were built on an uneven number of beats. We heard many different recordings by both Turks and Greeks, but he insisted that I should hear the musicians from the city of Smyrna/Izmir near the Aegean coast who really understood how these tunes should be played. He was rather scornful of musicians born on the Greek mainland who tried to play these tunes. He showed me examples of recordings of these different styles and gradually I came to see what he was referring to. Nikita's was a critical mind, and it elicited a critical response in mine.

Makam was not entirely new to me. This was what the cantors and community sang in the Sephardic synagogue in my neighborhood in the Bronx. What was most new to me on these old recordings were the instruments and the dazzling quality of many of the vocal performances, which were far beyond what I had heard at the synagogue.

One day my visit coincided with lunch break at the store. Aydın and Nikita never ate lunch out. I saw Aydın disappear into the back room and then I heard the sound of water boiling. After a little while he emerged with plates of spaghetti and tomato sauce, the bottom-line meal of working-class Greek America, without the feta cheese and olives that I would have expected at a restaurant. After our little meal, Aydın carried an oversized ancient disc into the back room, while Nikita cleared away the dishes. Aydın held up the disc like a sacred relic, anxious not to damage it or touch it with his not very clean hands. In order to view it better I followed him into the back room, where I could read the label of the oversized disc. The recording company was named "Pharos," and the label showed a drawing of a lighthouse sending its beams over the sea. The label was circumscribed by elegant Arabic script, and the same Turkish words in an orthography that I surmised must be French. The singer was not a Turk, however, but a Greek. He sang only in Turkish with a rich, full-throated voice whose pulsating vibrato was not really like anything I had heard before. I imagined his hair must have been as curly as his rapidly undulating voice. The accompaniment on the violin and the oud was rhythmically full and syncopated. Combined with the singer's clear and vibrant voice, the whole conveyed an image of stylish young men enjoying rakish nights in seaside tavernas.

Other recordings featured young Turkish male voices, hardly to be distinguished from the female timbre. Their songs were usually simple and voluptuous. Aydin would explain the rather artless words, which seemed always to be addressed to male beauties of roughly my age and seemed to request favors in none too delicate terms; one song was addressed to a butcher boy. Try as I might to penetrate this imagery, it remained totally opaque. Later, as I read the novels of Nikos Kazantzakis, I understood this to be the voice of the pasha's young plaything, little Yusufaki, who sang "World and dream are one, aman aman."

Meanwhile, I was amassing a collection of these antiques. I was encouraged in this by my Bessarabian father who enjoyed both Greek and Turkish music. Aydın was also able to sell me a series of "Cristea's Romanian Records" which were evidently recorded in Bucharest but produced in Detroit. They featured well-known Romanian Gypsy singers and musicians performing Gypsy songs whose passion seemed to explode from the discs. The frenetic tempos were exhausting even for one as young as I—they were much too taxing for my arthritic father, who seemed to feel tired just listening, much less trying to dance a *sîrba* to them. The violins shrieked in the shrillest tones, and the female and male singers employed vocal timbres that seemed as ritualized as those in a Japanese theatrical performance. The token Romanian that I had learned in order to honor my father put me in the good graces of Aydın, who nurtured fond memories of that country which my father had left and which I had never seen. Aydın encouraged me by frequently addressing me in Romanian, a language which he had spoken rarely for decades, and which I understood very partially. However, Nikita would laugh at times, saying, "My son not Greek, and you not Romanian." Nevertheless, Aydın persisted in his linguistic irredentism.

After almost two years, Aydın seemed to have thought that I might be ready to be initiated into a higher level of music. One day he reached under the glass counter and pulled out some ancient sheet music whose titles were written in a florid Arabic script. He read out for me, "Tanburi Djemil Bey." Aydin looked up solemnly and announced, "Turkish Beethoven!" From one of the shelves on the back wall he gently coaxed out a fragile 78 RPM disc. It was enveloped in its original brown-paper covering, through whose central disc-shaped cutout I viewed a label which was more elaborate than any I had hitherto seen. Ribbons of Ottoman calligraphy displayed their curving scimitars and staring eyes. These were translated below into smaller French writing, which explained the nature of the musical items being performed and named the performer. On the outer ring the businesslike Latin script announced the "Blumenthal Record and Talking Machine Company," and in the center "Orpheon Records." A clearly reproduced portrait photo was placed in a cameo amid this flood of commercial and musical information. From this cameo I met the sharp gaze of a thin, ascetic, yet handsome face emerging from a high formal collar and cravat, topped by an Ottoman fez. I accompanied Aydın to the back room as he placed this object on the turntable. After the initial rough bumps and scratches, a voice blurted out: "Orfeon Recooords," and then some incomprehensible Turkish in which I could make out the name of Tanburi Djemil Bey (Cemil Bey).

This record was older than anything that I had heard before, and at first I was blanketed by a sound like a heavy rainfall. From the midst of the downpour, I could distinguish a deep-voiced bowed instrument, apparently a cello. The bow drew out a slow, lugubrious, and meditative melody which reminded me of the elegiac prayers from the Sephardic High Holy Days. It was the most beautiful musical performance I had ever heard. On the reverse side the performer switched to a resonant, lute-like instrument, which lacked the rosewater sweetness of the familiar oud. Its sounds seemed not to be produced by the mere contact of plectrum and string; rather they were drawn down from another, unearthly realm. Despite the primitiveness of the recording, I could hear the sound of metallic strings and an ethereal aura surrounding the entire instrument.

Aydın said this was the *tanbûr*. No, he did not have one nor did he know of anyone who played it in this country. Much later, in Istanbul, I learned that the best musicians spent years listening to and imitating every phrase and nuance of these old records of Cemil. Indeed, Cemil's only son, Mesut Cemil Bey (1902–1963), had no recourse but to absorb his father's style through repeated listening to these recordings following his father's early death in 1916.

Some months later on a summer afternoon, an old man and two young men entered the shop, chattering loudly in Greek. Immediately the store was filled with sibilantine Hellenic speech as Aydın and Nikita joined into an enthusiastic conversation. They sat down and the old man opened a violin case in which he had stored two diminutive fiddles of an exotic type. They were pear-shaped and lighter-colored than violins. He pulled out one fiddle, set it on his knee, and drew the bow across it horizontally. His fingernails touched the sides of the metal strings, and he started to play a lively dance tune. After several minutes he looked up and sang out a few words in Greek. At once everyone was wreathed in smiles. He lowered his head and returned to the dance tune. Then he raised his head again and half sang, half spoke two more lines with the same rhythmic cadence as the previous ones. This time his listeners burst out laughing. The old fiddler continued this pattern until one of the young men who had been seated cross-legged at his feet, reached up, threw his arms around his neck, and kissed him on the cheek. Although I could understand not a word of what was being sung, I was enveloped in a new sequence of time, as the rhythmic excitement of the dance alternated with a musical and verbal stimulus provoking the audience in an anarchic, unpredictable manner. I gazed on in amazement and delight, totally forgetting my linguistic isolation.

After the music ended, we all drank Turkish coffee, and when the musician and his friends had made their departure Aydın pointed to an old photograph stuck under the glass counter. I saw a young man wearing a dark cap and a large dark cape, holding the same small fiddle. He was looking downward toward the little instrument that he bowed on his upraised knee. Aydin uttered the name "Kriti," Crete, an island I had read about in illustrated books on archaeology. The name also seemed to be reflected in the biblical "Pleiti ve Kreiti," the foreign troops used as bodyguards by King David. I was not surprised to learn that this was the music of these fierce mercenaries.

Then Aydın reached for an old recording, this time bearing his own "Balkan Phonograph" label. When he put it on the turntable, I heard the same tune that the old man had just played, this time accompanied by an oud and an hourglass drum. A young, bright male voice rang out, quite unlike the old voice I had just heard. When it was over Aydın picked up the disc and said: "That him and me, thirty-five years ago." Smiling, he handed me the disc. "For you, young man."

One day, the music moved closer to home than King David's bodyguards. Nikita showed me a group of very old discs whose Greek labels displayed a martial-looking man sporting a pleated white skirt and a short fez with a long tassel. This was Greek mountain music, in makams without any names. There was one singer and two instruments—a clarinet and a many-stringed dulcimer called the *santouri*. At the Club Khayyam in the East Village, I had seen the Iranian musician Nasser playing what he called a *santur*, and this seemed like a less-delicate relative. The singer's voice sounded wild, almost inebriated as befitted these songs about bandits and warriors. The clarinet had nothing of the silken tone of the Turkish style, nor the full-throated wail used by Greek and Armenian musicians in New York. Rather, this was a short, closed, cackling sound, expressing fast and staccato rhythms. I questioned Nikita and he replied:

"This really Greek music. Dance called *tsamiko*. Should be high off the ground, legs in air, and very fast. Not like you see here, slow, like belly dance. Must be fast, like in Romania."

"Had you seen much Romanian dancing?" I asked him.

"Not now, but many years ago, when I first come from Greece. I play many Romanian weddings. Jewish Romanian. They like Greek music. You know 'Di Greene Kuzine'?"

Nikita began to sing a famous Yiddish theater song, without the words but very accurately.

"There was one clarinetist, the best. I think must be Romanian. His name Pantuli, or Fanduri, or Naptuli, or something like that. He was wild. Play like fire, like crazy man. Always get into trouble because of the woman. But then he pick up his clarinet, and nobody mad no more."

All this sounded hard to believe, and I could not imagine how playing the clarinet could save one from a jealous husband or brother. But this must have been one of the mysteries of "That Time," which I had been born too late to witness. I was very young, and Nikita did not care to explain.

These words of Nikita's were my first introduction to the Galician klezmer clarinetist Naftule Brandwein (1884–1963), whose music would become so important in my life a decade or so later.

Chapter 5

♣♣♣

Greek Town

"BALKAN PHONOGRAPH" FURNISHED the sober, daytime face of Greek Town. Its nighttime face was the labyrinth of nightclubs lying in wait on every corner of Eighth Avenue and the upper 20s. I came to know both of these faces at the same time, with only some vague descriptions from Pyrrhus as my map. While Laszlo and Nasser had been my guides to the Armenian world of Harout's, no one filled that role in Greek Town. I sensed the reason why my older friends could feel at home at Harout's or at the Club Khayyam, but not in the "Istanbul," the "Port Said," or the "Egyptian Gardens." These Greek-owned nightclubs were commercial ventures whose central attraction were the bodies of the belly dancers; music and social conviviality were secondary. At the mention of one of these clubs, Pyrrhus and his brother Phillip would roll their eyes heavenward. Somehow, the austere musical world of Aydın and Nikita could only exist in symbiosis with these dens of iniquity. For my part, this blatant sexuality was not unwelcome titillation for my adolescent mind; the most serious transgression was the earsplitting volume of the mostly mediocre musical fare. But for my elders, the sexual charm had worn off long ago, and all they heard was the noise.

I had dropped in on one or another club with friends from high school, but all were soon repelled by the noise and the sleaze. Occasionally I would arrive just before showtime, carrying my ceramic *darabukka* in its case, hoping to be allowed to play on stage with the band. This approach had the best chance of success at the Club Istanbul, as its music seemed less prearranged than the other clubs. At times, after sitting quietly in a corner, I succeeded in making eye contact and entering into conversation with the owner or with one or another of the barely Anglophone musicians. And from time to time, depending on the musical cast of characters seated on stage, I would be allowed to sit next to one of the guitarists, especially during the belly dancers' shows, when there was a need for percussion. It was a rule of some Greek American nightclub owners never to waste a penny on a professional drummer since percussion held a minor role in Greek music. Of course, the music for the belly dancing was not Greek, but Turkish and Arabian, still they rarely granted any exceptions. However, there were occasions when one or more of the musicians, seeing a darabukka player willing to sit in, would argue to allow me to come on up. Their point, expressed mainly in Greek, with the odd English phrase thrown in, seemed to be since the owner would not hire a drummer, why not let this young boy have some practice and train him to follow the show?

Once I had established myself after a fashion at the Club Istanbul, I rarely ventured to Port Said or the Egyptian Gardens, although the music at the latter was probably the best on Eighth Avenue at that time. I regret not having listened more often to the *oud* playing of the talented, old Sephardic musician Louis Matalon, known as "Louie." Occasionally, first-rate players from abroad visited Club Istanbul; I recall the *bouzoukee* of Iordanis Tsomides, the Epirote clarinet of Phillip Rountas, and the Gypsy clarinet of Safvet Gündegör, but the weekday band was rather lackluster. Even at their worst, however, all of them were professional and competent on their instruments—notes were clear and tempos sharp. So, every couple of weeks, usually on a weekday, I would enter the sparsely populated club. On stage, the rows of musicians stared out at me like an icon depicting sinners on their way to Hell, that I had seen on the walls of the Greek Orthodox church in Washington Heights. Eyes bulging, foreheads creased, some with mouths distended in song, they seemed to cry out against the terrible fate soon to befall them. It took courage to listen to them, let alone to seat myself amid this chorus of the damned.

Weekends were more cheerful and chaotic. You could never predict who might enter the club: a group of celebratory Lebanese; a table of Syrian Jews from Brooklyn; Armenians from across town; or best of all, a troupe of Greek sailors, fresh off their ships for the weekend. These were a revelation to me. I could not really count them among the human race, they seemed to be a distantly related species, perhaps some form of large aquatic life, dancing dolphins or sharks. Their faces were unlike any others, their dancing unlike any I had seen. The sailors were all uniformly drunk even before entering the club, their eyes far away, they seemed incapable of conversation, even among themselves. And yet they never argued, never shouted. They started no brawls and broke no dishes. They had come to drink and to dance. Whenever such a group arrived, the musicians would leave off their insipid, lazily romantic bouzoukee songs—the kind that had replaced *reimbetiko*—and strike up Greek dance music, especially the martial *tsamiko*, the erotic *tsifte-telli*, and the mystical *zeimbekiko*.

For the first couple of years, I never dared play my drum for these sailors—my role was to watch and to learn. Each of these dances represented another mood of Greek manhood; what they had in common was the unrelenting energy of the sailors. Later on, I saw these dances performed in different ways by old men or by younger Greek Americans. Nikita had taught me his Old World zeimbekiko and tsamiko, but the sailors danced with an energy that was inimitable whether by Greek or barbarian. They all seemed to have lived only for this moment—their every movement was precise and full of meaning. The groups of sailors were never large—between four and ten men—and the dance floor was not wide enough to allow the tsamiko to present its full spatial character, which I would see only years later. In the club, the tsamiko became a fairly intimate ritual, centering on the relation of the leader and his second dancer, who supported him with his handkerchief as he leapt and somersaulted in place. The quick, three-quarter pace of the music kept the dancers off the ground—ideally the whole line was bouncing on the balls of their feet, their arms held high in victory, until the leader began to go into orbit. At that point he was accompanied in his celestial voyage by the solo playing of the clarinet, quickly gliding up a Jewish-sounding scale until he reached a rather high stopping point; then he opened the door of another mode, flattening notes, losing the rhythm, swimming in a Milky Way of slurs and cackles flowing from the horn of his instrument. Always seated close to the stage, I stared spellbound, watching the dancers' every move.

The tsifte-telli called for a different mood, as the music shifted to a rollicking four-four, repeated incessantly by the bouzoukees, while the clarinet wailed seductively, putting the sailors into a kind of trance as they raised their arms, shook, gyrated, and shimmied in place. The dance was usually performed by two men, and I was mystified by the nature of this "couple." I had already seen the *chifte-telli* of the young Armenians, but that was always danced by a heterosexual couple. While the sailors' movements somewhat resembled what I had seen in Harout's, the overall mood did not. Absent were the humor and seductiveness, or the elegant pathos of the Armenian couples. In their place was an utterly strange, almost

Dionysiac frenzy, which might permit one young sailor to leap between the legs of the other so that he continued to dance horizontally, swaying his arms while he was held tight by the other man's legs. At times a sailor danced solo, his hips and whole body swaying in place, as though he would drill himself into the feminine earth. I could only gaze on in wonderment and a little fear.

Nothing could prepare me for the zeimbekiko, a dance of pride, warfare, or else meditation and loneliness. I came to distinguish these moods as almost different dances, depending upon the mode of the music, its tempo and the breakup of its rhythm. Zeimbekikos were danced either by two men facing one another or by a lone soloist. There was the triumphant, hopping zeimbekiko, danced to a moderately quick tempo, its music in major, minor, or a mixture of the two modes. The rhythm and mood encouraged the dancers or dancer to hop, alternating between erect posture, arms raised, fingers snapping, or else bending low, slapping his foot raised high before him, or striking the ground with his palm. Unlike the old style zeimbekiko, really the Turkish *zeybek* taught me by Nikita, this Greek dance had no fixed steps, just an endlessly variable repertoire of movements on and off the floor. The dancers might permit themselves occasionally to smile, not a common facial expression for these Greek sailors.

The martial zeimbekiko was somewhat slower and seemed to use Turkish modes. In time I came to recognize *makams* like Hicaz and Saba. The dancing was closer to the old Turkish pattern, but it still avoided the fixed steps, featuring improvised dragging of feet while the dancers leaned forward and faced one another. These patterns required two dancers. Sometimes one of them stood almost still, his arms raised, while his opponent crouched low, sweeping his right hand before him as though slicing the air with an invisible *yataghan*.

And then there was the solo dance-meditation, almost always danced to a species of very slow songs in Greek, each section of which seemed like discrete units held together by little instrumental breaks in between the verses. This was always a solo performance. Perhaps performance is not the most appropriate word to describe it, because the dancer seemed to dance for himself alone, oblivious to anything around him. This zeimbekiko was a series of little dances, or movements, in some of which the dancer appeared almost drunk as he swayed from side to side, in others he was lost in thought, brooding on some hidden sorrow, while later he might break out of his mood, pounding the floor with his palm, leaping high in the air, even falling to his knees, while his back bent far behind, his shoulders touching the ground. These large movements might sound exhibitionistic, but the dancer always executed them as though he were alone, expressing his feelings in order to clarify some internal emotional process, not to impress an audience.

The music for the zeimbekiko might be either instrumental or vocal and had a varied character—the only thing that seemed to group these tunes together was their rhythm, always one of a small series totaling nine beats. I must have looked on, drinking in the dance for well over a year, until I sensed this hidden link uniting every separate expression named zeimbekiko. At that point, I took my query to Laszlo who had no difficulty demonstrating the various rhythmic patterns. On a weekday night, while I was sitting in, whenever the band struck up any zeimbekiko I would try to accompany them, not always successfully. Some of the slower patterns proved elusive, forcing one of the musicians not otherwise engaged, to beat out the rhythm for me on his thigh. It was only some years later, when I was able to study the dance with the Turkish Zeybek mountaineers, inland from Izmir, that I finally gained a better understanding. Back then in the club, I avoided playing zeimbekiko for the sailors where any mistake on my part might spoil their ecstasy—what a heavy responsibility to bear!

I imagine most other customers had not come to watch the sailors—and here I must confess that I also could not ignore the writhing, almost nude female limbs that appeared on the stage at intervals of an hour or so. This was another big difference between the Club Istanbul and Harout's. Although I was only perhaps six months older when I began to frequent Greek Town, my relation to sexuality differed in the Armenian and Greek environments. At Harout's, dancing was always in couples or lines, and the absence of solo performances gave even the couple dancing a less erotic meaning. There were some attractive Armenian young women and girls, but not one of them ever exhibited herself—the chifte-telli always functioned as an erotic dialogue, never a monologue. This dialogue afforded each couple a certain privacy—one could only eavesdrop. It was impossible to focus exclusively on one partner, both because of the constant changes in their spatial positioning and because so much of the communication was a response to a particular bodily statement that even a keen and experienced observer could not always catch from a distance. And so, nothing I saw at Harout's struck me as truly erotic. In Greek Town I could not relate and empathize with most of the belly dancers, but there was no doubt that their sexuality was directed toward me as much as to any male in the audience, and this carnal assault triggered a reaction that I had already begun to experience for several years previously, first of all in art school.

I was eleven years old and had won a scholarship to the Art Students

League on 57th Street in Manhattan, near Carnegie Hall. On my first day my nostrils were assaulted by the acrid smell, almost a taste of turpentine and acrylic paints. I walked down the marble hall and opened a heavy door. An elderly male teacher showed me an easel and I unpacked my brushes and paints. I had dressed myself in a rather chic, green, cotton artist's smock my mother had sewn for me. But suddenly my eyes were blinded by a flash of light coming from the center of the large studio—a broad expanse of an almost white color tinged with pink was shimmering, attracting my attention. Instinctively I cast my eyes down. My second reaction—why doesn't someone give a coat or a towel to cover up this poor naked woman? Could she have been surprised in her bath? Finally, I understood. We were allowed to look. In fact, we were supposed to look, that is why we were there. Slowly I raised my eyes. I looked at her calmly. She was a tall, long-limbed, rather pretty, youngish woman with long blonde hair. Her breasts were a moderate size but well formed with large red nipples. So, this was it—this will be mine. My long look, my proprietorial gaze, changed everything. Perhaps it came too soon.

And now, as the belly dancer writhed and shimmied, I raised my head, opened my eyes wide, and looked out calmly. If she would stay a little more still, I knew I could paint her—anything else was too disturbing, and at age fourteen, still unimaginable for me. Something was upsetting me, but I could hardly identify it. Only in one case could I connect something like erotic yearning with a particular body and face—she was called "Beba."

Beba may have been the oldest dancer at the club—I could estimate now that she was no younger than forty. But none of the dancers in their twenties could compare with her. On weekend nights at the Club Istanbul, Beba sat majestically on a chair at the front of the stage. Already in her costume, she invariably sat with her legs folded, swinging her crossed legs in time to the music, perhaps also tapping her little brass finger cymbals. She was tall, with long and beautifully sculpted legs and feet, and she sat with a relaxed and dignified posture. Her dark hair was long and a little thin—a suggestion of her age—and her roundish face was formed by strong cheekbones. Her lips were large and her mouth none too delicate. Her large and beautiful eyes were usually shielded by dark glasses. At that time all the dancers were Greek—I could never follow a word of their conversation. They usually scurried about looking preoccupied, but nothing could ruffle Beba's serenity, which did not seem particularly open or good-natured, simply unconcerned and proud.

And then she would dance. Finally, to see Beba without her dark glasses as she raised her arms in the air, finger cymbals clacking out the chifte-telli, her black eyes fixed on the ground, for if she ever were to raise them not many men there could have withstood their accusations. But the split-second glimpses she did shoot out sufficed to convey her angry mood, and a sexuality boundless as the ocean, although she was somehow tired and listless, perhaps hinting that not now, but later, she might be ignited again. The best moment came when she hurled herself to her knees, leaning backward until she could pound out the slow, seductive rhythm on the floor with her cymbals. Then her stomach would tighten; beautiful muscles glistened with sweat in the spotlight. Her face invisible—she had surrendered her personality so we could contemplate the animal underpinnings of her female sexual being. Each time I saw this performance it was too much to bear. When it ended, I was exhausted—could Beba have known that a fourteen-year-old boy in the front row was as drained as she was? And utterly confused.

I could never have imagined that five years later, Beba and I would be neighbors on the Upper West Side of Manhattan! I had moved into a studio apartment on Riverside Drive at 80th Street, while she lived on 72nd Street and West End Avenue. Prior to my first trip to Turkey in 1969, I had stopped by the Club Istanbul to announce my plans to the few people with whom I chatted there, Beba among them. Immediately she offered to take me out for coffee to celebrate my upcoming trip. When we finally met at a Greek coffeeshop at 72nd Street, she was full of smiles and laughter at my impending journey to the real Istanbul. She was also impressed that I had already learned some Turkish. She was sure that I would enjoy myself and come back with much knowledge.

Chapter 6

⫴

Journey to Byzantium
in Washington Heights

THE GREEKS WERE also offering me an antidote to the sweet poison of the nightclubs and quite a separate social route led me to the other pole of Greek American life—to the austere yet sensual music and painting of the Greek Orthodox Church. There I found a powerful aesthetic substitute for the raw sexuality of the clubs. My interest had been piqued by my visits to my mentor Pyrrhus when I had noticed the icons adorning several walls and corners of his bedroom, along with his Ottoman calligraphed ceramic plates and ornamental *yataghans*. It was there that I had first listened to recordings of Greek and Syrian Orthodox cantors. Yet despite my host's deep appreciation for the chant, his knowledge of theological doctrine, and general sympathy for the church, I sensed that he was a spiritual but not a religiously involved man. I had grown up among religious people and I was not yet comfortable with the aestheticization of religion that such a mature intellectual represented. My opportunity to experience the Greek Orthodox Church as a living organism came not through my ethnic and musical circles but, unexpectedly, through my high school.

I was in my first year at the High School of Music and Art—which was then an institution of unbridled fantasy. In accordance with some bureaucratic custom, all private parochial schools ended one year earlier than New York City's public schools. And so, the first-year entering class of Music and Art always had a large percentage of graduates of religious schools, Jewish Talmud Torahs, or yeshivas, but also from the Protestant, Catholic, and Orthodox Christian schools. I was not unhappy with this arrangement because the presence of these children from other parochial schools cushioned the shock of being thrown suddenly into a totally secular environment. The first class had a fair number of children from wealthy backgrounds—mostly Jews and some Protestants—coming in from their secular private schools. Then there was an odd assortment of Roman Catholics—Hispanics, Italians, Irish, Poles (or various mixtures of these last three ethnicities), and the odd African American. There were also a few West Indian Protestants, some Greeks, one or two Armenians.

My neighbor in homeroom was a very handsome boy with chocolate-colored skin who invariably spent his free time reading books with titles like *Christian Liturgy*. At that time, I was plowing my way through Abraham Idelsohn's *Jewish Liturgy and Its Development*, so I could figure out at last why I had been repeating those particular prayers all those years. One day we turned toward each other, looked at the covers of our respective books, and burst out laughing—we seemed like mirror images! This led to a long friendship. Tony Yearwood had come in from a Lutheran school in the Bronx, where he had been brought up among Swedes and Germans. He had inherited his religion from a German ancestor who had settled on the West Indian island of Barbados, where his father had been born. The apparent malleability of culture and race that had led to his own ancestral and personal environment left him with a curiosity about Europe and the variety of its religious legacies. Although his mother came from a deeply religious Southern family, this branch of Christianity was less appealing to him.

By the middle of our stay in high school I began to notice a change in Tony's reading matter. Lutheranism disappeared entirely and was replaced by tomes by Gregory of Nazianzus and John Chrysostom, or general works on the mysticism of the Orthodox Church. Tony had crossed the Elbe and was journeying to Byzantium. One day he confessed to me that he was contemplating conversion to Eastern Orthodoxy. I began to see him often in the company of the principal instrument of this change in religious outlook—a short blond boy with large blue eyes set in a head shaped like a thinner version of Aydın's egg. Sure enough, like Pyrrhus, Christopher Kosma was the son of an Albanian-speaking Epirote family—in New York that meant that he attended a Greek church. Chris turned out to be very bright and talkative; Tony informed me that he was a fine religious painter as well. I discovered the truth of this claim one fall day as the three of us made one of our frequent pilgrimages to the Met Cloisters, the medieval museum in Fort Tryon Park in Upper Manhattan. While we lounged on the stone walls of the park, Chris opened a satchel and pulled out a carefully wrapped package. When he unwrapped it I saw a painting on wood, an icon depicting the Virgin Mary, her hair covered by a dark blue cowl, and holding the baby Jesus in her arms. The lines were elegant and the colors vibrant—I liked it immediately. I expressed my admiration to him. Chris then invited me to visit his church for a Sunday service—I could see several respectable modern icons and frescos and a few older icons. He knew I liked Turkish and Sephardic music, and he suggested some of the modes and melodies might seem somewhat familiar to me. This invitation had no hint of religious proselytizing—Christopher was a technician of the sacred, reaching out to a potential colleague.

I was accustomed to visiting Roman Catholic and High Protestant churches to observe the architecture and religious paintings, but for the most part I found the pale derivation of the Italian Baroque and the attempts at Gothic Revival not very compelling. I also noted that Gothic marked Catholicism in the United States, but when I visited my mother's family in Montreal, the Catholic churches were more likely to be in the Baroque style. Indeed, the symbol of Quebec Catholicism, the Shrine of Saint Joseph on the Mountain, was built in the grandest Italianate manner. In New York, Tony had taken me to many Baroque concerts held at Anglican and Lutheran churches, and these were wonderful. But I did not attend Protestant church services. The walls, arches, and stained glass windows did not seem to come from a living religious community but from a priestly bureaucracy or from an aesthetic nostalgia. I was contemplating something dead. In both cases my still active religious instincts warned me to stay away.

Saint Spyridon's Greek Orthodox Church in Washington Heights, however, was a church unlike any other I had entered. My first visit was for a Sunday Mass, which offered me plenty of priestly bureaucracy, but the community seemed equally strong. These Greek men and women were no passive Roman Catholic flock—at times they were so obstreperous they appeared ready to conduct the service themselves. The atmosphere lacked the self-absorption of the Orthodox Ashkenazic *shtibls* I had known and had more of the cheer of the Levantine Sephardic synagogue. Physically the congregation resembled the Sephardim somewhat, except they were usually not as handsome—their faces were often asymmetrical and their complexion oily and uneven. And for all their noise they were not as free as the Levantine Jews; they seemed to chafe under the watchful eyes of the priests. On the other hand, the Greek women were much more prominent than those at the Sephardi service. The Jewish service was still basically an affair of the men. Here it looked almost like a contest between the male priests and cantors and the pious, female congregants—the husbands were caught in the middle. But through all this competition my senses were caressed by the almost continuous singing of the cantors, the *psaltes*, usually one powerful leader and two alternating drones—the *ison*. This was the finest cantorial singing I had yet heard in person—they made both our Ashkenazi and Sephardi prayer leaders seem like the amateurs they were. These Greek cantors were not leading or representing the prayers of the people, as our precentors did. They were clearly on the side of the priests, reenacting a sacred mystery beyond the ken of the congregation, who were kept behind the barrier of the *iconostasis*.

At the close of the service Christopher emerged, resplendent in the golden robes of an altar boy. He urged me to look around the church and he pointed out the better paintings. Now I could open my eyes again—during the service I was all but oblivious to my physical surroundings. I could see this was a light and airy space, constructed somewhat like a Byzantine building. It was capacious by Greek standards. Some of the frescoes intrigued me, although frequently the colors had a modern, synthetic look. Gone were the fleshy faces of the Italian Baroque paintings; as a rule the saints here had to scowl. Strange lines were incised along the cheeks, under the eyes, and cleaving the foreheads of the saints, prophets, and martyrs. But the congregation must have judged them not too stern to be propitiated because they had hung little sculpted arms, legs, ears, eyes, and hearts over them. As Chris explained, this was to ask the saint to heal the afflicted body part.

From that Sunday on, while hardly a member of the congregation, I was a frequent visitor, coming for occasional Sundays, special feasts and fasts, and of course, for Easter. I even learned the Greek words of the Resurrection Hymn so I could walk with the midnight procession on the street near the church, carrying my lit candle. Chris assured me it was all right. If I did not speak Greek, no one would suspect a thing. The congregation was peppered with the odd Romanian or Serb who had memorized the Greek words just as I had—and I was Romanian, wasn't I? That would be sufficient if anyone were to ask, but no one ever did.

I had never been exposed to a body of music expressing the mystery of the relation between God and man. Our synagogue songs, even our finest hymns and cantorial improvisations, represented the crying out of man for God, of Israel, the most forsaken, abandoned of men who could express the human condition most precisely. But in the Greek church I discovered the music of faith—man had found God and the two were mysteriously united in the personality of Christ. Many of the Byzantine hymns sang magisterially of the exaltation man could attain in partnership with God if only he could surrender his wayward will. But if he would not, this faith might carry a hard edge—the world of man was corrupt, and God would judge it most harshly. Especially in the weeks leading up to Easter the hymns sounded angry, accusatory. While the words, as explained to me by Christopher and Pyrrhus—usually accused the Jews, most intelligent Greeks knew that the fault could not be so simply palmed off on one particular group of men— but was shared by all humanity.

Prior to Easter, these Byzantine hymns lamented humanity's failure, their somber music suggesting darkly that there could be no atonement for the terrible crime of deicide. "Guilty! guilty! guilty!" hissed the bearded chorus of the saints. Over and over this congregation must learn how unworthy they were, how unfit for the life eternal that God offered to the truly good and faithful, to those who could love His son in human form. Perhaps at times I came to understand, even to feel the frustration and despair of those Christians who became eager to vent their anger on those even more guilty than they—on the Jews, the tribe of Judas.

Chapter 7

▥

Limberis

Revelation of the Greek Cimbalom

During the summer of 1971, I made my second trip to the Balkans—Romania and Yugoslavia—and Turkey, this time traveling through Anatolia as far as Erzurum in the north and Diyarbekir in the south. Two years before I had bought a *tsambal* in Romania, and now I thought I would purchase a *santur* by crossing the border from Erzurum into Iran. Before going abroad, I consulted Nasser Rastegar-Nejad (1939–2018), the Iranian santur player whom I had known since those early days in the Club Khayyam. He had taken a daytime job at the admission's office at Columbia University, where he worked while listening to Persian music through his Walkman. I marveled at how swiftly his English had improved—he had become fluent within the past five years. When I visited him at his office, I asked whether I might be able to find a santur in Tabriz, capital of Azerbaijan province, and the first major Iranian city across the border from Turkey. He smiled at my request—imagine going to Iran and stopping only at a Turkish-speaking city! Besides, he knew of no santur maker there, where the instrument was not very popular. But he obliged me by constructing a crude Turkish sentence asking for a santur. As it turned out, however, I never took the bus from Erzurum to Tabriz and so I returned home with no santur.

The week of my return to New York I enrolled for my second year at Columbia graduate school. As I walked through the main campus gate, I almost passed Nasser on his way out toward Broadway. He asked me about my trip to Turkey and whether I had found a santur in Tabriz. On learning that I had not gone there he suggested that I buy his old instrument—the price would be nominal, practically the price of the case alone. So, within a week of my return from Turkey I owned a fine Persian santur.

I loved this instrument and was thrilled to get to know its beautiful sound. Rather than Persian music, I played Anatolian and Caucasian dances on it, as the Armenians had done. Nevertheless, within the year I understood that this santur was not constructed to play Turkish *makams*— it lacked the flexibility in modulation. On both trips to Romania (in 1969 and 1971) I had returned with tsambals, (in Yiddish, *tsimbl*), or *cimbalom*, the East European version of the santur, which the Greeks call *santouri*. My first Romanian tsambal, a factory-made instrument, came with instructions like "Do not leave in the sun" and "Do not expose to the rain." It was capable of producing almost no sound, and I sold it within the year. On this second trip I purchased a homemade tsambal from a young Gypsy. It sounded a lot better, but it would not stay in tune well. Also, I could not adjust the bridges to create microtones, as I could on the Persian instrument.

I presented this problem to Aydın, and he understood immediately. He replied that I could not play the makams perfectly on the tsambal, but I could perform them in a somewhat Europeanized manner, something like the Greeks did on their santouri. After all, he judged, I was neither a Turk nor an Armenian, so why shouldn't I play Turkish music in this Balkan fashion? He would help me with the makams, and for the santouri there was a friend of his to assist. He produced a piece of paper and wrote out the phone number of Paul Limberis, a Greek santouri player from one of the islands, who played both the santouri and the large concert cimbalom. Armed with the number, I called Mr. Limberis that week. An elderly Greek voice answered, speaking English rather like Nikita had done. Aydın's name proved to be an adequate introduction, and I was invited out to Queens that very weekend.

Saturday, a breezy day full of sunshine in early spring, clouds scampering swiftly across a blue sky. I emerged from the subway in a section of northern Astoria that I had never seen before. Unlike Pyrrhus's cramped and box-like neighborhood, the houses here were very low, and the streets wide and green. There were none of the symbols of Greek America so evident in Manhattan's Greek Town, with its pseudo-Hellenic pottery and massive crystal chandeliers. Instead, the commercial avenue featured a variety of small shops arranged in a strangely non-American style—handmade signs in Greek announced olives and feta cheese stored in large barrels. I had not yet been to Greece, but I sensed that a small Greek city's commercial street had been reassembled in Queens.

I walked several blocks to an apartment house resembling Pyrrhus's in lower Astoria. But the man who greeted me was no eccentric intellectual in a Manchurian cap, like Pyrrhus, nor a working-class type in a crumpled, open white shirt, like Nikita. Pavlo (or Paul) Limberis stood before me; a tall, thin, elderly man wearing a tie tucked into a well-pressed and starched white shirt. His dark slacks were neat and trim. His long face seemed as much European as Greek but without any striking features, except for the usual shock of white hair. His blue eyes were shielded by wire-rimmed glasses. We shook hands as we exchanged names—I became "Mr. Friedman," retaining that surname throughout our relationship, which remained on a formal basis. Limberis ushered me into his simple two-bedroom apartment, where, in the crowded living room on an upholstered chair near a window facing the avenue, a squat female figure greeted me with a crooked smile exuding distrust. He introduced this plump redhead as his wife. Glancing to my right at their bedroom I noticed a monumental Russian crucifix hanging over the doorway. Mrs. Limberis's face, her figure, and the prominent cross suggested a bedtime purgatory. When the three of us were introduced, Limberis explained that his wife was of Russian origin. Judging from her American working-class accent I did not think it likely that she was from an aristocratic family who had fled the Bolsheviks. After our introductions she trundled off to the kitchen.

Mr. Limberis seated me on a couch from where I could see the object dominating the entire apartment—a Hungarian concert cimbalom, set on four sculptured legs; looking like a grand piano without its top and keyboard. I had never seen such a contraption, but somehow it struck me as constituting an affront to the sensibilities of all the musical instruments of the Eastern Mediterranean, including its little relative, the santouri. Limberis seated himself on the broad cushioned seat near the cimbalom and turned around to face me. He seemed most comfortable in that seat. Mrs. Limberis returned from the kitchen with a tray of Turkish coffee, water, and candies. She sat again near the window and the two of them proceeded to question me about my musical interests. On hearing that I had been studying the *darabukka*, Limberis stood up and opened a closet door where he took out a typical Syrian copper drum. He wondered whether I might want to buy it from him. I declined, explaining that I already owned more or less the identical instrument. When we spoke about Aydın, both of them laughed, Limberis recalling how often he was drunk at his musical jobs, even before the music began. When they played together for Albanians, Limberis would hold the same chords endlessly while Aydın improvised on the clarinet. He said the Albanians loved this sort of music, but for the santouri there was almost nothing to do. I tried to visualize Aydın in this unaccustomed role, musical, passionate, and intoxicated. Perhaps he relied on alcohol to reach that emotional abandon so absent from his everyday dealings at his shop.

Limberis then asked me if I had ever heard the concert cimbalom. When I replied that I had heard it only on recordings from Hungary and Romania, he laughed, saying the sound of this instrument could never be captured on a recording. He rose and went again to the closet, this time removing a box containing a reel-to-reel tape. He told me someone had recorded it almost twenty years ago, so that there might be a document of how he played. But, lacking a playback machine, Limberis was now unable to hear it. His wife added that Paul's heart was weak, so he should not play much music anymore. For my part I had never heard this medical theory, and looking at their two shapes I reckoned that she was probably in more imminent danger of coronary complications than he was. In fact, he outlived her by several years.

But now Limberis thought it was time for a little musical demonstration. He turned around toward the instrument, lifted his two long, cotton-tipped hammers, and commenced to strike the strings. A series of chords crashed and resounded, only occasionally dampened by the pedals at his feet. Then he stopped while he adjusted a book of notations balanced between the wall and the head of the cimbalom. Suddenly the hammers set up a rhythm of rollicking triplets, and then they flew up to the highest notes on the instrument to carve out a melody, evidently a dance tune, using the peculiar, minor-like scale, its fourth degree alternating as major or minor, held in common by Greek, Romanian, Jewish, and some other musics of Southeast Europe. But the tune itself was almost obscured by the crashing chords and arpeggiated runs that the musician added between the phrases. Limberis's playing was somewhat rigid but still masterful, and when he finished, I applauded loudly. He turned around and explained "that was Bulgarian," pointing to the book from which he had been playing. I stood up, walked over to the instrument, and read *Bulgar*. Then he showed me the book's cover: *Hebrew Wedding Melodies*, Wolf Kostakowsky, Brooklyn, New York, 1916. So, this was the music for the famous bulgar that my father used to dance, first in Bessarabia and then in New York.

When I returned to my seat, Limberis began another tune, whose structure and mood were utterly different from the last. Instead of pulsing triplets and crashing chords, I heard a delicate, sad tune in a Turkish mode, slowly stretched over a broken nine-beat rhythm. I recognized this tune as one of the *zeybeks* from the Aegean coast of Anatolia; it was one of the tunes I had listened to with Nikita. But Paul's rendition was not the old Turkish style Nikita had so much admired. Its jumpy, nervous, rhythmic phrasing announced it as Greek, no longer a Turkish zeybek, but a Greek *zeimbekiko*. Paul turned to me and announced: "Ayvaliatiko, from Ayvali near Smyrna."

I told him how beautiful I thought it was. Then I asked him, in that makam (which I remembered Nikita referring to as "Saba") wasn't the fourth degree supposed to be somehow neither flat nor natural but something in between? Yet I was sure he had played it throughout as a flat. Yes, he admitted, in Turkish music it would be played that way, and even in Greece some violinists and clarinetists played that neutral note. But on the santouri or the *bouzoukee* that note did not exist—there was only the flat or the natural, and the same was true for the cimbalom. In Greece they understood that the tune was in the Saba mode but without that characteristic note. I accepted this explanation but was a little disappointed.

I asked him where in Greece he was from. I learned that Limberis grew up on a small island in the same group of islands where Nikita had been born. It was there on the island of Lesbos that he had learned to play the little santouri from an old musician. He used to carry the instrument slung over his shoulder in a common sack. But, he added, the santouri was such a simple, primitive instrument—it had no pedals, only a few bass notes, and its tone was weak. He had immigrated to America when he was a young man and was already a good santouri player, but when he came to New York he heard Hungarian musicians playing the concert cimbalom, and this experience changed his life. He found a Hungarian musician willing to teach him and within a few years he adopted the cimbalom and ceased playing the santouri entirely. Now he was able to vary his accompaniment more richly than he could have done on the little Greek instrument, and as a result he became much in demand at wealthier Greek weddings and at nightclubs. Paul showed me old photographs, several of them framed, in which he and his concert cimbalom were flanked by a group of prosperous-looking Greek men and women in tuxedos and low-cut evening dresses. It seems he was the only Greek musician in New York who had mastered the Hungarian instrument after the 1930s. He had corned the market, leading a comfortable musician's life. It seemed to me that his dress and comportment were meant to be in keeping with the social demands of a prosperous Greek, upper-middle-class clientele. They still wanted to hear their island syrtos and *zeibekikos*, but played in a more elevated and pompous style, along with a repertoire of the more northerly East European musical cultures that they admired, especially the Romanian, the Hungarian, and the Jewish.

In order to demonstrate the difference between the Hungarian technique he had adopted and the Greek method he had abandoned, Limberis went into the hallway and emerged carrying a canvas-covered trapezoidal object. Setting it on the couch, he removed the cover, revealing a larger version of the tsambal I had brought back from Romania. Reaching into his pile of sticks he picked out a short, dark pair, their bulging, curved heads naked of any cotton wrapping. Rapidly beating the strings, he thumped out a *kalamatiano* dance, alternately playing the melody and the accompaniment. He seemed to be trying to play in a simple, almost perfunctory manner, but his youthful enthusiasm for these tunes came through—he looked younger and utterly carefree.

At that point, Mrs. Limberis came in again with more coffee, indicating that her husband had played enough for one day. After drinking my coffee, I thanked both of them and left.

That season I visited Limberis several times, until my ears became full of the hammering resonance of his glorified Balkan and Jewish dance tunes with their thundering arpeggios, and the tinkling, bittersweet nostalgia for lost Smyrna. As I drank it all in, I learned how he had developed the techniques of these musics, but it seemed to me that he had trodden a path for himself alone. Limberis's music was of a time and place—the New York of my father's time, but not of his place. This was not simply the music of struggling immigrants, but of bourgeois, self-satisfied Greeks who wanted it dignified and prettified. As much as it was a pleasure to hear and watch him, Limberis was at the end of a musical road. I could see no path extending any further. I could not really take up Aydın's offer to teach me the makams using this cimbalom technique as a base. I needed to find the root of this music and not only one large and colorful flower.

Limberis was much more active and healthier than Nikita, but his wife hovered over him, convincing him of his weakness, age, and imminent demise. Every time he struck his cimbalom, he seemed to be recreating a performance of the past or trying to hold onto something soon to be lost. Whenever it seemed as though his music might let out a cry, notes shaping themselves in the here and now, the wife was always there to lay her heavy hand over his, reminding him of his fragility.

I tended to see more of Limberis in the spring and summer. In those seasons the window in the living room was always open, admitting a sharp wind that ruffled the pale curtains so that they seemed like portals to a world beyond. As I looked at the somber Russian crucifix guarding the bedroom, the open window came to appear to me as the gateway to the afterlife, the exit whence the old musician's soul one day would fly like two cimbalom mallets, wrapped in wings of white cotton.

I brought Limberis the little tsambal I had bought from a young Gypsy in Romania, an instrument almost identical to the little santouris from the Greek Islands. He looked at it in amusement, almost chuckling to himself at why anyone in this country would want to play such a crude and feeble instrument. Finally accepting my unaccountable taste, he produced the pair of short sticks he had played with earlier on his own santouri. He demonstrated them on his instrument and on mine, saying that these were the kind of sticks I needed. He sold them to me for ten dollars. They were superbly sculpted, and I play with them on occasion to this day.

By then I was reading the novels of Kazantzakis, and I recalled the many descriptions of Zorba and his santouri. In this passage it is Zorba himself speaking:

> I was twenty. I heard this santouri for the first time at one of my village fetes, over there at the foot of Olympus. It took my breath away. I couldn't eat anything for three days.

But in the New York of our time, who would want to hear the sound of the old santouri, or of the tsambal, an unending roar of hypnotic melody and rhythm, strong and relentless? It was only years later, on my slow path toward Klezmer Island, that I gradually learned to tame this unruly sound and to discover some of the lost secrets of the klezmer *cimbal*. I would struggle with that most elusive of musical styles—that of the klezmer cimbalist.

Chapter 8

⧉

Balkan Phonograph II

The Later Days of Aydın and Nikita

"MARRY HIM! DON'T let him get away!"

Nikita, the old fiddler, uttered these words in Greek, urgently leaning close to her on the bench, his clouded, cataract-covered eyes twinkling behind his thick glasses. Despina's eighteen-year-old, black, almond-shaped eyes tensed in surprise. With Nikita sitting between him and the girl, old Aydın jutted out his bald, egg-shaped head, his usually expressionless blue eyes fixing on those of the voluptuous young woman: "Don't worry that he's a Jew—Jews make the best husbands, better than any Greek you could find."

Sitting at Despina's side, and entirely innocent of Greek, I could not make any sense of the sudden commotion surrounding us. In contrast to her soft, shapely body, Despina's sharp nose jutted forward, lending poignancy to her facial expressions and gesticulations. But now she restrained herself, deferring to whatever was provoking this almost unseemly display of emotion from her elders. I had never seen the two old men so animated.

After drinking a quiet cup of Turkish coffee with them, the two of us walked out into 29th Street. On the way to the subway, I asked her what the commotion had been about. Despina's voice rang out huskily above the traffic: "They wanted me to marry you!"

Then came the translation of the Greek conversation. My eyes lingered over her wide hips, her full breasts, remembering that perhaps it was only my friend, her current beau, who prevented such a transformation of our rather casual friendship. But at eighteen, what was marriage to me? Or to her, rebellious little Greek sprite that she was? But old Nikita and Aydın had been eager to give up one of their own for me. I could not expect greater loyalty. Their enthusiastic recommendation of my marital qualifications confirmed my status in a welcoming way. Not that I had taken Despina along with this in mind—I had thought the place might amuse her.

I had grown over the last three years and my relationship to the Balkan Phonograph shop had changed. I no longer entered the store's narrow passage as though I were partaking of a mystery, a zone where the time of the outside world ceased to flow. Now every detail of the two old men's appearances, the location of each shelf of 78 RPM records, labeled in French, Ottoman, or Greek was known, familiar. I came by rather frequently, perhaps once a month or more, whenever I had some free time in Manhattan. I understood that Nikita saw me as a kind of student, but Aydın's position as the proprietor, coupled with the poverty of his English and his general reticence, made his position toward me less clear. Nikita sometimes punned on my name, calling me "Zeus," in modern Greek pronounced "Zef," while Aydın knew me only as "young man." I rarely brought any of my friends to the shop—what would my classmates from the High School of Music and Art make of this narrow, dusty booth? The shop was part of my own private world, and I felt no need to justify it to my friends who would not have understood it.

The shop was located in the heart of Greek Town, directly west of the old Armenian neighborhood in the East 20s, which still offered employment to many of these players of the violin, clarinet, *oud*, and *kanun*. More often it was not mine, but Aydın's and Nikita's friends and musical colleagues who appeared in the Balkan Phonograph. In addition to the younger, ethnic Americans who seemed to be the main customers for the shop's merchandise, elderly musicians, mainly Greeks or Armenians, came in occasionally to pass the time with the proprietor and his almost sightless assistant. When one of them arrived, Nikita might go to the back of the store to put on Turkish coffee. Cigarettes would be smoked, a snatch of song might be sung, someone might even dance a *zeybek*, a *chifte-telli*, or a *halay*. Time and again I saw how, for these musicians, national and ethnic boundaries were less important than the world of music and dance they conjured up. All of them spoke several languages and knew the basic dances from each region. I can recall an old Greek clarinetist demonstrating the shaking, stamping movements of the halay of Armenian Kurdistan—that he had evidently learned here in New York—his tall form bubbling humorously.

When a paying customer chanced to come in, the two shopkeepers went into action. Despite his limited English, it was always Aydın who stood behind the counter. It seemed to be Nikita's job to scour the store looking for a customer's requests, and whenever this might require an expedition to an upper shelf, Nikita would move slowly and deliberately, occasionally employing a short ladder. Once, when Nikita seemed reluctant to climb up, Aydın smiled, and issued a series of comments, whose mixed Greek and English contents seemed to be "once in a while you may have to do something in this store." Another day, Nikita summed up his position in life to me: "We are soldiers who have done our duty."

One day, as I sat chatting with Nikita, Aydın appeared in the doorway next to a man about his age. In addition to the usual broad moustache, the man's white hair hung down beside his face in stringy, loose clumps. His white shirt, de rigueur for the old musicians, was even more soiled and crumpled than expected. His irregular teeth were stained yellow from cigarettes. The conversation was mainly in Greek, with some phrases in Turkish, which I was beginning to understand. Seeing a young American in the shop, the visitor introduced himself as "Nick," and to my surprise, he spoke English somewhat better than Nikita. Under the disheveled hair, his face and expression held a savage grace. He began by questioning me about what I liked in the store and the music in it. I explained as best I could, referring in particular to the *makam* modality of much of the repertoire. He looked at me piercingly: "The makam is music for the millionaires, for the beys and effendis. You should listen to the music of the people!" As an example, he began to sing in a shaky voice a song I had heard on an old record:

> *Ben bir kasap seviyorum.*
> I love a butcher boy.
> I gave you bread,
> I gave you cheese,
> Do you want to make me kill you?

Or:

> Young lad, pretty lad,
> my arm is your pillow,
> my hair your blanket,
> pretty lad, mercy, pretty lad!

Both songs were sung to straightforward little tunes in a minor key, echoing the simplicity of the words, which expressed sentiments I was not accustomed to hearing. Aydın sat down next to us, hugged "Nick" around the shoulders, and said in Turkish: "Leave the boy alone. It's enough that he loves our music." Nick smiled at me and said, "I no really 'Nick.' My name Ahmet—I am Turk. But in this country I wash dishes with Greeks. The workers all Greek, so now I am 'Nick.'" After a cup of coffee we all escorted him outside. As we passed by the Greek barbershop next door, the two barbers saw Nick's hair and began to wave their clippers wildly over the bewildered heads of their customers: "Why not cut hair? You man or woman?" they shouted out the door.

A few weeks after Nick's appearance, I was sitting alone with Aydın. As usual, customers were rare, and Nikita had gone out on an errand. Aydın put on an old recording, on which an unusually resonant tenor voice sang above the loud and piercing accompaniment of a double-reed shawm, a *zurna*, while a low-sounding drum beat out a simple binary rhythm. Aydın explained, "This no makam. This folk music from the north, from Erzurum." The singer pronounced the words of the song in a peculiar regional accent. Aydin translated them as best he could, coming to the refrain: "*Chemerim altunlari . . .* the money in my sash." Aydın pantomimed the wide woolen sashes, *chemer* (or *kemer*), that men used to wear in Anatolia and Albania. Many things could be stuck into the sash—money, hashish, knives, pistols. I recalled the soft leather money belt my father had brought to America. It was very well-made and must have been both comfortable and invisible under his jacket—a higher technology than the sash. But I liked the woven sash and all it represented. Aydın smiled and said in Turkish: "You like the old world." He pointed to my sprouting moustache and pretended to curl the ends of invisible hair over his upper lip: "The old world not so easy. Many wars. Look at Ahmet. Communist. In Turkey had nothing, here has nothing." He paused. "This good country." I had always seen Aydın as a small capitalist, but I was intrigued by his friendship with this Turkish Communist, of whom he evidently disapproved. That summer I worked in a nearby housing project, distributing food to the mainly Hispanic residents. Often, I would drop in to the shop and when Aydin learned of the nature of my job he commented enigmatically: "You feel sorry for the poor people." Aydın's deadpan delivery of this comment left me doubting whether I should interpret it as "and so you are a good person," or "but you really should not waste your time."

The next year was my third at The City College of New York. I mortified my parents by moving out of our Bronx apartment and renting a tiny studio in a historic Dutch brownstone at 80th Street and Riverside Drive. On their first visit, my father looked resigned, but my mother wept, announcing: "It's so small, so dark; you must have been so unhappy with us!" I knew that this lament issued from her heart, but it was also the kind of maternal rhetoric with which I was familiar. I replied that I was not unhappy at home, but despite its small dimensions I liked this little apartment. I also preferred its location, so much nearer to my school, to my friends, and to almost everything I did. Surely, she had noticed how often I had been traveling to Manhattan over the past five years. Did she really want me to spend half my days riding the subways? I had not moved so far away, and certainly I would see them every week. As it turned out, our relationship improved now that I had left home; in particular my father and I could speak more freely than before: those two years between my moving out and his untimely death were the closest period we spent together.

Now that I was living in Manhattan, however, I did not see more of Aydın and Nikita. I was now an actor in life and was not in the mood to absorb passively the lessons of my elders. That summer of 1969 I traveled abroad for the first time, visiting Romania, Bulgaria, Yugoslavia, and Istanbul. When I returned, I did not go to the Balkan Phonograph shop until late in the fall. When I stopped there, I was shocked to find the store boarded up. Worried, I phoned Pyrrhus, who had never liked Aydın, calling him the "Old Gypsy." He told me not to worry, the shop would reopen soon. Several months passed when Laszlo told me that Balkan Phonograph had reopened only three blocks from its old location.

By now I had become accustomed to not thinking about Aydın and Nikita. A month went by before I followed Lazslo's instructions to find the new store. It was a dark, windy winter afternoon when I made the trip to Greek Town. The shop was now in a basement, and I circled around the neighborhood several times before noticing the Balkan Phonograph sign. The sight that greeted me differed in several ways from what I remembered. The new shop was almost square. There was no long bench, only wooden chairs, and instead of the sun streaming in from the south side of 27th Street the light came from a few overhead bulbs. Aydin was sitting in a chair in front of the counter, wearing a faded, navy blue suit, his hands folded peacefully before him. His dark blue eyes seemed further away, resigned. He rose to greet me: "Hello young man."

We shook hands and as I complimented him on the neat appearance of the new store, my eyes quickly noted the absence of the other denizen of the old Balkan Phonograph.

"Where is Nikita?" I asked.

"Nikita cannot see, he went back to Greece, to his family. He writes that he is happy there."

I could glean no clue as to how this might have happened, or how Aydın felt about it. I asked naïvely whether Nikita might return. The answer was a definitive no. We were both silent and Aydın resumed his seat. I wandered about the store, not wanting to reveal the depth of my surprise, disappointment, and sorrow. Even the previous year I had noticed Nikita's sight fading; he could no longer help me read the Ottoman labels on the oldest 78 RPM records. I felt a lament rising up inside me, but I forced it to be silent.

Wanting to appear interested, I looked around the shelves. There was another lack—no more manila paper sleeves for the 78 RPM records. The stock was composed mainly of LP recordings issued in this country, including "Balkan Phonograph," "Guirak," "Colonial," and other Balkan American reissues of old recordings. My eyes were caught by the colorful and well-designed 45 RPM records from Yugoslavia, each featuring a color photograph of a group of musicians in peasant costumes of different regions of the republics—Serbs, Croatians, Bosnians, Macedonians, even Albanians from Kosovo. I had seen some of the same records in the shops in Skoplje that summer. There were a few records of the Macedonian clarinetist Ogenovski from Monastir, who sounded mysteriously like our klezmer clarinetist Dave Tarras. I bought a couple of these to add to the collection I had begun in Macedonia. The new Yugoslav recordings were exciting, but they could not compare with the endless adventure of the old recordings, now banished to who knows what warehouse.

It was difficult to accustom myself to the new Balkan Phonograph minus the sunlight, the bench, the old 78 RPMs—and minus Nikita. I did not return for more than six months. Then, later that summer, came the shock of my father's sudden and unexpected death.

It may have been close to a year before I returned to the shop. Once again, I asked Aydın about Nikita. He replied, "I don't know. Six months now I send letter, it come back unopened."

Compared to the loss of my father, Nikita's disappearance was distant, less a death than an evaporation of something insubstantial, vaporous: to use his own image of the soldier, he was missing in action. Yet I knew something solid that had supported me, was gone forever.

Without Nikita, Balkan Phonograph reflected the presence of Aydın more than it had before. The old, slow-paced hospitality was replaced by a somewhat harder business sense. Just as the old 78 RPM records had disappeared, so too did the old musicians cease to come by. Those who did come were usually younger American-born Greeks or Armenians, or recently arrived Greeks, and none of them knew Aydın well. In the new shop, lunches were no longer cooked in the back, nor was Turkish coffee served. Aydın remained alone, without an assistant. His decision to get rid of his oldest recordings and to bring a new stock from abroad made one thing clear—he had no intention of fading into a memory of the Old World. For all his old ways he was a survivor, and he would survive right here—there would be no going back to the Old Country to die.

These business-like calculations did not prevent Aydın from remaining affable to me. He seemed to appreciate my increasingly serious attempts to learn both Turkish and Romanian. I would sometimes try to practice my Turkish with him, but at the first mistake the short conversation ceased while he corrected my grammar. He was more forgiving with Romanian, which he had learned later in his life.

That year was the first time I saw Aydın's entrepreneurial skills. An ethnic arts association run by two friends of mine—Ethel Raim and Martin Koenig—was sponsoring a Balkan musical event. They asked Aydın to put together the Albanian component. He called on a variety of old and new immigrant musicians from Albania and Kosovo for the concert that was given at McMillan Theater at Columbia University. I smiled to see an octogenarian Aydın sitting on stage with his oud, surrounded by younger men playing clarinet, *lauto,* and *bouzoukee.* In honor of the occasion, I wore an embroidered bolero jacket I had acquired from the Zeybeks in Aegean Turkey and a broad kemer woven sash. When I came up to congratulate him his eyes remarked humorously on my Old World garb. This concert seemed to be the high point of Aydın's later days and a gratifying sight for me. Later that year the same arts organization sponsored another dance party where Aydın's band performed. I danced chifte-telli with a tall Armenian beauty, then working at Columbia, who was coming to be my dancing partner at these events. I chuckled at the thought that we were dancing to Aydın's music: he was a true survivor.

Yet, away from the concerts and parties, with Nikita gone, nothing bound me anymore to Balkan Phonograph. Aydın certainly did not need my company. He appreciated good music, but his aim in life had not been to perform music but to organize, preserve, and exchange it on the market. I did not share these aims, and, much as I owed him for the enchantment of those early years, I did not feel he had much place in my life, or I in his. Perhaps since I was an amateur myself, I failed to appreciate that all the older musicians I had met staked their lives on their music remaining viable within a marketplace. Aydın and Nikita might admire the *taksims* and *peshrevs* of Tanburi Cemil Bey, but they were not going to play this repertoire in New York, where there was little demand for it. As I got to know the Turkish Armenian musicians, I came to recognize how this market process had shaped their repertoire and style toward only the ecstatic and the sentimental. But in a sense, Aydın took even fewer risks. He had no personal style as a musician; his uncle Selim may have been a masterful clarinetist, but he himself was at heart an entrepreneur, an organizer of music. I was not sure what it was, but I was looking for something else.

A couple of years passed in which I rarely entered the shop. By then I was playing Armenian and other old Anatolian tunes on my Persian *santur,* and I was asked to do a radio show for WBAI. At the studio I met the program director—a diminutive Jewish boy several years my junior. After the show he asked me some questions and he wondered whether I knew about the Balkan Phonograph shop. I looked at him sharply. Thinking I might not have understood the question, he repeated it, mentioning the name of the owner. Before answering, I sat dumbly. Aside from a couple of professionals in public-sector folklore presentations, never in all these nine years had any normal, white, European American shown any awareness of the Balkan Phonograph and what it represented. That was strictly for Greek and Balkan types and strange hybrids like me. Not only did this young fellow know Aydın, but he had found a teacher, with whom to study Turkish makam singing—a medical doctor who sang classical Ottoman music. Dr. Irfan Doğrusöz had left Istanbul several years ago, first for Virginia and then New York. From then on, the young man and I kept in touch, and he became my source of news about Aydın.

Within the year the news became alarming. Aydın was ill. The nature of the illness never became clear to me, but now he could open his shop only irregularly. Soon he was spending long periods in the hospital. The young student had gotten him together with Dr. Doğrusöz, who was taken with this elderly Albanian from Istanbul who had represented Turkish music in America for so many years. Through his hospital contacts Dr. Doğrusöz arranged for a bed in a small, private French hospital just a few blocks from Aydın's shop.

One evening I went to visit Aydın in the hospital. As I walked up the marble stairway amid tasteful Baroque statues and vases, I marveled at Aydın's good fortune even in his illness. He did not have a private room, however, but shared a space with several other men. Entering the quiet room, the first person I saw was not Aydın but old Perikles Halkias, that indestructible symbol of the clarinet of Epirus, whose pentatonic mountain melodies had wailed for so many years throughout Greek Town. Still basically ignorant of English, Halkias pantomimed his condition, pointing to his belly, indicating where he had been operated on. He smiled that all was well. Nodding across the room toward Aydın he knitted his brow and puckered his lips.

Aydin sat up in bed, wearing a blue hospital gown. He had grown somewhat thinner, but his eyes were as sharp as ever. Spotting me, he spread his arms in greeting: "Ce mai face?" He spoke this greeting in soft but clear Romanian. After uttering these words he looked into the distance, deeply preoccupied. Speaking in Turkish, he began to tell me about Dr. Irfan, how much he had helped him and how happy he was to be here. After fifteen minutes he thanked me for coming and asked me to come again.

Dr. Doğrusöz's student went to the hospital as well and kept me informed of Aydın's condition. I returned a couple of weeks later on a weekday night after my classes Uptown. Once again, the hospital was as dark and quiet as Bruno Schultz's sanatorium. No guard sat downstairs, and the nurse was away from her desk. I entered through the main door and walked up the wide marble staircase, glancing at the urns and religious statues. Going directly up to Aydın's ward, I was greeted by a half dozen men, most of them snoring softly in bed. Halkias had returned home. Only Aydın sat up on his bed, in the same position as before, his egg-shaped head somewhat thinner and bonier.

He saw me enter and barely acknowledged my presence by a whispered Romanian greeting, while he continued to look straight ahead. He did not smile, and his speech shifted from Romanian to Turkish. I could barely make out a few words of a prayer in Arabic. Around him were the bodies of the sleeping men and the darkness. I pulled up a chair but found no way to enter his conversation, whose occasional sentences in Romanian were the only sign that he was conscious of my presence. I could not touch him but looked at his face intently. Finally, I wished him farewell. I rose and walked down the staircase to the dark street off Eighth Avenue. It was our last meeting.

Chapter 1: Meshilim Feldman, Romanian Passport, 1920

Chapter 1: Meshilim Feldman and Friends, Edinets, ca. 1934 (photographer unknown)

Chapter 1: Zev Feldman, Edinets, 2013 (photo: Christina Crowder)

Chapter 2: Sephardic Jewish Center, 120 E. 169 St. Bronx, New York (photo: Zev Feldman, ca. 1970)

Chapter 4: Roza Eskenazi, Istanbul, 1955. (Balkan Phonograph LP-881)

Chapter 4: Tanburi Cemil (Djemil)
Bey, Mahour Taksim avec
Violoncello (Orpheon Records)

Chapter 5: Serena Wilson,
Egyptian Gardens,
1960s (photo: James J.
Kiregsmann, courtesy of
Scott Wilson)

Chapter 5: Zev Feldman with Zeybeks, Tavas Village, Denizli Province, 1971 (photographer unknown)

Chapter 6: St. Spyridon Greek Orthodox Church, 124 Wadsworth Avenue, New York

Chapter 7: Santouri made by Speros Mamais, Athens (photo: Zev Feldman, Abu Dhabi, 2015)

Chapter 9: Zebulon Avshalomov, Armenian Christmas Celebration, Tehran, 1941. Zebulon is the second kemanche from the right.

Chapter 11: Antranik Aroustamian, ca. 1987 (Dr. Homayoon Beigi Archive)

Η "ΠΑΛΙΟΠΑΡΕΑ"
ΣΕ ΛΑΪΚΗ ΣΥΝΑΥΛΙΑ
ΜΕ ΡΕΜΠΕΤΙΚΑ ΚΑΙ ΤΡΑΓΟΥΔΙΑ ΣΥΓΧΡΟΝΩΝ ΕΛΛΗΝΩΝ ΣΥΝΘΕΤΩΝ

ANDREW STATMAN, PERICLES MICHALITSIANOS, THANASSIS GALANOPOULOS, ZEV FELDMAN
CHRISTOS TSIAMIS, LIVIA DRAPKIN, GEORGE VIKOS

"PALIOPAREA"
IN CONCERT OF
GREEK FOLK MUSIC

FRIDAY, JUNE 10, 1977 AT 8:00 P.M.
at
CAMI HALL
165 WEST 57th STREET • ACROSS CARNEGIE HALL
NEW YORK CITY

For Information and Reservations Call: 691-0075

Chapter 12: Paleoparea with Zev Feldman and Andy Statman (Cami Hall, 1977)

Chapter 13: Dave Tarras, Sam Beckerman, Irving Gratz in Studio, (EFAC and CTMD, 1979)

Music
of the
Ottoman Court

NECDET YAŞAR, *tanbur*
NIYAZI SAYIN, *ney*

THE CATHEDRAL CHURCH OF ST. JOHN THE DIVINE
112th Street and Amsterdam Avenue

FRIDAY, FEBRUARY 20th
8:30 P.M.
tickets at the door - $5.00

Postlude: Necdet Yaşar, Niyazi Sayin flyer, 1980 (Phillip Schuyler}

Postlude: Tanbur, Charles Fonton, 1751 (Feldman, *Music of the Ottoman Court*, p. 149. Brill, 2024)

Postlude: Khevrisa, 1999 (Steven Greenman, Zev Feldman, Alicia Svigals, Michael Alpert, Stuart Brotman at home of Zev Feldman, New York, photo: by Jeri Drucker)

Chapter 9

⫯⫯⫯

Zebulon

A Survivor from the Caucasus in Brooklyn

ON A SUNDAY afternoon in spring in the early 1970s, I stroll through the quiet streets of a Brooklyn neighborhood consisting of two-story brick houses. As I pass close to one of them, I notice a Hebrew sign announcing the office of a *sofer*, a Torah scribe, and simultaneously see the scribe himself, a white-bearded man in a black yarmulke and a clean white shirt, gazing out of the window. There are few people on the street. The Hebrew and Yiddish signs are small and decorous. There are no hard sells for cut-rate gaberdines, announcements about the war against intermarriage, or the advent of the Messiah. As it was not the Sabbath, one would have to look closely to discover the Hasidic character of this neighborhood. However, my destination was not a prayer *shtibl*, a group of *nign* singers, or wedding *badkhonim*. I had heard about the existence of a member of a much smaller Jewish tribe living unobtrusively, probably unnoticed among this community.

So much of the domestic architecture of Brooklyn and the Bronx is completely uniform, but the building that I now entered conformed to none of the familiar patterns. I went through a small door on a side street and walked up a narrow dark stairway. At the top of the stairs, I rang a doorbell. A young boy let me into a very spacious top-floor apartment with a skylight illuminating the middle room which did not face a street. As I entered, I heard the sharp, thin voice of the *kemanche*, the Persian spike fiddle, the sound resonating from its skin-covered body. An elderly, rather hoarse voice was singing a lilting tune whose lugubrious words were in Caucasian Turkish:

> With one wayward glance you took my soul,
> You held it, then threw it into the desert.
> Come to me, don't put on airs,
> O wild mountain doe!

The room through which I passed was stacked with freshly stuffed pillows covered with cheap, gaudy, machine embroidery. Leaning on several of the pillows I noticed musical instruments of the Caucasus, some of them encrusted with an inlay of mother-of-pearl. Soft, delicate Caucasian riding boots lay curled up in one corner.

The singing was coming from a room that faced the street near the outer doorway. Several women and children, as well as a couple of men, were seated on chairs or pillows. They listened to the music half-attentively, the women making comments and issuing commands to their children in Hebrew. The musician was not clearly visible behind the table piled with food and bottles of vodka, but presently he put down his fiddle and raised a Caucasian frame drum whose brass rings jingled loudly. Its skin was taut and bright. Already beating a ferocious rhythm, the musician stood up, his head cocked to one side toward the large drum that almost obscured his face. Over his thin body, of medium height, he wore a faded gray suit and an open-collared white shirt, and when his face became visible, I could see his rather thick black hair, his brownish skin, and his enormous aquiline nose. His black eyes seemed to squint, and their whites showed mild alcoholic intoxication. As his hands beat out the relentless rhythm, he shouted a high-pitched humorous song in Turkish.

His audience chattered away in Hebrew, and I sensed that most of them probably did not understand the language of the songs but had heard them many times before; they viewed this entertainment with bemused indulgence. Nobody clapped, danced, or revealed any sign of involvement. This attitude on their part did not seem to stop the singer who sang each new verse in full and increasingly loud tones. He frequently turned, swiveled, and even tossed the drum into the air. When his face turned my way, I saw a mask impossible to interpret—energy, rage, sadness, and a seemingly shamanic trance mingled in one changeless expression. Finally, he put down the drum. There was a little token of applause—apparently a ritual of hospitality had been completed. The Israeli families rose to take their leave, showering their host with profuse good wishes. He responded with a bright smile and some well-turned Hebrew phrases. A man wearing glasses and a short leather jacket led the way, and the whole group rushed, buffalo-like toward the exit.

As soon as the Israeli guests had left, he turned to me:

"Shalom. You speak Hebrew, Russian, Turkish?"

I answered, "Turkish."

"Good," he continued in the Caucasian dialect of that language. "Are you Ze'ev?"

He gave my name the Semitic glottal pronunciation used by Oriental Israelis.

"Steve told me about you. You like music from Turkey, Persia, Kavkaz? Good."

Steve Wolownik (1946–2000) was a Russian musician of Ukrainian American origin then living in Los Angeles. He had phoned me from there telling me that the "Old Man" had moved from California to New York and that I should not miss an opportunity to meet him. Steve described him as a part of the pre-Soviet culture of the Caucasus, something like a living Oriental rug, he said.

My host went on: "These people are from Israel. I knew their parents, their uncles, so when they come to America, they know they must visit me, and I must entertain them." He went on, "You see this *daf*?" pointing to the frame drum, "This *kemanche*, the *tar* over there? All my work." Then pointing to the other room, "Those pillows and the boots. All my work."

He continued:

"If you want to learn music, that is good. Or if you want just to listen, that too is good. Come again, any time. Now I will rest. Shalom."

After that initial meeting, everything that occurred for the next two years seemed to be subject to different interpretations. This was an elderly, vulnerable, lonely, immigrant artist, who was also an aggressive, predatory survivor. Nothing was simple, and few things were as they seemed.

My host had two names. His Hebrew name was Zebulon. His Muslim name was Sha'ban Khan. I learned that he did not take the Muslim name for the sake of cultural conformity, but that he had begun to use it after he had left his home in the Caucasus and journeyed through Iran. While crossing a desert, he had been beset by bandits and he knew that he had a better chance of survival if he appeared as a Shiite Muslim. As he told me, "I no tell lie, but if you put gun to head, I no tell truth."

Language too was malleable. Zebulon spoke many, such as Tati, his native language, Azerbaijani Turkish, Armenian, Russian, Persian, and Hebrew. English came too late, and while he spoke it after a fashion, more often than not it was a kind of mortar holding together the other elements of the sentence. These other elements changed according to the language of his interlocutors. I had seen him in conversation with speakers of Azerbaijani Turkish, Russian, Hebrew, or English, adding words in each language as he turned to that speaker. When the two of us were alone we usually conversed in a kind of Turkish. I did not know his Caucasian dialect, which was certainly not that of the Azerbaijani capital, Baku, but I could usually follow his meaning. He understood my Istanbul Turkish quite well. After a couple of months, I also began to find his English almost perfectly intelligible, but Anglophone newcomers were usually perplexed.

His conversational technique was that of a salesman—first he excited interest; after that, the details could be negotiated. Selective mispronunciation could also be enlisted. One of his best English creations was the word "tundred." It was a number, which could stand either for a hundred or a thousand, as in: "How much do you want for this kemanche?" "Two tundred dollar."

During the ensuing conversation Zebulon could raise and lower the price several times, and the prospective customer could not be sure what the opening price had been.

Zebulon was now living alone in his second-story apartment in Brooklyn. When I met him, he was sixty-six years old. To construct a narrative of how he reached this point in his life I need to enlist the help of several people who had known him. To me he spoke mainly about the earliest years, in the Caucasus and Iran. Some sections of the narrative seem clear, others have more than one version. Perhaps the later events will be more understandable if I set down what is known of the earlier years of his biography.

Zebulon was a Tat, or Caucasian Mountain Jew from Dagestan. In this part of the world, origins count for much, so I will set down a few notes on Zebulon's people.

The Mountain Jews, as the Russians called them, claim to descend from the Ten Lost Tribes of Israel who had been sent into exile by the ancient Assyrians. Zebulon was named after one of these Lost Tribes. From Assyria, mainly south of modern Iraqi Kurdistan, the Israelites had moved northeastward to Media and then Caucasian Albania, much later called Azerbaijan. At some point in their history, they must have mixed with exiled Judeans, because despite their Israelite tribal consciousness, for over a thousand years the Mountain Jews have practiced Rabbinic Judaism. Their west Iranian language, Tati, related to Persian and not to one of the local Iranian languages, also suggests a movement from the south northward. In time they had moved north of Albania—modern Azerbaijan—into the high mountains that the Muslims came to call by the Turkish name Dagestan, or the Land of Mountains. Jewish travelers who visited them almost a thousand years ago were impressed by their political independence, buttressed by their policy of alliances with the still-pagan Turks against the Muslim Persians. Since that time, they have been accustomed to carrying arms, and after the Russian conquest the Tsarist government thought it wiser not to attempt to enforce the anti-Semitic legislation that they enacted elsewhere in the Empire. Besides settling in fortified mountain villages, the Jews had long since predominated in the city of Derbent, located on the shores of the Caspian Sea at the foothills of the mountains.

Zebulon was born in Derbent. He would speak to me about the high, Cyclopean boulders of its walls. He felt that they were of ancient construction, perhaps from the time of King David, and much older than the Greeks and Romans. Looking at Zebulon's eagle-eyes and hawk-like beak I saw an image of Jews of his character, unwilling to endure the humiliations visited on them by the Gentiles of the plains, growing huge wings and alighting on the mountain peaks. From there they could scan the horizon on every side, and hurl down boulders on any potential foe who would consider sneaking up on them.

Zebulon's childhood had coincided with the First World War, a time of suffering and deprivation for the entire Caucasus. Cholera had spread to Derbent. Perhaps it spared the mountain villages somewhat, but the city was decimated. Among the many victims were Zebulon's parents, whom he can no longer remember. Somewhere between the ages of six and ten he was forced to earn his living as a *hammal*, a porter in the bazaar. Little Zebulon must have known well the boulders of the city walls, for they may have sheltered him on snowy winter nights. He told me this tale only once. As he closed his description, his eyes reddened and he said: "Two days I worked for one loaf of bread."

After the war he moved south to Baku, the capital of Russian Azerbaijan. In Baku he had heard a performance of a blind Armenian musician with a high reputation in those parts. The Armenian, Vartan Mangasarian, was a virtuoso on the lute tar, and was so adept that it was said that whenever he broke a string during a performance, he replaced it and tuned it without interrupting his melody. In Baku at that time Vartan was one of the masters of what was called the *mugham*. This term, related to the Arabic and Turkish word *maqam*, referred to an entirely instrumental performance of a musical mode. The Azerbaijanis usually preferred to listen to a singer reciting classical poetry in their Turkish language, accompanied by a tar and a kemanche. It was the Armenians who had perfected this purely instrumental style of performance.

I do not know how the blind Armenian maestro was persuaded to accept this penniless Jewish orphan as his student. The child worked as a servant in Vartan's house and in return he received his room and board. He was allowed to listen to the master teach the older students. However, Zebulon was not privileged to learn all of Vartan's repertoire. Vartan was known principally for his renditions of the classical mugham, which he performed both at weddings and at private seances at the homes of the wealthy Muslim and Armenian merchants of oil-rich Baku. Although Zebulon was not trained to be the successor to his teacher, he learned enough to be a professional musician, and he always spoke of Vartan with the sincerest gratitude. Without the latter's compassion and generosity, he might have ended his days as a day laborer in the bazaar.

Zebulon spoke little of the march of the Red Army into Baku, but he did mention that the Communists reorganized the musical life of the city. Now all kemanchists were expected to pass an examination consisting of a solo performance, and more importantly, a performance with a tarist and a tarist and a singer. Vartan also played the kemanche, and Zebulon had learned both the tar and the kemanche from him. Zebulon's knowledge of the mughams and his performing ability were sufficient for him to pass the examination.

Zebulon related little about his years as a musician in the Caucasus. His repertoire included mughams, *ashoog* minstrel songs, as well as lighter songs and the fast and difficult Azerbaijani dances. He had a large, popular repertoire which he sang in Tati, Azerbaijani, and Armenian. He used to go up to the Jewish villages in the hills near Derbent, where he performed at weddings. On some occasions there he would sing an epic that related the tale of the captivity and exile of the Israelites by the Assyrians—"Dastan Melekh Ashshur," or "The Tale of the King of Assyria." He had made the same claim in Israel for twenty-five years, but he never allowed any ethnomusicologist to record or even hear any part of it. He never explained from whom he had learned this, as it could not have been part of Vartan's repertoire, and it was too specialized to have been in the general folklore of the Mountain Jews. Although Zebulon had sung for me several Jewish songs in Tati, and some fragments of the Azerbaijanian minstrel tales "Ashiq Gharib" and "Ashiq Kerem," he never performed a note of the "Dastan Melekh Ashshur." Who were the characters in this epic? Assurbanipal may have been the villain, but who was the hero? Was there an Israelite heroine like Esther in the Megillah of Purim? Since I did not understand the Tati language of the epic, I thought it was futile to press him on this point. I came to suspect that Zebulon would carry this epic with him to the grave. He did.

Meanwhile, the war was over, but the Bolshevik regime brought more woes to the local economy. Zebulon found he could not make a living as a musician, so he began to smuggle textiles from Azerbaijan to Russia. In order to avoid being questioned by the customs officers on the train, he hit upon a foolproof plan. Whenever there seemed any likelihood of an official boarding the train, he took out his kemanche and initiated a tanz-fest, attracting the passengers of every nationality—Russian, Ukrainian, Tatar, Chechen, or Armenian. He remembers the younger Ukrainian women as being particularly irrepressible. Once he began to play the Hopak or Kozachok he knew that he would be surrounded for hours by dancing and singing Ukrainian femininity.

By the end of the New Economic Policy everything began to tighten up, and Zebulon could not risk being caught and labeled a saboteur. Rather than wait to see which branch of the Bolsheviks would prevail, he decided to find a way out of the Workers' Paradise. He was around eighteen at the time and was inducted into the Red Army. Military service actually facilitated his plan, as his unit was stationed near the Aras River which forms the border with Iran. One day he accompanied a Russian sergeant walking close to the river who pointed out how loosely defended the Iranian border seemed to be. Taking this as an invitation or as a challenge, that night Zebulon strapped his kemanche to his back and swam across the river. As he had thought, there were no Iranian soldiers anywhere near the border. By the time he was missed by his comrades, he had walked several kilometers into Iranian Azerbaijan.

The first Iranians whom he met were bandits who took his money but not, it seems, his kemanche. It was also then that Zebulon felt it necessary to deny his Jewishness. In the Caucasus this had never seemed crucial, but in Iran he judged that in unknown situations it was safer to be a Shiite Muslim. As he crossed the desert leading to the city of Tabriz he created his second identity as Sha'ban Khan, a Shiite Azerbaijani ashoog. Where he was well-known to his patrons he remained Zebulon the Jew, but elsewhere he appeared as Sha'ban Khan. Much later in New York I encountered Iranian Jews who had known him primarily by his Muslim name.

Zebulon arrived in Tabriz penniless and without contacts. He did not yet speak Persian, but in any case, Tabriz was essentially a Turkish-speaking city. He looked for the Jewish quarter and went directly to the synagogue, where he asked the beadle for permission to sleep in the building. The following morning, he located the *chay-khana*, the teahouse in which the musicians congregated, waiting for customers to arrive with plans for weddings, circumcisions, or other celebrations. Most of the musicians were Armenians, but the repertoire required was mainly held in common by all the musicians, whether Armenian, Azeri, or Jewish. Zebulon already spoke Armenian and knew much of the specifically Armenian repertoire.

As soon as the police noticed a new face in the teahouse they approached and requested papers. Zebulon had destroyed his Soviet papers but, in this case, he appeared as a Jew. When the policeman asked where he was living, he replied "In God's house," indicating the synagogue. The policeman evidently approved of Zebulon's answer, and that was the last official interrogation that he underwent in Tabriz.

Zebulon created a good reputation for himself, the more so as many of the musicians at the teahouse were smokers or eaters of opium and could not always be relied upon to appear or to perform properly. He spent over a year in Tabriz, and he claimed that his only reason for leaving was the jealousy of the Armenian musicians who were plotting to murder him. So, he moved on to Tehran, which seems to have been his home for the next twenty years. From what he related it does not seem that he lived there continuously, but only made it his base for extended sojourns as far afield as Baghdad, Damascus, and Jerusalem.

He still had in his possession a memento of those Tehran years. In a dresser, he kept a large professional photograph of the musical ensemble that had performed at a celebration at the largest Armenian church in Tehran in the winter of 1941. The formally posed photograph showed three female vocalists, fifteen instrumentalists, and three dancers. Despite the formal setting, the photographer, whether by intent or ineptness, allowed each figure to retain his or her own personal expression, all of whom differ fundamentally from one another. The central position on the carpet was occupied by the player of the *santur*, whose hair was parted down the middle in the style of Rudolph Valentino. On his right was a rather timorous-looking young vocalist, while on his left was seated a Caucasian dancer wearing an overcoat, a *chuha*, adorned with bullet cartridges, and soft white boots. His handsome mustachioed face bore a noticeable resemblance to that of Stalin/Djugashvili. These three were flanked by two lithe, youthful figures sprawled over pillows on the carpet. Their longish hair was tucked under visored Russian peasant caps, their costume an Orientalized version of male Russian garments, while their pretty, smiling faces revealed the sexual ambiguity of Turkish *köçek* dancing boys.

The seated and standing musicians were all dressed in identical black suits and bow ties, and they all held Caucasian rather than Iranian instruments. Seated among the kemanchists I noticed a stern-looking young man with a shock of black hair and a mustache—none other than Zebulon/Sha'ban Khan.

Zebulon spent the war years out of harm's way in Tehran. In 1948 he immigrated to the new State of Israel. He related certain aspects of his life there to me, but I was only able to piece together some important events with the aid of others in Brooklyn.

For roughly twenty-five years Zebulon prospered in Israel. He had married a Caucasian woman who bore him two sons. Although he was by no means a virtuoso, Zebulon had become the representative of the secular music of the Caucasian Mountain Jews in Israel. There was little competition, as few of that small community had immigrated to the Jewish State. Zebulon's mixed repertoire was well-suited to the radio and other modern venues—neither too "primitive" nor too artistic and classical. He showed me an article from a Hebrew newspaper displaying a photo of his three-man ensemble, dressed in Caucasian shirts and fur hats. No doubt this Cossack-like outfit increased the appreciation of the general Israeli public, who, despite the bloodthirsty pogroms, harbored a grudging respect for the "manliness" of these Ukrainian warriors. In Israel there was also a certain charisma surrounding the Mountain Jews. They were the only Jewish community of modern times with an unbroken history of militant activism and some degree of political independence, perhaps the "proto-Israelis" of the Caucasus.

Zebulon benefited from all this favorable publicity, which he had never known in Iran, where he had been just another competent player of an international repertoire. In Israel he became the preserver of the music of a small and distinctive Jewish culture. Zebulon also had the extramusical skills needed to exploit this new situation. He was himself a fine instrument maker, selling his instruments not only to his own students and accompanists, but to musicians of other communities who played similar instruments but had no musical craftsmen among them. He was fond of telling me how the more numerous Bukharan Jewish musicians from Russian Central Asia were obliged to come to him for their kemanches and tars. In Tehran he had worn suits or tuxedoes, but in Israel he understood the value of Caucasian costumes and he quickly learned how to manufacture the required chuhas, boots, and fur hats. He boasted to me that he could learn any trade if he could watch it being done for two days.

Zebulon also caught the attention of the ethnomusicologists of Israel, but from the very beginning he was suspicious of any attempt to record or document his repertoire. To him it was all a case of specialists of one trade stealing the "merchandise" of another. Perhaps it was even worse; musicologists were parasites with no trade at all. He described one of the senior ethnomusicologists in Israel as being in need of "material," to obtain which she used to "grease him up."

A recurrent problem in his professional life in Israel was his fundamental disagreement with the musical establishment about the nature of folklore and the "oral tradition." Zebulon was not a composer, so the directors of the state radio felt that they could learn any part of his repertoire and teach it to the radio musicians. Many of Zebulon's frequent radio appearances led to squabbles about pieces of his repertoire that became regular radio fare. Although he had not created or even extensively altered any part of this repertoire, Zebulon considered it his property because in Israel he was the unique source of most of it. After almost two decades of quarrels, he finally brought a legal suit against the musical director of the Oriental section of the Israeli radio. When he lost the case, he became violent, publicly assaulting the musical director and privately subjecting his own wife to savage beatings. In fear for her life, she notified the police and had Zebulon committed to a mental institution. When he was released after a few months he returned home, then divorced her and left the country. Somehow, he managed to become a landed immigrant in the United States. I often wondered about this absent, divorced wife, whose name Zebulon never mentioned, and whose image appeared nowhere in his house.

The one family member whom I met was his son, named Zion, who was what his father described as a "playboy" in Las Vegas. Zebulon had tried to make him into a musician or else a practitioner of a useful trade, but all in vain. Whenever Zebulon spoke of his son he adopted a tone of amused frustration. During one of my visits, I met Zion—the handsome image of his father from the photograph of thirty years earlier, except that instead of a tuxedo and bow tie he wore an open shirt revealing a large Star of David on a golden chain, while his eyes were shaded by stylish sunglasses. Zion quickly decided that I was beneath his attention and left his father's apartment without a word to me.

Zebulon lived for less than two years in Los Angeles, whose Mediterranean climate and large Iranian population, including Persians, Azerbaijanis, Armenians, and Jews, had initially attracted him. He had visited Canada—where another son had settled—but found Montreal to be absolutely uninhabitable. He described it to me as a city of eternal snow whose people did not dare venture into the streets. I cannot readily explain his decision to leave sunny California, except that it seems he never learned to drive an automobile. Possibly the move had also been connected in some way with a young man who became his student in Los Angeles, and who came to assume a large role in his life. This person, a young American named Jeffrey Werbock, had moved to Los Angeles from Philadelphia. Still in his twenties, he had tried to establish himself as a rock guitarist. He had also become involved with the Gurdjieff Work, the self-improvement group which had been begun by George Gurdjieff (1867–1949), the son of a Greco-Armenian ashoog from a South Caucasian province of the Russian Empire. Closer to home, one of my old Bronx neighbors, Sultan Catto—now a professor of physics and a fine poet—hailed from the North Caucasian Turkic Karachay people. According to family tradition his great-uncle had actually been a disciple of Gurdjieff during one of his journeys to the mountains nearby.

By means of the axiom "wisdom is found in remote and inaccessible places" one can easily arrive at the conclusion "remote and inaccessible places contain wisdom." Because of its sheer height, the belligerence of its numerous tribes, and its political seclusion throughout both medieval and modern times, the Caucasus Mountain region is one of the least accessible places in the world. To my knowledge, apart from Gurdjieff, at least one other Caucasian native who is currently residing in Vancouver, has traded this reputation for a position as a spiritual teacher in the West—an Abkhazian prince from Turkey, trained in the wisdom of the Nart spirits.

But during the following few years, this fame remained confined to a handful of members or ex-members of the Gurdjieff Work. The most dedicated followers became students of Zebulon, under the direct supervision of Jeffrey who retained his status as senior disciple. Most of the time I succeeded in keeping my relationship with Zebulon distinct from the "music school" so I was only partially aware of the inner workings of the structure. Zebulon never discussed anything related to the students other than the specific problems of the teaching aspects of the repertoire.

Occasionally my visits coincided with the end of a lesson with one or another of the students. Zebulon taught in the traditional manner of the Caucasian mugham, imparting discrete sections of the free-rhythm melodies with all their ornaments broken up into precise tonal units. Jeffrey showed great capacity both as a kemanchist and as a singer, and Zebulon sometimes had to be coaxed to part with so much of his repertoire so quickly. He expressed astonishment to me about Jeffrey's ability, which was much greater than any student he had taught in Israel. Many years afterward it became clear that Jeffrey Werbock would become a masterful

performer of both the instrumental and vocal repertoire of the Azerbaijanian mugham. He would be acknowledged in Azerbaijan, and eventually
taught this repertoire academically in the United States.

Meanwhile, Zebulon supplemented his income from the lessons with
occasional sales of instruments to his students. While outside of the
Brooklyn apartment the demand for these instruments was nil, for the
new students there was absolutely no other source for the Caucasian tar,
kemanche, or daf. These were all rather different from their more available Iranian counterparts. Zebulon scoffed at the latter, claiming that even
the Iranians did not like the dull sound of the Iranian instruments. The
purchasing of instruments became a kind of ritual act by which the student
pledged his allegiance to Zebulon and to the mugham of the Caucasus. All
of this was essential for Zebulon's survival, as Caucasian weddings were
infrequent in the New York area at that time—Caucasian Jews began to
arrive in numbers only toward the end of the Soviet era, almost twenty
years later.

After the first year, Zebulon felt that the students were good enough
to perform with him, but for this they needed Caucasian boots, chuhas,
and fur hats. Of course, he was the sole local source for all of these items.
As I watched this system unfolding it seemed essential for me not to have
any financial dealings with Zebulon whatsoever. I was able to keep to this
vow scrupulously. The only service, other than hospitality that ever passed
between us, was a haircut that Zebulon performed for me when he felt my
hair was becoming too long—he was also a good professional barber. He
would accept no money in this case and seemed pleased with his work.

My typical visits with Zebulon usually took place on Sunday or sometimes a weekday afternoon and extended into the evening. When he was
in Manhattan he came to my apartment as well, but this was rare. It was
more usual for me to go to him. During the day we were frequently alone,
and I used much of the time to question him about the music and the
musical life of the Caucasus. At times we listened to recordings together;
occasionally he demonstrated music on the kemanche. By the early evening one or more of the students and sometimes others would arrive.
Music would invariably be played, and I usually kept rhythm with the daf.
During the evenings Zebulon would cook a light meal, more American
than Caucasian, and he would pass around moderate quantities of vodka.
After dinner, the music began. Zebulon had an extraordinary ability to give
of himself even in these casual performances, and to stimulate the emotions of everyone around him. While he was never overly intoxicated or in
any way undisciplined, his musical expression took precedence over other

hierarchies. No amount of emotion or pathos in his music was allowed to create an atmosphere of sentimentality or weakness. For those evenings Zebulon was able to drop his identity as teacher and to throw his entire technical and emotional capacities into the performance.

I was then a graduate student in Middle Eastern studies at Columbia University, specializing in the Turkic cultures of Central Asia. Zebulon was able to make something of these cultures come alive for me. I was coming to specialize in the poetry and music of the oral bards of that region, the famous singers of tales, who had caught the imagination of Western and Russian scholars from Milman Parry (1902–1935) to Viktor Zhirmunsky (1891–1971). While Zebulon's skills were on the periphery of that cultural complex, there was no doubt that he had known something of the art of the ashoog, the Caucasian folk bard. I knew that he would not be an appropriate subject for my own research, but nevertheless Zebulon united in his person a source of emotional and aesthetic delight as well as a degree of intellectual fascination.

Perhaps it was those evenings of music and dance during which he was willing to open himself somewhat to us youngsters, that most endeared Zebulon to me. I had not found this quality in my other musical mentors. These men were sober, friendly, and welcoming, but always insisted on the hierarchy of age and professional status. While I accepted these cultural assumptions—which fit so well with my own upbringing—Zebulon offered me something more. Here was a man who had spent much of his life deep in the ecstasy of the music, song, and dance of one of the most exotic parts of the Orient; he had been a tireless traveler, an adventurous troubadour. Every Sunday night as I returned on the subway from Brooklyn to Manhattan, my ears still rang with the sound of the kemanche, of his high-pitched, hoarse voice, singing simple verses in Azeri Turkish, a language that I was coming to understand.

By any standards Zebulon's repertoire was not large. I heard him perform and teach only four mughams (Shur, Chahargâh, Mahur, and Shustari), and even these he seemed to know only in their abbreviated instrumental versions. It is probable that he had never accompanied a professional mugham singer since he left Iran in 1948, or perhaps even earlier. He sang a number of minstrel songs, and he knew at least the melodies of several of the *tasnif* songs of the rhythmical "zarbî" mughams. He also remembered a few Tati folk songs of the Jews. I never heard him pray, so I do not know how much he had learned of any type of Jewish religious music. I know that some Georgian Jews had sung the Hebrew prayers to the melodies of the Caucasian mugham, but I was not sure that this had been the practice in Derbent. Much later on, when Mountain Jews began to immigrate to New York, I visited their synagogue, and I learned that it was not.

Although in Iran he was able to interact with Caucasian musicians of several ethnicities, in Israel he was restricted to the very few Caucasian musicians of Jewish origin. The Iranian Jewish community in Israel was considerably larger, but Zebulon had rejected any association with Iranian music, despite and partly because of its structural similarity to the mugham of the Caucasus. While another musician (such as the kemanchist Antranik Aroustamian, see Chapter 11) might have developed a mixed Perso-Caucasian style, Zebulon rejected any intrusion of the Persian musical aesthetic. When I played him recordings of younger musicians living in Baku who had developed something of such a style—which seems to have considerable historical precedent—he reacted indignantly at the breaking of what he regarded as traditional musical boundaries. Zebulon played nothing Iranian—his twenty-year sojourn in Iran left no mark on his music. Furthermore, he resented the fact that the Persians had abandoned the kemanche for the violin, although he felt that that the Persian kemanche was an inferior instrument in any case. Rather than picking up the Western violin he had urged instrument makers in Tehran to adopt the superior Caucasian instrument-making techniques. He even claimed that the best Persian craftsmen had learned these Caucasian methods from him.

With this attitude toward the kindred Persian music, it should be obvious that Zebulon had no interest in learning music from other nearby parts of the world. Whatever music he had heard in Baghdad, Damascus, or Jerusalem had no effect on him. He was fond of saying that the mugham/maqam whether in the Caucasus, Iran, Iraq, Syria, or Palestine was all one, only the voice was different in every country. He interpreted this axiom to mean that a Caucasian musician should perform only the type of maqam that was suitable to his "voice" in the broadest sense. Any other approach would result in a bastardized patois, like his English speech, which was strictly functional and boasted none of the style and authenticity of his many other spoken languages. However, within the Caucasus he insisted on the unity of all the national substyles; he never spoke of the music of Azerbaijan but rather of the "Kavkaz," the Caucasus. The only exception for him was the polyphonic singing and playing of the Georgians, which he viewed as basically a village tradition not relevant to the commonly held urban mugham.

Zebulon could recall many specific weddings where particular tunes were much in demand. His favorite expression was how he had "burned them up" with a certain dance tune. In order to "burn up" the dancers, Zebulon had employed several techniques. He emphasized the sharpest contrasts within the rhythm of the dance tune, directing his drummer or drummers to highlight specific points in the melody. He also superimposed a fragment of mugham over the rhythm of the dance. He observed the dancers closely and could discern when several of them had worked up sufficient emotion to need the release of the soaring mugham melody, freeing them from the repetitive constraints of the dance rhythm which their bodies continued to execute. It was for this reason that he came to feel possessive about particular dance tunes because no one else played them quite in his style. He often criticized any Caucasian tune that I had learned from other sources without an elaborate style, saying that I had done nothing with the tune. In contrast, each of his dance tunes was a masterpiece. His expertise in dancing certainly aided his understanding of the needs of dancers. He demonstrated for me almost all of the dances that he played. He was expert in several forms of the Lezghi, called by the Russians "Lezghinka," the great virtuoso men's solo dance which had originated in Dagestan, but which had become a transnational dance of the eastern and central Caucasus.

I can well remember Zebulon's melody for the Lezghi dance of the Chechen people of the northern Caucasus. No melody can better express the unconditional, spiritual independence demanded by the dwellers of the Caucasian highlands. Floating, almost rubato melodies alternate with quick and highly syncopated sections. The scale switches from the broad pentatonism of the Caucasus mountains to the narrow tetrachords of the Iranian cultures of the south Caucasus. I glimpsed a vision of a ferocious world in which each individual was beautiful, proud, and lean, bent not on destruction (at least not at first) but only on displaying his or her beauty to the maximum. These are the dances of the eternally young; they demand the suppleness and stamina of the youthful body. It is fortunate that the mountaineers retain their youth for well over eighty years. As the Abkhazians say, a man is a man up until the age of one hundred. There is nothing self-indulgent or even trance-inducing about these dances. Each dancer must be aware of an intricate succession of steps and sometimes arm movements executed at great speed. The moment of ecstasy for the man comes when he lifts himself up onto the knuckles of his toes, a move allowed but not supported by soft leather riding boots. Even at home, at rehearsals, or simply after dinner Zebulon would sometimes spin around the room, finally lifting his weight onto the impossible support of two or even one toe. At times he added to the effect by pulling a real dagger from his belt into his teeth, then spitting it out so that the blade stuck upright in the floor!

As a musician, Zebulon was most proud of his Azerbaijani dances, which provided him with the maximum scope for ornamentation and melodic improvisation. These tunes, named after flowers or women were a hybrid of the sensuality and mysticism of Iran and the vigor and ferocity of the Caucasus. This seemingly unlikely match gave birth to a wealth of music redolent of saffron and nutmeg and glimmering with flashes of dyed silk. The dances themselves were almost uniform except for small differences in arm movements and tempo, which gave each dance its own character. This dance music was a major part of the after-dinner "rehearsals" with the students and the frequent rituals of hospitality.

Over a year later I was dating a professor from California, ten years my senior, who spoke excellent Russian. We arrived in the afternoon and Zebulon conversed with her quite soberly in Russian. After the students came and the meal was served, Zebulon toned down the drinking and conveyed the appropriate degree of emotional abandon. My friend came away with just the right impression from the encounter.

During the winter one of the students had announced that while traveling on the West Coast he had met a young woman of Russian descent who was intrigued by their group and wished to learn to sing with them. Within a month the young lady showed up to investigate the Caucasian music scene in Brooklyn. She was more ravishing than I had expected, an exquisite blend of Russian and Turkic features, coming from her family's rather long sojourn in Central Asia. During the spring she moved to New York, renting an apartment a few blocks from mine, and getting a job in the neighborhood. Unfortunately, within a couple of months she discovered that Zebulon was incapable of coaching a female vocalist. She quickly lost interest in the group.

I visited Zebulon in Brooklyn one weekday afternoon, and he was friendly and gracious as always, but seemed very tired. He had spent some time at the bank, and he did a pantomime of himself standing behind the "old Ashkenazim" doddering their way to the teller. He added in Hebrew that he had no patience for these wrecks. Moreover, he seemed to have exhausted all our topics of conversation—he was not brimming over with new plans to sell instruments or pillows, or with news about the ensemble. In the evening, we walked the streets together, hardly speaking a word. Zebulon became fatigued, and we both squatted near a wall. He lit up a cigarette and we gazed silently at the Hasidim and a few Turkish women passing by in their raincoats and headscarves. We were silent. Some good-will remained between us, but no unfinished business. We did not meet again for several years.

Soon after, I performed at an Armenian club in Colorado—which I describe in Chapter 10. Later that year (1975) I began a long series of travels to California, France, Holland, Ireland, and Turkey. Over the course of these journeys, I met my first wife—Siobhan Gibbons—whom I later married in Dublin. By 1981 I began my first academic position at Princeton University and lived with Siobhan on campus.

One weekend I came back to New York to attend a concert given by Zebulon and the ensemble. The lads were all dressed up in their gaudy stage costumes. While Jeffrey gave a modified version of his standard speech, an Armenian in the audience noticed that Zebulon's teacher had been named Mangasarian. He immediately interrupted, and he asked whether Zebulon's repertoire was not really Armenian. Jeffrey responded with a dismissive remark. The other Armenians objected, and the situation looked as though peacekeeping forces from the Commonwealth of Independent States might have to be called in. At that moment, Zebulon seized the microphone and hissed, "This no wedding, this concert!"—silencing the discussion.

Zebulon performed wonderfully during the concert, even dancing on his toes, and the audience treated him like a national treasure. During intermission I took the opportunity to speak with the Armenians and explain something about Zebulon's repertoire. I also mentioned the very old Armenian recordings from Tabriz, New York, and Boston that were in my collection. When I spoke the names "Stepan and Haigiz," "Harputlu Kerakin," or the tar virtuoso "Shah Nazarian" their eyes lit up, as their parents and grandparents had owned these same 78 RPM discs. Peace was effectively made.

When the concert was over Zebulon stood to one side smoking a cigarette while the students collected their instruments and costumes. I went up to him. He was friendly and matter-of-fact, asking me about my life, family, and work, but there was something mechanical and dead in his eyes. He did not reproach me for abandoning him, nor press an invitation to visit. He was glad that I appeared to be doing well, and I sincerely complimented the ensemble; they had turned out to be good students. There was now a new young drummer with them who was becoming well-known in the New Age music circles. Evidently, he had learned what he needed from Zebulon and went on to use it for himself. Although I was pleased to see that Zebulon was in good health and apparently flourishing, I could not summon up much emotion. I was a little perplexed at how distant I had become from him.

Now I can see that the emotional vulnerability of Zebulon was not what I needed to enter the world of Ivy League academia. Over the last two summers I had resumed my travels to Istanbul, where I had the good fortune to be accepted by some of the very best classical Ottoman musicians in Turkey. They were all either performing on the radio, with the State Turkish Music Chorus, or arranging international tours. Although these musicians were usually supported by their music, their employment was always of the most "honorable" kind. They received steady salaries and held it as a point of honor never to perform in nightclubs, let alone weddings. Nor would they accept any money for lessons. An old spiritual philosophy obligated them to share their art with any talented younger person who could carry it on into the future, regardless of his religion or social class. Even playing music for guests in one's own house was considered to be in poor taste—as they were a captive audience. When I returned to the United States, I resolved that I would still maintain my contacts with musicians, but only of the most sober and accomplished type. Zebulon was not among them.

This concert turned out to be our last meeting. Within a year I received the unexpected news that Zebulon had returned to Israel. I could not fathom this decision; Israel was too small to live a new, anonymous life. And what of the student ensemble here?

A few years later my employment at Princeton—and my marriage—both ended, and I moved back to New York. Three years passed with no thought in my mind about Zebulon. One evening, in 1987, as I was about to take my seat at a Persian concert at Columbia University, Jeffrey quickly strode up to me: "Have you heard? Zebulon is dead."

I could register the pain in Jeffrey's voice, but my own was cold and unfeeling. Whatever reply I gave must have given scant comfort. Something in my heart wanted to rise up and cry, but another feeling, heavy and cold, suppressed this sharp desire. My years of admiration and enchantment had given way to indifference. I pushed him away from me like an orphan boy in the bazaar whose large eyes begged for a crust of bread.

Part III

COLORADO INTERLUDE

ııı

Yerevan in the Rockies

An Armenian Winter's Tale

I

Bill Budinsky and I were both part of the ethnic music scene at City College New York in the late 1960s, and so we came to meet and get to know one another. I had often wondered how Bill could see over his globular, protruding belly to find the strings of the tiny round *dombra* resting on his lap. Seated on a chair, his left leg crossed before him, the face of the instrument became invisible beneath the folds of the polyester Russian peasant blouse covering his massive trunk. I could make out the fat, stubby fingers of his left hand working busily across the short neck of the little lute while, judging from the sound, the diminutive pick held in his right hand must have made contact with the bright-sounding plastic strings. Usually his round, blond head leaned over his instrument but from time to time he showed us his smiling face with its tiny, almost Mongol blue eyes.

These Russian tunes, alternately brisk and aggressive or slobbering their lugubrious tremolos, held no interest for me. This rotund Jewish boy from Brooklyn was one of the most pleasant characters I had ever met, so I tried to conceal from him my dislike of the music he played. At that age, though, I had not yet developed any diplomacy, so my true opinion tended to come out, much to our mutual embarrassment. Still, he never seemed to hold it against me, and it was to his good offices that I owed my winter's employment at the Armenian nightclub, the Erevan, high among the Rocky Mountains of Colorado.

Bill knew that I had been learning the Caucasian frame drum, the def, from an Azerbaijani dancer who was a scholarship student of physics. The *balalaika* ensemble with whom Bill performed was planning to present a Dagestani dance and a suite of Crimean Tatar melodies at their next concert at Town Hall. Bill thought I might add a more authentic touch than their regular drummer. So, he asked if I would volunteer, as it was to be a benefit concert for I do not know which Russian old-age association. I did not expect much from this or from any other balalaika ensemble, but I could not refuse Bill. At the rehearsal I did not pay attention to much except for the medley called "Crimean Sketches." Over the years I came to understand that the Crimean Tatars were somehow very close musical kin to our more southern Jews in Eastern Europe, although at that age I could not begin to explain why. The Crimean khans—descendants of Genghis— had ruled parts of Southern Bessarabia, and in Romanian balladry it was described as "the Land of the Tatars," Tara Tatarului. At any rate, the Crimean tunes sounded Jewish enough but performed now by these Russian musicians in such a cold and monotonous style that could not be rescued entirely by my minimal part on the frame drum. Everything went fine at the performance, a Sunday matinee where I could be spared most of the music by remaining backstage until my two numbers were called.

This service put me in Bill's good graces, but over the next five years, other than casual meetings at school, Bill reappeared only rarely in my life. We met perhaps once or twice a year at parties and then we graduated from college. I went on to graduate study at Columbia and Bill became a nightclub musician, strumming his Russian Gypsy tunes at hotel restaurants. Then I heard that he had left New York and was making his way as a musician throughout the West. In 1974, I finished my coursework and passed the qualifying examinations for my doctorate in Central Asian Turkic studies. I now faced the numbing prospect of beginning research on my dissertation. At this juncture it was mildly salutary to receive a phone call from Bill, the first in three years. Where was he? In Aspen, Colorado, working nights at a small folk club with a Russian trio. He had called not only to greet me from the Rockies but to let me know that the local Armenian nightclub—there was one—was in need of a musician with an authentic Near Eastern repertoire who could also drum for their belly dance show. Bill had thought of me and wondered if he should mention my name to the owner. He added an enigmatic joke: "Out in California there's an Armenian mafia—they make you an offer you can't understand." I appreciated the offer and the joke, but I was not sure I wanted to spend a season so far away—I would think about it and get back to him. Bill added that the money was very good and that I would get a taste for life out West, where I had never been. And I would only need to be gone from mid-January to April.

By Christmas I felt I would like to get away from my PhD research. I phoned Bill and asked if his Armenian offer was still open. He said he thought it was—he would speak to Souren, the owner of the nightclub. Two days later Bill phoned back; Souren would be delighted to have me. I would stay on an entire furnished floor of his country home, and play only from 8 p.m. until midnight, with standard breaks, six nights a week for ten weeks. The rest of the time was my own and he was sure I would enjoy Aspen. Altogether this situation seemed ideal.

Although by this time I had traveled twice to England, Scotland, the Balkans, and Turkey I had never been out West and was somehow hesitant to go there. My background and environment in New York and Montreal (home of my mother's family) drew me easily enough to Europe and to Turkey, but Colorado represented a deep America about which I knew next to nothing. Nevertheless, all of my musician friends in New York thought it was a real opportunity, so I accepted Bill's offer.

II

I was cheered when the tickets for Aspen arrived in the mail one week after the New Year. Following my father's death four years earlier, my mother had moved back to Montreal, so there was nothing pressing to keep me in New York. As I embarked on the plane, several older male passengers asked my destination, and to a man their eyes glazed over with envy and respect. I was on my way to a three-month stay in Aspen during ski season!

We flew by way of Denver whose unvarying flatness was hardly auspicious—I found it difficult to imagine where the lofty peaks of the Rockies might be hiding. But soon I boarded a small aircraft that skimmed the tops of the wooded, snowcapped mountains, shaking me and my fellow passengers to within an inch of our lives. I touched down more dead than alive and leaned against a wall, too queasy to walk. But then I was met by a red-haired woman of perhaps thirty years old, speaking in a hard, upper-class English accent: "Oh hello. My name is Victoria, and you must be Zev Feldman, the new musician for the Erevan. How do you do?"

Seeing that I barely replied, she went on: "Oh, I see you are a tad under the weather. We all are after our first flight in here. Don't pay it too much heed—it will pass presently. I'll ride you over to the house—Souren is eager to make your acquaintance."

During the ride, Victoria's one-sided conversation flew over my head like a bird's chattering. I was exhausted, yet all around me my eyes were assaulted by the bright sunlight glancing off the fallen snow, and by the intense blueness of the sky. We turned up a hill and as I looked out, I saw the peaks of the Rockies towering above, surrounding the little town. Then I was face-to-face with a nondescript suburban house, shining glassily in its familiar modernity. Victoria helped me get my suitcase and my *santur* into the vestibule and directed me toward Souren's office. As I walked toward the office, I was assailed by a feeling of alienness and vulnerability, which were only partially dispelled when I met my host. Souren Santurian sat in the sunbathed far end of the office, sporting a dark sweater and a vaguely Middle Eastern, black, sheepskin fur cap, perched askew on his head. I was struck first by his eyes, which were black, very large, and somehow poorly aligned—one of them seemed to focus somewhere off to one side as the other stared at me. His expression could be described as a stare—intense yet divorced from his processes of thought. These were evidently occupied elsewhere, leaving his face dominated by his eyes whose huge size seemed to result from their largely ornamental function—disengaged, as they were, from processing anything that might cross their field of vision. The club owner was not smiling, but as soon as I entered the room he rose, took my hand and declared:

"Come in my friend. Bill told me so much about you—I thought you would never decide to come out here. I am sure you will enjoy yourself and will not regret your decision."

He went on: "Almost no one here understands the music. Since I left Chicago I've missed the sound of the *oud*, the *kanun*, all of our music. I have a cousin down in Denver who is picking up the oud and teaches me what he knows, but we can't find anyone around here to learn from. Armenian musicians from California or from back East come through so rarely."

I noted the expression "the music" that all the American-born Armenian and Greek musicians used to refer to a variety of mostly Turkish musical forms and styles. Members of every ethnicity in a vaguely delineated area from Syria to Romania knew this as a musical lingua franca. Although I had been brought up on the klezmer music and Bessarabian dances of my father's country, I had come to adopt this larger Near Eastern musical world as my own. By this time, I had already made two trips to Romania, Bulgaria, Macedonia, and Turkey to get a closer look at this music and dance in their original surroundings. Whatever my own ethnic origin, however Bill might have presented it, for my Armenian host I was somehow included.

Now I focused on Souren's squarish face. White, clean-shaven skin, thick lips, a moderate-sized nose. Not an unattractive face but displaying an aggressive energy I remembered from Harout, the tall Armenian club owner from the New York of my early teen years. Souren went on, "Bill told me you play the santur. That's amazing. Did you notice my name, Santurian, 'son of the santur player'?" Of course I had. Over the past six years I had been playing a santur acquired from my Iranian teacher, Nasser.

"Look, let me show you something." Souren reached into a drawer and pulled out an album filled with old photographs. Taking the book in both hands he opened it and laid it down on his desk. In an old photo I could see an American indoor scene perhaps from the 1920s. Several young women dressed in old Turkish-Armenian costumes, their heads wreathed in silken scarves hung with gold or silver coins, stood around an elderly-looking man with a long, drooping moustache who sat behind an instrument perched on a little table. The instrument was something very like my own Persian *santur*, yet it was somehow deeper and displayed a few bridges at the bottom, evidently designed to support the bass strings that were absent from my little instrument. This was the first picture I had ever seen of the Anatolian *santur*, which was now extinct.

Souren said, "That's my grandfather's brother. He was born in Sepastia, or Sivas, as the Turks call it. He came here just before the First World War and the massacres. The picture was taken in Chicago where he used to play for the local Armenian dance group sponsored by one of the churches. I never knew him and nobody in our family, or in the whole Armenian community there can play santur anymore."

I volunteered, "Do you know the old recordings of the santur player Harputlu Kerakin? Or the violin santur duet of Stepan and Haigiz?" [I mentioned these very old recordings that I had purchased long ago.]

"Yes, of course. A few of my relatives owned these old records. They must have been some of the earliest Armenian recordings made in the US."

I replied, "When I was playing santur in Boston an old man approached me and introduced himself as the son of santuri Haigiz. The family had lived in Watertown since before the first War. But he didn't play santur or any other musical instrument."

Souren frowned. "Yes, that's how it is. Most Armenians don't even know what a santur is. They think my name means 'son of the prince' or some such nonsense."

I would recall this conversation less than a year later as I played my way across Europe. I was in a Turkish restaurant in Amsterdam, where I had been recommended by a friendly hotel owner in the Sultan Ahmet quarter of Istanbul with whom I had spent several afternoons smoking a water pipe. He was the cousin of the restaurant owner in Amsterdam, and he thought that the restaurant might be a good venue for my Anatolian santur melodies. A few months later I found myself in the Netherlands and I decided to look up this Turkish restaurant. Sure enough, the owner was a cousin of the hotel owner from Sultan Ahmet. The restaurant owner was a suave and subtle Istanbul gentleman of remote Anatolian origin, and he seemed to enjoy the music I played for him. But he informed me that, as I could see, he already had a musician. Later in the evening I listened to the performance of this man, an *ashik*—a Turkish minstrel—from the Sivas/Sepastia region who played a wonderful old village repertoire of the Alevi sect. Between sets I played a bit for the owner and the ashik. At one point I looked up and noticed someone, apparently the restaurant mana-ger, shooting me hard and hostile looks from over his moustache. He said to the *ashik* in Turkish, "That's what the Armenians used to play, isn't it?" From his tone of voice, I instinctively waited for the unspoken remainder of the sentence—"and I thought we were rid of them forever."

Now Souren put back the album. "You must be tired now. I look for-ward to hearing your santur tomorrow. Meanwhile, get some rest. Victoria will show you to where you are staying downstairs."

The basement was both openly accessible and secluded. It could be reached through a large door on the ground level near the garage, just beyond a pile of logs for firewood. But from the rest of the house, it could only be entered by means of a ladder built into a wall; especially in winter this was the normal way to reach it. As I descended, the strong sunlight pouring through the windows revealed no ordinary suburban basement but an Oriental treasure trove, a storehouse for some of the goods Souren had imported from Beirut and points East. One corner was occupied by a divan-like structure, evidently a bed, covered by a rich Iranian tribal *kilim* in deep reds, blues, and white. Large Persian rugs covered the floor and in one corner stood an elegant brass tray of Syrian workmanship, lying atop a pearl-inlaid wooden stand. Carpets and kilims lay stacked in piles next to boxes filled with antique Turkish pistols and inlaid daggers. A cozy fire burned in the fireplace. I was too tired to explore more thoroughly, but as I unmade the bed I noticed a powerful stereo system built into the wall facing it, so that one (or two) could adjust the musical entertainment without getting up.

I slept soundly and long through the remainder of the afternoon and the entire night. When I awoke, Victoria had already breakfasted but Souren seemed quite ready to have another cup of coffee while he put some plates of white cheese and olives, a boiled egg, and jam before me. As I had expected, his manner was a mixture of friendliness and distracted brooding, so similar to my businessman cousin in Montreal—he was then, by the way, working for a local Lebanese firm—and several Greek and Armenian American musicians I had come to know. For me, social intercourse was a time to open up and listen, to gain a sense of the other and learn how to speak to him, until gradually the conversation would pour forth as though on its own. Not so for these types—hard sustained work was difficult for them, but they were always conscious of some aspect of work during much of their socializing. They always seemed to be waiting to hear something they could use to their own advantage. Perhaps this too was a kind of work, some kind of business.

When I asked Souren some questions about the club and about his import business he answered in a disjointed, almost distracted manner, partly out of laziness, and partly, I suspect, because there were aspects of his work that he was not willing to discuss so openly. I understood he had been traveling to Lebanon since his late teens. He had also visited Turkey, Egypt, and Iran. Over the years he had imported a variety of items, from carpets to various antiques, and perhaps other things as well. He described the difficulty of buying rugs from Iranian dealers—he was pleased to see I had formed a similar opinion of that group—they were so devious that even Armenians had cause to complain. Although I had never been to Lebanon I had visited Turkey twice. Souren was impressed to learn that I had traveled to the eastern provinces, from the old Armenian city of Karin/Erzurum to Diyarbekir, which the Armenians called "Dikrankert," after the ancient Armenian king Tigranes. And he was impressed that I was able to speak and read Turkish—while his only usable foreign language was Armenian. I had not thought it possible to get around Lebanon with only English and Armenian as a protection against the difficulties of life, as the Irish humorist Flann O'Brien would put it, but evidently it was.

I inquired how long the Erevan nightclub had been in existence. Souren replied that he had never run a restaurant, but he had owned a rug shop and had done other kinds of buying and selling. He had tired of Chicago and had frequently visited various relatives on his mother's side—they were originally from Kharpet—now in the Fresno area. One of his mother's sisters, Aunt Harriet, was an excellent cook and she was eager to try her hand at business. Her husband had lost several businesses, including a restaurant or two, and she had urged her nephew to come out West so they could attempt something together. She felt that California was saturated with Armenian businesses and restaurants, but that the Southwest was almost virgin territory. So, five years ago they had bought a nightclub in Aspen and converted it into an Armenian restaurant with belly dancing several nights a week. Here they had absolutely no competition and business had been very good. Tonight, he would introduce me to his aunt. I would get a feel for the place, and we could start working the following night.

III

After our breakfast I wanted to get out and see the town. Souren told me this would be a forty minute walk from his place, but I was eager to do it. First, I explored the vacant area near his house, and ascending a small hill I found myself facing a sky that was bluer and seemingly much lower than any I had seen. Even in January the light had a dazzling intensity—the opposite of the pale ethereal light of New England or Quebec, wrapped in its gauzy sheath of white clouds. The light in Aspen shone with the blueness of polished turquoise. And all around me rose the mighty heights of the Rocky Mountains, a sight of a sublimity not to be imagined by an Easterner like me. I could not conceive of myself ever scaling these threatening fastnesses.

All day I amused myself with the varied delights and curiosities of Aspen, not least of which was the sight of healthy young blondes of both sexes limping through town on their crutches, casualties of downhill skiing. At 7:00 p.m. I met Souren and we went together to the Erevan. The club was situated in a wing of a moderately large, Old West-style hotel. We entered a spacious room of a size that would bespeak luxury back East, but here seemed normal for most enterprises. A few young waiters were setting tables as we walked toward the kitchen. Souren seated me at a table and went inside to fetch his aunt. In a few moments he reappeared at the side of a short woman of perhaps sixty years. As they sat down it became clear to me that Aunt Harriet was not in the habit of smiling—her facial lines indicated that she might not have attempted it in years. Her round-headed, aquiline features and large black eyes adopted a blank expression that perhaps was among her friendlier poses. Souren now introduced me to her in a few sentences to which Harriet nodded. Even his mention of the santur elicited no more than a slightly raised eyebrow. After listening politely Harriet hurried off to the kitchen. While I chatted with her nephew she reappeared with one of the evening's dishes—baked mushrooms, spinach, and white cheese with *bulgur* on the side, an exquisite Eastern Anatolian specialty that I had never tasted in Turkey.

Afterward Souren and I retired to the dressing room, where he kept his oud and a couple of hourglass drums, *darabukkas*, of the standard Syrian aluminum and nickel variety. Sitting in the cramped room, he picked up the oud and asked me to accompany him in a couple of Armenian tunes. The first was a typical dance of the rollicking *jurjina* variety in ten-eighths rhythm; it was called "the apple orchard," "khunazarin zar" in Armenian. With the darabukka, I accompanied the music with thoughtless ease, as his performance was absolutely regular, without nuance or acceleration. Putting down the oud he exclaimed: "You are the first *otar* who has ever been able to play this with me! Over the years I've tried to teach other otar musicians in Chicago, in LA and here, but they never get it, let alone keep it up for a whole piece. How did you learn it?" I really did not see anything special; I told him I had been playing it for the last eight years or so. I had first heard it in Harout's club in New York and later worked it out with the drummer Laszlo, who was, after all, another otar—in Armenian terms, a "goy." I could dance it as well. Souren looked at me with disbelief. Over the years I had come to love this rhythm, which the Armenians believe to define their music. In America it is Armenian, but it is also a staple of the music of Mesopotamia, stretching from the Anatolian sources of the Tigris and Euphrates to the Persian Gulf. Years later, I would lead a line of dancers in the jurjina in a riotous caravansarai turned nightclub in prewar Baghdad, recalling the lessons I had learned from the Armenians.

Just then I heard a swishing of fabric, signaling the appearance in the doorway of a shapely female body. Souren introduced Rachel; her delicate features and beautiful green eyes smiled at me.

An hour later, Souren was playing the oud for Rachel's dance—he was barely competent, but Rachel performed well in a graceful, subdued style; her legs and torso were a marvel to behold and although she was no taller than I, she seemed to gain in stature while she danced. The audience looked on with good-natured appreciation. These were different people than any I had met elsewhere in the States; somehow more trusting and easier to entertain. And so, our routine got under way. Although Souren's musical level was unlikely to improve much, the audience seemed content. My own santur style, while hardly the product of one tradition, and on no great technical level, had the virtues of impeccable rhythm and a certain musicality of phrasing. And my drumming could be either solid or electrifying—more than adequate for Aspen's Erevan nightclub.

IV

From time to time, I would pay a visit to Bill Budinsky after our show ended at the Erevan. Bill played six nights a week at a small, subterranean cafe in the heart of Aspen. The first night I came by he was on stage alone, playing tunes on the dombra and relating little humorous anecdotes about the Russian musicians back East. He had grown even fatter over the past four years, and he had lost his childlike shyness. Now his manner and speech were decisive, powerful and humorous; he radiated a likable *chutzpa*. After fifteen minutes performing solo, he introduced his accompanists: "And now, let me bring on the band, the *Mamzerim*."

Bill, you have gone too far, I thought. The Yiddish name he had given his band meant "The Bastards." A tall, thin, dark young man walked on with a bass balalaika, followed by a small, pretty, equally dark girl carrying a standard instrument. Both wore Russian peasant blouses, but their appearance was not Russian, Gypsy, or Jewish. Once the music started, they accompanied Bill with the most leaden, clubfooted chords I could imagine for Russian Gypsy music. The audience loved it. Afterward Bill and I sat together over our Coors beers.

"Bill, you have too much chutzpa. Why 'mamzerim'?" I asked.

Bill answered: "Zev, you heard what these Chicanos are doing to my music. What would you call them? Don't worry, there isn't another Jew in the whole building."

V

Rachel's dinner was served after closing time, so as not to interfere with her dancing, and sometimes I sat with her at her meals. Gradually she began to interest me more than our shows. Apart from her physical beauty I came to appreciate her trustingness, artlessness, and her quiet sense of humor. By our second dinner, however, she presented the shocking news that she had already been married for ten years and was the mother of three children. I almost gasped—not only in disappointment but at the thought of her retaining her shape and energy so completely. She invited me to visit their home—they lived high up in the mountains, so she advised me to take a taxi to the end of the road, where her husband would meet me. There was no show on Sunday so we agreed I would spend the afternoon and night with them.

That Sunday Souren had a guest—his cousin Arthur from Denver. Arthur arrived late Friday night, and when I awoke Saturday morning, I could hear the strains of the oud coming from upstairs. When I went up, I found the two cousins seated on the carpet wearing white Egyptian peasant robes, *galabiya*, while burly, bearded Arthur demonstrated a couple of phrases to Souren. Arthur's stroke on the oud was not at all like his rotund shape—he played with real delicacy. Moreover, Arthur projected a relaxed kindliness that was quite alien to Souren. With his eyes shielded behind his glasses and the rest of his face behind a dark curly beard, the Armenian from Denver sank totally into his music. The three of us spent the day together and he came to the club that night. But at the Erevan, so unlike Harout's, or any real Armenian club, there was no dancing—the entirely WASP audience had come mainly for the belly dancing. I was sorry to see Arthur leave the next morning; he never returned during my stay in Aspen.

I had my own adventure planned for the next day. At 2:00 p.m. I boarded a taxi and directed the driver according to the map Rachel had drawn for me. We were to go far up the mountain, following a winding road until its end. Not far ahead, the road was replaced by a narrow path, virtually a ledge between two mountain peaks. An American automobile could negotiate it only at great risk, if at all. I assured the driver that he had taken me far enough. I got out and he turned back down the road to Aspen. Now I stood facing the most beautiful and majestic scene I had ever witnessed. My eyes were somewhat uncomfortable in the glaring snow, but all around me I was overwhelmed with the view from an elevation of 8,000 feet and the quality of light that accompanied it. I felt myself losing touch with what I had known as reality; if I stayed there much longer, I would start to believe I could fly. Fortunately, just then I noticed a figure coming toward me from across the ledge, walking in long strides, barely paying attention to the sharp drop-off yawning to one side of him.

Soon I was face-to-face with a bearded, fairly Jewish-looking man of perhaps thirty years, only one of whose eyes appeared to be sighted. He introduced himself as Jerry, Rachel's husband. Then he turned and led me in silence across the ledge. While I had been standing at the end of the road the view of the gorge was breathtaking, but as I walked over it on the narrow path, I quickly became insensitive to its aesthetic attractions; what had been a magnificent landscape became a vertiginous chasm, beckoning me to destruction. Ten minutes later the gorge was behind us, and we were surrounded by aspen trees on a flat, table-like surface. We walked a further ten minutes in total silence until smoke could be seen rising from the midst of a clump of aspen trees. As we approached, I was shocked to see not a house but a teepee, shining white on the snow. But this was a very large structure, as large as some of the ceremonial teepees I had seen in western films or in old photographs. Outside the tent, near an outhouse, a black goat stood tethered to a post, surrounded by her pellet-like droppings. As we pulled back the tent flap a transformed Rachel greeted us. She was no longer an enticing, seminude belly dancer; her legs were covered by a long print skirt, her top by a bulky sweater, and her straight, fine brown hair flowed over her shoulders. Rachel smiled her greetings, her hands holding the lettuce she was drying for our salad. An impish blond tot of perhaps three years began hopping and shouting, and a girl of perhaps ten raised her head from a book, revealing elegant Jewish or Gypsy features, with bushy, arched eyebrows and long straight hair, similar to her mother's. A slightly younger blond boy with a long head and delicate Nordic face stared silently from a corner.

As I looked around, I observed most of the fixtures of a stationary house, including a wooden platform floor, and a sink placed under a plastic-covered window. Above me was a wooden ceiling pierced by a kind of trapdoor through which a tall ladder led upstairs—this was a three-story teepee! Seeing my amazement Rachel laughed: "No Zev, it's not what you've seen in John Wayne movies!"

As we sat down to lunch my questions produced a lot of information. The teepee was a unique structure designed by Jerry himself, who had been trained as an architect in his native Philadelphia. He had even worked on one of the stations of the Montreal Metro; we agreed that system was a masterpiece of elegant design using the cheapest materials—mostly concrete and steel. While Jerry's career had seemed to be going well, during the sixties he had been bitten by that bug that traveled so widely around America in those days. But in his case, it was not a search for community but a more traditional American longing to commune with God in nature, all alone with his own nuclear family. About six years earlier he had reached the point where he had to decide whether to continue his career as an architect and to remain back East. He and Rachel, who was about five years his junior, decided no to both questions. They already had two small children and Rachel wanted very much to raise them in a natural environment. Jerry knew something about solar heating, and he thought he might be able to install such systems in a region that got lots of sun, like Colorado. He now worked out of an office in town, and he was getting clients. He had worked out an arrangement with a local forest ranger so that he fulfilled some inspection duties, gratis, in return for which he rented a small plot of land.

Rachel had taken belly dancing lessons in Philadelphia from the dancer Barbara Siegel—known as Habiba—who had traveled widely in Egypt and Tunisia, but she had never danced professionally. When the Erevan opened, she saw an opportunity to exercise her skills and earn some income. Jerry had raised no objections. She was not the only dancer at the club—I would probably meet the other girls, both from back East. Rachel now asked me how I was getting along with Souren. I told her I thought our relationship was quite satisfactory. She seemed pleased but she asked:

"Does he know you are Jewish?"

"Of course, I use my Hebrew name."

"It hasn't been a problem?"

Well, so far it had not seemed to be, I replied. Of course, now I wanted to know more. Rachel explained that it had not occurred to Souren that she might be Jewish until after she had worked there for almost a year. Souren went to Lebanon almost every summer and was deeply involved with the Arab-Israeli conflict. By the early 1970s, Lebanon was inching its way to its terrible civil war. And while the local sects and political parties created enough dissension on their own, the presence of a large and well-armed Palestinian refugee population had altered the balance among the factions. One day a couple of years ago, while sitting at the club before showtime, Souren had been reading a local newspaper that carried some news item about Lebanon. Suddenly he slapped the paper down on the table and began cursing Israel and the Jews everywhere who were destroying the whole Middle East. Rachel had gotten angry and told him what he was saying was nonsense. Souren glared at her, his face growing red. There was silence, and then he asked her if she was Jewish—she told him she was and why did he ask? At that Souren fell silent. He rose from the table, taking the newspaper with him. An hour later, Aunt Harriet came out of the kitchen and told Rachel that Souren did not feel well tonight, so she could go home. Rachel had not returned to the club for six months. Then she bumped into Souren in town. He stopped her, looking down, and asked her why she had not been by the club lately. Rachel answered that he must know the reason. Souren made an attempt to smile and said that he missed her dancing and that he hoped she would come back. When she came back that week everything was as before, and there had been no problem since.

In the musicians' world I knew back East, where Greeks, Armenians, Turks, Albanians, and Sephardic Jews all performed together, I had not encountered such behavior. And in Bill's Russian musical environment it was the same. The unspoken rule was, whatever your loyalties, sorrows, or anxieties as a member of an ethnic group, you should never allow it to affect how you behave toward an individual member of another, even a historically hostile, group; you were all musicians. But Souren was primarily an Armenian entrepreneur, not a musician, so his attitude might reflect more mainstream social opinion among Armenians, I thought. And when he traveled in Lebanon, his dealings were not with musicians but with merchants. It seemed somehow incongruous 8,000 feet high in the Colorado Rockies, with no other human habitation in sight, to be reminded of this dark side of human nature. Jerry interrupted my ruminations by finding a deeper meaning for these ethnic squabbles:

"As long as man does not raise his consciousness, he will always be lost in the dark imaginings of illusion. But to raise his consciousness he must follow the teachings of a Perfect Master."

I was a little surprised to hear this interpretation of the issue. As I turned to Rachel she stared up at Jerry like a student at an adored teacher. Then I noticed a portrait hanging on one side of the teepee—a Middle Eastern-looking man with long hair and a very long moustache. I had seen that rather theatrical-looking face before—I recalled a pin on the collar of an attractive, dark Greek girl who worked in one of the offices of my undergraduate college. I had meant to ask her about it when I invited her to lunch, but my romantic life had led me in other directions, so the girl and her pin remained enigmas.

We passed onto other topics and Jerry wanted to show me around the mountain. Pointing to some skis standing in a corner he asked: "Do you know how to use these?"

Of course, I did not. He explained that this was the best way to get around up there and fitted me immediately—I got my first lesson in cross-country skiing. It was a delight and within an hour the two of us were gliding silently through mountain paths and forests. The weather in the sun was so warm I could be comfortable in only a sweater, and I gave no thought to the breeze rushing across my face.

When we came home Jerry showed me to a place in the corner of the teepee where I could rest while Rachel prepared dinner. Once I felt rested, I walked out again to see the sun as it disappeared over the peaks of the mountains. When I came back inside a vegetarian meal was awaiting me which we ate to the accompaniment of the wails of the coyotes deep in the forest. Immediately afterward Rachel put the children to bed upstairs. When she returned, Jerry opened a thick, hardcovered book. It was their custom, he explained, to read every night from the teachings of the Perfect Master, Meher Baba.

As he read, Jerry's good eye shone ferociously in the light of the kerosene lamp; I could see he was reading a text in which he placed absolute faith. Rachel soon began to doze, a beatific smile on her face. The warmth of the wood fire after the hot meal induced sleep in me, as well. Jerry continued to read aloud with undiminished intensity. I think I fell asleep, because sometime later Rachel roused me and led me to a bed along the side of the teepee. She and her husband slept on the far side of the dwelling. As I dozed off again, I could hear only the crackling of the fire and the distant howling of the coyotes.

In the morning, the teepee became a flurry of activity as the two older children prepared for school. Jerry seated me behind him on his motorcycle while the boy and girl were dragged behind on a sled tied to the back of the vehicle. Their father drove recklessly fast, right over the narrow ledge peering over the gorge, even though he had mentioned to me last night that he had lost sight in one eye after a motorcycle accident. Once on the main road he unhitched the children so they could walk the rest of the way while he drove me to town. When we parted, he urged me to come back and stay for a few days whenever I could.

VI

Souren was at home when I returned, and he did not seem pleased that I had spent the night with Jerry and Rachel. He asked how they were in a perfunctory manner. I quickly recalled their earlier conflict—as related to me by Rachel—based on nothing personal but only on their respective group identities. Of course, it was no secret that I was an otar—a non-Armenian—now perhaps I was being classed with that particularly inconvenient group of otars, the Jews. Or perhaps Souren only wanted me more under his control. In any case, I paid no more than a moment's attention to the issue.

He then suggested we spend some time working on the fireplace together, as I had little experience either in tending fires or chopping wood. The weather would be turning colder by next week and I might want to put up and adjust the fire on my own. Chicago-born Souren was only a novice himself, but he could offer me a few tips. Once we began on the logs I enjoyed swinging the axe, but it did become tiring after twenty minutes or so. We spent over an hour on this task.

Afterward my host wondered if I could help him with an Armenian tune he was learning from a record by John Berberian, the New York oud virtuoso. Souren and I worked for over an hour, but the rhythmic phrasing in five-eighths time proved too elusive for him, and he could not concentrate any longer. He told me that years ago he had hosted the renowned, blind, Armenian oudist Hrand Kenkulian (1901–1978) in Chicago on a visit from

Istanbul. He had been fascinated by a *taksim* improvisation Hrand had recorded on an American jazz label and begged the old master to teach it to him. The oudist swore that they must lock themselves in a room until the young man learned it. They tried this method for half a day, stopping only briefly for coffee—but alas, today Souren could not remember more than a few imperfectly learned phrases.

He and Victoria had planned a grilled meat feast. A few hours later the aroma of lamb was wafting from the fireplace in the basement. We took the food upstairs—it was delicious, but I was surprised by the total absence of alcohol. I had never noticed Souren drink, and this temperance seemed somehow out of character. But I soon learned that his intoxicant of choice was hashish—he had brought some back from Beirut and he now urged me to smoke with the two of them. I could not help but notice that he was becoming rather more hospitable after my night with Jerry and Rachel. Had a subtle competition begun between the Armenian nightclub owner and his Jewish belly dancer? Following our leisurely smoke, we set out for the Erevan.

After only one week at the club my professional responsibilities were becoming routine, resembling my experiences of the past few years in Greek, Armenian, or Israeli clubs in New York, except that in Aspen my performance was more central. Back East an oudist like Souren would not have appeared on stage, but here in Aspen the nightly shows at the Erevan partook of that sense of newness, of youthful improvisation that was the hallmark of a town still in the process of building itself. In New York, a performance at any Middle Eastern nightclub displayed a ritualism shaped by decades of tradition. But in Aspen one could sense the inexperience and gullibility of the clientele who wanted just enough exoticism to add some color. A nightclub routine imported directly from New York's Greek Town, complete with hypnotized Greek sailors, would probably have provoked an intolerable level of social, cultural, and erotic anxiety here in Aspen.

Souren ran his show in the nonchalant, improvised style he affected in his other business dealings. Perhaps that is why, in speaking to me of his travels in the Middle East, he usually characterized most of the male popu-lation as *chingenes*, "Gypsies," by which term I understood him to mean lazy, disorganized, and irresponsible folk. Souren wanted to appear as the opposite of the chingenes, the ordinary Muslim Turks or Arabs. This may also have explained his choice of a prim, upper-class English paramour; the mind behind the restaurant business lay under Aunt Harriet's auburn hair, and it was clear to me that it was precisely those slovenly chingene-like qualities that had attracted Victoria to him.

Among the reading I had taken with me was a book in Turkish—*The So-cial Structure of Eastern Anatolia*—that I had picked up a couple of years ago in Istanbul. First published in 1969, the book was a breakthrough at the time; so much so that its author, Ismail Beşikçi (b. 1939), was promptly jailed for treason. When Souren noticed me reading it backstage one night he asked about its contents. This led to a prolonged discussion of Armenian issues. Of course, he was bitter about the Turks' role in forcing his mother's family to leave Anatolia. His father had emigrated before the First World War from a relatively peaceful Central Anatolian Sivas prov-ince where the Armenians had maintained rather good relations with the heterodox Alevi Turkish population. His mother's family originated in the region of Kharpet, or Harput, near El-Aziz (Elaziğ), and had been rescued from the genocide by American missionaries. In William Saroyan's time the Armenians of Kharpet held an unsavory reputation as dishonest carpet dealers, and Souren seemed to identify more with his father's family from Sepastia, or Sivas as it is called today. Politically he could not agree with the extreme Armenian nationalists, some of whom were then training with militant Palestinians in Lebanon. Unlike the vast majority of Armenian Americans, he had visited present-day Turkey and had developed a rather nuanced view of its people, at least during those moods when he was not describing them as chingenes. And he had no intention of moving back to Sepastia, even if it were under an Armenian government. He had evi-dently gone through the inner conflict that William Saroyan (1908–1981) had described years before in his visit to his father's hometown of Bitlis. Saroyan was overwhelmed with nostalgia and claimed to want to move back there. His Armenian hosts from Istanbul, however, pointed out how unreal and impossible his desire was. But some Armenians from Lebanon, who had grown up in a country just over the border from the East Anato-lian provinces of Turkey, felt otherwise. They really might move back to their ancestral homes if they could. Souren concluded:

"I may walk around in pajamas and slippers like my father, and I can speak Armenian, but I am not a man from Sepastia, I'm an American. I have been to Sivas, and I know I couldn't live there no matter who was in charge. So, a lot of Armenians in America are fooling themselves—they say they want Armenia, but they don't. They want to make trouble, to take some kind of revenge. That doesn't get anyone anywhere."

Later that week I noticed the unusual sight of Aunt Harriet sitting at a table in the restaurant speaking with a guest. Souren came up and asked me to sit, explaining that the guest was a Turkish engineer touring the west-ern United States with his attractive, and much younger, blond American wife. The man looked to me about Harriet's age. What is more, Souren went on, he was from Harput. Apparently, he had enjoyed the meal and the ambience so much that he wanted to convey his appreciation to the chef.

The Turk spoke English fluently, which was just as well for Aunt Harriet knew only a few phrases of Turkish. He was a handsome, casually attired man with a full head of white hair, sporting wire-rimmed glasses, and exuding a self-confident energy that I later came to associate with the bourgeoisie of the southeastern towns in Turkey, such as Aynteb, Kilis, or Urfa. This was something quite different from the quiet, suave, deferential style of the Istanbul middle class. The man had left Harput as a child and moved to Ankara. He returned to his hometown only rarely and most of his relatives had moved westward to Ankara or Istanbul. His nostalgia for Harput was entirely centered around food—his older female relatives had cooked the many specialties of the region, and now that most of them were deceased or very elderly he rarely had the chance to reawaken his culinary memories. Finding old-fashioned Harput cooking in the middle of the American Rocky Mountains seemed little short of a miracle to him. Throughout this speech Aunt Harriet remained almost silent, forcing her mouth into something resembling a smile.

The rest of the conversation was essentially an exchange of recipes, a few ingredients were mentioned by the Turk or by Aunt Harriet, prompting instant recognition by the other. It really did seem as though religion and language had made very little difference to eating habits in his East Anatolian town. Or perhaps the Armenian haute cuisine had been accepted by the small Turkish merchant and the bureaucratic middle class—after all, before the First World War Kharpet had been a predominantly Armenian city. I followed all this with some interest, but I noted that the word Armenian never came up once in the conversation—the Turk spoke as though Harriet's family had simply been old neighbors of his kin. Aunt Harriet's face took on a mask-like quality, her eyes glaring more sharply as her mouth maintained its rigid pose in which one could read as one wanted—a smile, a shriek of pain, or a bloodthirsty grimace.

VII

By the following Sunday I had learned how to walk up the mountain from town by following a devious trail, half-hidden in the trees. Rachel explained it to me—it was how she usually went home after work—Jerry did not normally pick her up. Aspen was so completely safe no one thought twice about a beautiful young woman climbing a deserted forest trail alone after midnight. And at midday the landmarks were clear, so that after resting awhile by the banks of a mountain stream, I came out quite near the mountain ledge I had crossed the previous week. I could not help marveling at the utter perfection of the scene, with no sign of man's baleful presence. I arrived at the teepee in time for more silent cross-country skiing with Jerry, followed by a simple vegetarian meal with the family.

The three children were all physically beautiful, but with completely diverse features and characters. Jessica, the eldest, was quiet but very self-confident, almost telepathically attuned to her mother's moods and wishes. The blond boy Peter was not nearly as intelligent as his older sister, often appearing confused and disoriented. He usually followed Jessica's lead but at times became sulky and uncooperative. Baby Stephanie was a blonde with pronounced Russo-Tatar features, her large head was as round as a grapefruit; her slanted blue eyes shone with intelligence. But I came to see she had the character of a young camel, insisting on her own way with her older siblings and even with her parents, and if she did not get it, she was capable of screaming, kicking, and even biting. At those times only her father could quiet her with a mixture of warmth and warning emanating from his one, sighted eye.

After the meal, Jerry took me aside to show me several books by Meher Baba (1894–1969) and explain why he considered him the Perfect Master. I was struck by the many photos of Baba with his long hair, heroic moustache, and delightfully enigmatic smile, looking like a handsome version of Gurdjieff. Jerry owned a library of these books but before he could begin his lecture, I asked him whether these were his principle means of learning Baba's teachings. Yes, he answered, all of Meher Baba's teachings were contained in these volumes. I asked, are there no people alive today who had known him personally? Yes, I was told, principally in India, but Baba did not appoint a successor. There is no church or even a Sufi order of Meher Baba. Besides, Baba ceased to speak for many years and that is why his books remain the principal source of learning his wisdom.

This clarified something, but my yeshiva training got the better of me. According to what principles, I asked, do you interpret his words? Are there never contradictions between a statement found in one of his books and one found in others? Did he write in English, and if not, who translated the books? And who was responsible for editing them? Jerry had never thought of any of these questions. He only answered that as one followed the teachings one's heart would become purer, enabling one to understand the teachings more perfectly. And for that, one had only to apply them—alone or in one's family, no exegesis was necessary.

I was curious about Baba's name—it sounded Persian, was he not some kind of Sufi? Jerry answered that Baba was no kind of Muslim at all, he had been born into a family of Parsees, Indians of Iranian Zoroastrian origin. But he had ceased to belong to the Zoroastrian faith; as he matured, he reached the conclusion that his ancestral religion had become an empty shell, a series of rituals with an ancient scripture that the community it-self no longer understood. While there had once been wisdom there, it was now buried beyond the reach of anyone. Baba's own teachings were the result of his personal enlightenment—it certainly was not necessary or even useful to become a Zoroastrian in order to learn Baba's wisdom. According to Baba no modern religion in its present form represented the teachings of a Perfect Master. Some might have been so, long ages ago, like the teachings of Jesus or of the Buddha. Islam was even less true to a spiritual source because Muhammad had never been a Perfect Master, so his religion was flawed from the start.

What exactly was a Perfect Master? I asked Jerry. That is a fundamental question, he answered. A Perfect Master comes to the world rarely, per-haps once in a millennium. He is a human being who has spiritualized his own nature; he is able to lead others along the path to their own spiritu-alization; and he understands how the spirit has manifested itself through time, that is, in human history and society.

To illustrate the second point Jerry opened a book that seemed a kind of catalog. In it, Meher Baba listed over 1,000 Hindu, Jain, and Muslim ascetics living throughout India, described the nature of their individual ascetic practices, and assigned each one a level along the universal path of spiritual progress. I was incredulous. The point, said Jerry, was that Baba could see into another human being's spiritual state and estimate how far he might progress before his mortal body wore out.

This brought Jerry to the third point. Baba, as Perfect Master, could extrapolate from the spiritual level of particular individuals to the spiritual characteristics of a nation or a historical age. For example, in faraway India Baba had lived through the rise of Nazism and the Second World War, and he followed these world events very closely. He even appointed certain followers of his to carry within themselves the current spiritual state of nations or of whole continents, and by communing with them Baba was able to learn the tendency of world events. Jerry opened another book containing a photograph of the disciples representing each continent. In one photo, dating from the early 1940s, Baba stood next to a thin, very old man, his hair disheveled, grinding his teeth in the most vicious expression of anger while his eyes shot out a look of utterly deranged hatred. I read the caption: "The Master's disciple in charge of the continent of Europe."

VIII

Jerry's lesson continued while Rachel put the children to bed and then went to bed herself. I awoke to the usual bustle, but today I stayed on after Jerry and the children went to town. I sat with Rachel having a second cup of coffee. Light streamed into the teepee and Rachel spoke more calmly than she had on any other day:

"You know Zev, you remind me so much of my father."

I had not yet asked anything about Rachel's family. She went on:

"My father died when I was thirteen years old. But I can remember him so well. He was very quiet, and he always listened to me so carefully. And he liked joking, eating, and music. My mother never remarried after he died."

"How did your parents meet?" I asked.

"They met in England, during the war. My mother was from Ireland, and she was working in London. My father had arrived as a refugee somehow just before the war broke out. He came from a little town in Polish Galicia."

"Do you recall the name?" I inquired.

"Yes. Czortkow, near Susnowicz. Of course, I've never been there. Have you?"

"No, I've been only as far as Suceava in Romanian Moldavia, considerably to the south, but I have heard of it. Now it is in the Ukraine."

As I looked more closely at Rachel's face, I realized I had seen that face before, not once but three times. The features on this archetypical face had a childlike softness. The head seemed neither markedly round nor long, and the features were placed with the most pleasing proportions. Rachel's face belonged to Beatrice, a good friend of mine from high school. She had been born in France after her parents had survived the deportation from Susnowicz. Beatrice had almost the same lithe body as Rachel but was a little taller. And there were the two Israeli brothers I knew, identical twins exactly my age. Their parents were both born in Czortkow. We often joked that the Galicianers, as we called them, were so inbred you could spot one at first meeting. Whereas most other East European Jewish communities had been destroyed and reconstituted over the last few centuries or had experienced an economic boom that attracted new immigrants, many

Galician communities had stayed put for five or six hundred years, and the economy had become so stagnant no one would move there. There was something poignant to me in seeing this very beautiful face so far from its origin, and recognizable even through the medium of an Irish mother.

"My father's whole family was killed by the Nazis. No one came back to Czortkow from Auschwitz or the other camps. My parents married during the war and afterward they immigrated to Philadelphia where I was born."

She paused for a moment and became more thoughtful:

"In America my mother converted to Judaism, and we lived in a Jewish neighborhood. She still lives there, and we all go back to visit every year. Her Irish family disowned her, so I never knew them. I was an only child. If only my father had lived longer. I really needed him in those years. And even now."

Rachel's green eyes filled with tears. I looked down at the table. Now she spoke somewhat more quickly:

"I know I'm so lucky to have Jerry and these three wonderful kids. And I am so happy that we live here in nature, it's so much better than it was back East. Jerry is so strong and decisive. I don't have to worry about anything." She paused again. "Of course we try to live by the Master's teachings." She stopped speaking for what seemed like a long time. "But I wish there were more men like my father."

Rachel lowered her head, and we were both silent. An additional word by either of us would send us down a spiritual abyss as deep as the 8,000-foot drop-off beside the nearby path. Strong as my feelings for Rachel had become, I did not dare to even look into her eyes. I was afraid that what I might read in them would destroy the life that she had built for herself in the beautiful and remote Rockies.

Then Rachel turned and looked out the window. "Zev, you'd better go out for a ski now. I can see it will probably snow later. You'll be lucky if you can get down to the club. I'll have lunch ready when you come back."

When I went out, I could see clouds gathering in a corner of the sky, but I was able to have a long ski while I brooded on Rachel's story, on Rachel's beauty, on the hopeless affinity we felt for one another. My personal ties were few now and nowhere did I feel more alone than high up on this mountain plateau, watching the sky darken; the wind growing stronger, driving the snow that filled the endless gray sky.

When I returned to the teepee, I was surprised to find a guest seated at the table. A very tall young man, perhaps five years my senior, his thin face framed by long, straight, dark hair and an equally long beard was speaking to Rachel in a very soft voice. They both rose to greet me. "Zev, this is our neighbor Ivo. He and his wife Jane live just over the next hill. He had some business here and he also wanted to meet you."

The three of us sat down and I confessed my surprise that there were any neighbors—I had never noticed any sign of human habitation. The guest smiled shyly and explained that he and his wife had worked out an arrangement with the Forest Commission similar to Jerry's. They had arrived about a year later than Jerry and Rachel. Ivo was a violinist, and he worked several nights a week at a restaurant in town. We might even walk down together tonight, as Rachel would not be working at the Erevan until tomorrow. Rachel explained that tonight I would be playing for a belly dancer from New York whom I had met around the club a few days before.

Ivo rose to leave, saying he would return around 6:00 p.m., which would give us an hour to walk down the mountain. He doubted the snowfall would be very severe.

I spent the remainder of the afternoon reading the works of Meher Baba, occasionally stopping to ask Rachel a few questions. By 4:00 p.m. Jerry had returned with the children. He was pleased that I had met Ivo and was sure we would find something in common.

At 6:00 p.m. Ivo appeared at the teepee and the snow had died down to a flurry. As we walked it tingled cold and wet on our faces but posed no impediment to our talking. Like Jerry, Ivo tended to remain silent, but I sensed that this silence was of a different type, somehow softer and slower. Ivo spoke first, asking me about my involvement in music. I told him about my background and my life back East. Ivo told me he was from a farming community in the northern Midwest. There were no Moldavians there but many Croats, Serbs, Slovenes, and some Macedonians. Both of his parents had grown up in a small village in the interior of Croatia. He himself had played fiddle in a *tamburitza* band, but he felt he had to choose between the music of the community and the classics. He had been studying violin since childhood and in the past ten years had ceased to play with the tamburitza group. His greatest love was Bach. He invited me to visit him in his own teepee, about a half-hour walk from Jerry and Rachel.

At the foot of the mountain Ivo and I went our separate ways. I promised I would come to see him and his wife on my next trip up the mountain.

IX

Elaine was younger than Rachel, closer to my age. Like me, she was a New Yorker—in fact, a born Manhattanite. She was slightly taller than I was, and curly black hair framed her smooth white face and dark-brown, almond-shaped eyes. She was also Jewish, but many more generations American. Tonight, we sat together at the club while I had my dinner; this would be our first show together.

Back home we had been neighbors—we both lived between 72nd Street and 86th Street west of Broadway—but we had never met. I thought it was a dear neighborhood, full of eighty-year-old brownstones, little restaurants, small cinemas, and bookstores. Although life and general security seemed to be declining in the mid-1970s, the neighborhood retained some of its charm. Elaine and I spoke nostalgically about the Citarella fish market on Broadway and the nearby vegetable grocer. She seemed to be a more adventurous cook than I was at that age, and she really availed herself of the culinary resources of Manhattan. Yet, within an hour I knew instinctively that I could not form a friendship with this attractive, intelligent, former neighbor. Elaine's eyes never engaged mine. I felt an invisible protective shield enveloping her face; I began to sense that her sexual preference was not for my gender. As the conversation developed, I learned that she had moved out West, permanently it seemed, with another woman of our age, who was also a belly dancer—I would meet her sometime next week.

At that point, Souren came up to us with friendly but clouded eyes and, muttering a few words, he beckoned me backstage. Once in the dressing room he closed the door. "Zev, have you ever smoked opium?" he asked.

I confessed I had not. Souren told me that he had just received a shipment from Beirut, and he urged me to try it. Opium held so many cultural and literary associations for me that I quickly overcame any scruples I might have held. Souren opened a drawer and took out two little brass pipes. Inserting some black substance into each one, he proceeded to heat one of them over a cigarette lighter. Within a few minutes he judged it to be ready and handed it to me while he worked on his own pipe. I put the pipe to my lips—it smoked very smoothly. Soon, time began to slow down, and I became deeply relaxed without being at all sleepy. As the two of us walked out of the dressing room and onto the stage our movements felt strangely languorous. We played a few Armenian tunes together on santur and oud, and I sensed our lingering over certain sections, spontaneously creating a few ornamental turns of phrase that had not been there on previous nights. I played my solo santur pieces with effortless control.

When Elaine came out in her skimpy costume, I was pleased to see her shapely form, yet I was curiously calm and serene. Our playing may have been a bit slower than usual—in any case it seemed that way—although the dancer was comfortable with it. My intoxication continued into the next set and on into the night. Back at Souren's, when I settled into my well-carpeted basement abode, I filled the darkened space with a treasured recording—an Azerbaijani master of the *kemanche* conjured up a world of romance and deep feeling against an unending background of the *demkesh*—a discrete drone on an oboe—and the delicate tapping and snapping of a high-pitched frame drum. I followed the arc of his bow into a deep, untroubled sleep.

X

That week proceeded in the same way, with Elaine's dancing and Souren's opium smoking, so I was relieved to go up to Rachel and Jerry's on Friday night after work. When I told Rachel about my new narcotic delights, she looked concerned, warning me to be careful—Souren was not an addict, but he did use opium rather heavily in some seasons. She could not predict how my system would react to it over several weeks. Of course, as followers of Meher Baba she and Jerry never used any narcotics or alcohol, and they also kept their sexual contact to the minimum. I expected to hear the first set of rules, but the last stricture took me by surprise. Yes, Rachel went on, the Master taught that sex was only to be used for reproduction. In that context sex was good, but for anything else it was evil, or at the very least distracting from spiritual progress.

We spent Saturday the usual way—in the morning I skied with Jerry, then spent the afternoon and evening with the family. The evening ended, as always, with readings from Meher Baba's teachings. The next day after lunch I was greeted by Ivo and his wife Jane. They had come to take me to their teepee for the day. Jane was a small woman with friendly, delicate features, and evidently, she was a few months pregnant. After half an hour of friendly small talk we left, and I followed the two of them across to the next valley.

All around us the snow glittered in the sunshine—this was a landscape I was accustomed to viewing from my skis and now it was wonderful to dwell on the details of the trees, rocks, and distant mountains as we walked at a slow pace. Ivo looked around him as we walked, seemingly responding to the beauty of nature surrounding us, but Jane put her hands to her hips and looked down, appearing to give herself support for the journey. Gradually she adopted a rather graceful posture—the measured gait of a pregnant woman covering a distance on foot. As she felt more secure, her back straightened while her hands remained on her hips—a picture of grace that seemed both practiced and unselfconscious.

After half an hour, a small teepee came into view near a clump of aspen trees. Smoke wafted up from the smoke hole. This was no architectural tour de force but a simple tent the size of the smallest Native American shelter. When we entered there was hardly any room for the three of us. Jane reclined on the futon, while Ivo and I sat on the felt spread over the ground. A violin in its case was propped against one side of the tent and a few books were stacked on the floor. There were some cooking utensils and crockery. One large, wicker chest held all of their clothing. There was nothing else to be seen inside. Ivo motioned me outside—we would allow Jane to rest for a spell.

Ivo gave me a tour of his neck of the mountain. The view was different from what I had seen from Rachel and Jerry's, whose teepee was shielded by the aspens on a wide mountain plateau. Here, there was almost no flat surface, one was continually walking upward or downward, and trees were sparse. But standing in front of Ivo's teepee we could see the entire expanse of the mountains and the town, tucked into a valley far below. Ivo smiled silently as we looked out together, then we set out walking.

As we walked, I asked a few more questions about him and his wife. Ivo told me Jane was born in the same Midwestern farming community, but her parents came from Macedonia, so they spoke a language more like Bulgarian than Serbo-Croatian. They went to the Orthodox church, attended mainly by the local Serbs. But these things did not matter, he said, back home all those Old World squabbles had been almost forgotten, and his parents did not mind him marrying an Orthodox girl. In any case, neither he nor Jane carried on any form of the Christian religion. Ivo spoke slowly and shyly. He began to speak critically of all forms of religion and even New Age spirituality: "By now Jane and I are a little tired of hearing about the Perfect Master—actually we might spend more time with Jerry and Rachel if it weren't for that preoccupation of theirs."

He looked out at the mountains and went on: "This is the teaching, right here in these trees, in these mountains. The Indians who lived here before us knew it best. Anything that comes between us and these mountains is a trap."

Now he looked down at the snow and when he looked up again his face seemed a bit harder: "Does Jerry really think that reading those repetitive books will bring him enlightenment while he lives in that three-story house he calls a 'teepee,' stuffed with every gadget that can run on batteries?"

Ivo's face wore a look of embarrassment at having expressed himself so critically. He was silent for several minutes. He seemed to concentrate again and continued, even more strongly:

"They are good people, good neighbors, and we are their friends—we don't have any conflicts living close by. But I think they carry the city with them wherever they go. It's a real burden for them and they try to disguise it with this spiritual teaching of theirs. And what does it all amount to? That poor Rachel hasn't had a moment of physical pleasure with her husband for the last three or four years! With all the junk in that 'teepee' of theirs that's the one thing they give up."

Ivo seemed genuinely embarrassed by his outburst and fell totally silent for the rest of the way. We walked on together without a word for more than two hours, until the sun began to fade.

When we returned to the teepee Jane was awake and had prepared a small repast—homemade bread, apples, peanut butter, and herbal tea. The interior of the teepee was bare, yet it reflected a warm feminine presence. Jane made no conversation. I looked effortlessly into her blue eyes—they were open, unguarded, and shining with quiet satisfaction. My mind took me to a small house on the outskirts of Erzurum, on the high plateau of old Armenia, where I had traveled three summers ago. A baby was rocking in a kilim-covered cradle suspended from the ceiling and from time to time an older woman, his grandmother, put her hand to the cradle. When the old woman's glance fell on me, I was transfixed—I looked into the eyes of a handsome woman who was far from young, her white hair covered by a thin cotton scarf, but at once I sensed the strong lines of her face as they must have been decades ago. Out of my left eye I caught the glance of an elderly, bearded man wearing a knitted woolen cap, her husband, smiling at her and at me.

XI

With the passing weeks I felt myself more secure in my niche within the natural and social ecology of Aspen. I learned to chop wood and to make my way up the mountain to Rachel and Ivo. From time to time a mishap occurred, as when I neglected to wait for sunrise before breaking through the ice covering the stream a short walk from Jerry and Rachel's teepee. The sun had not yet risen over the trees when I smashed the ice with a hatchet and thrust my hand in to scoop up water with which to wash my face. I could never have predicted the burning pain that engulfed me at that moment, and I endured the excruciating thawing out of my hand all that Sunday. Some weeks later, I tried to imitate the downhill skiers by taking a low slope on my cross-country skis. But they were not designed for this and were unable to protect my legs even at a moderate speed and angle—and as a result one of my knees was wrenched backward when the ski caught in the snow. I crawled uphill toward the teepee and found Rachel at home. She heated up a stone, wrapped it in a towel, and placed it under my knee. Still groaning with pain, I finally slept for almost twenty-four hours. Fortunately, these two accidents, both caused by my foolish ignorance of local conditions, left no permanent damage.

The social ecology proved to be stable, and I did not make any miscalculations as I had done with the frozen stream and the skis. Souren was content with the musical practice I furnished him and with our little performances at the club. His suspicion of Rachel never revealed itself. Israel and Lebanon, Turks and Armenians, never became serious issues for us; Jerry's and Ivo's approaches to life and family never confronted one another; and Meher Baba's role as Perfect Master was never challenged at the big teepee. Souren and Victoria were content to let me come and go as I pleased and as a result I felt at home in my basement space, not being obligated to share more of their lives than seemed natural to the three of us. I did spend increasingly extended stints with Rachel and Jerry. Much as I liked to be with Ivo and Jane, their tent was too small for a guest and their life was so self-contained that too much of anyone's company seemed an intrusion. So, I made my peace with Meher Baba.

During the final two weeks of my stay in Aspen, Elaine left town for a while and Rachel divided the week's dancing with Elaine's friend Leftheri, a tall and very well-formed Greek girl from New York. I never got to know her, but I appreciated her dancing and her elegant shape and stature that emphasized her command of rhythm. Just as a tall stature magnifies poor posture and rhythmic imprecision, long and full limbs moving with precision and grace overwhelm the viewer. After over two months, my musical performances as an accompanist to Souren's oud playing for Rachel and Elaine's dancing had become fairly routine, but on my last weekend at the Erevan, Leftheri's putting into motion her lithe limbs and tall back—her neat, pretty face ringed with dark curls—urged my playing to transcend itself. Over the last weeks my steady accompaniment on darabukka had helped Souren's oud to become more reliable so I now felt free to vary my percussion. Leftheri was responding well and after fifteen minutes of our normal routine I nodded to Souren—I would perform a drum solo. We had been playing the one Turkish song that Souren knew for the dance *karshilama*, that ingenious blend of Turkmen tribal rhythm and Anatolian Gypsy dance in the nine-eighths rhythm, known as *aksak*. Leftheri rarely performed it, but she had danced it occasionally at Greek parties and weddings back home, where it is known as the *karsilamades*. She was able to improvise on the basic choreographic pattern.

Ideally, I picture the karshilama executed by a woman of ample proportions whose full, round bosom would shake and bounce provocatively to the asymmetric, nine-eighths rhythm—that magical pattern called by the Turks aksak or "limping." I had first seen it when I was fifteen years old at a Greek nightclub in New York performed by a short, squat, buxom, and homely middle-aged Greek woman from the audience. I watched in amazement as she transformed herself into a voracious female animal, wild yet somehow graceful as she stooped forward, delineating a charmed circle with her rapid and repetitive steps.

Now as Souren's oud dropped out, I raised my volume on the darabukka but did not accelerate the tempo—at this moderate speed the aksak rhythm broke up into angular slivers of time, their sharp edges polished by my clear snapping on the drum's rim or my thumping on its face. Leftheri turned to me for an instant, smiling—she understood what I was up to. Now I could subdivide, syncopate the slow, innocent, first part of the rhythmic cycle, and then close with the hard, insistent stamping of the final three beats of the nine.

As I played, I recalled having performed this same rhythm several years before at a dance studio of a witty and cultured Anglo-Saxon woman who had learned the karshilama from the Turkish, Greek, and Armenian musicians in New York. I had met this dancer at one of the Greek clubs on Eighth Avenue, and she had invited me to drum for her dance class from time to time. I had been amazed and intimidated to realize that a WASP woman, somewhat my senior, had sought out an earlier, more authentic version of the Near Eastern dance and music that thrilled me. It was only years later that I had learned her true identity; she was the famous dancer and author Serena Wilson (1933–2007), and she had invited me to her Serena Studios on Eighth Avenue. A few years later she would be presenting *The Serena Show* on TV, featuring belly dancing!

But now I was viewing not wise maturity but exuberant youth. Leftheri had left the performing area in front of the stage and had taken to the aisles, alternately shimmying and arresting the motions of her hips as she glided between the red candles lighting each table. Our blonde Rocky Mountain audience was tongue-tied; sometimes gaping, sometimes squirming with embarrassment. Even scowling Aunt Harriet emerged from the kitchen. Leftheri and I lost all sense of time; we responded only to the unexpected twists of the rhythm as they produced graceful and seductive motions of her body, so tall I could see it easily no matter how deep into the relative darkness she wandered. By now it was no longer a game; and we were all struck silent as the girl let out a shrill scream, a ululation of delight, of desire, of triumph. Then she turned to the stage, and by the candlelight I could make out her sweat-drenched body gyrating its way back to us. I turned to Souren, and we switched to a fast, simple Arab tune to bring Leftheri home.

XII

That week I spent some days at the big teepee. I parted gratefully from my hosts, whom I felt I would see again. I said goodbye as well to Ivo and Jane, wishing them luck for their new baby. Back in town, Souren and I somehow knew that this phase of our lives would not be repeated. As a musical environment Aspen was too isolated for me, and the lonely Erevan provided no musical relief. Other than the brief visit of Souren's cousin, no other Armenian musician came by the town all winter, and my host showed neither much talent nor the discipline to improve his music. For all his nostalgia for his santur-playing ancestors, a steady diet of the delicate, fine, metallic strains of this instrument proved unsettling to Souren Santurian. For his part it seemed that he would have preferred an Armenian boy with whom he could joke and whose musical horizons were safely contained within the thumping *dumbek* and amplified *kef* sound of the Fresno beat. But on the whole, the winter had been well-spent by both of us—he had found me of interest at times and now he prepared for my imminent departure a celebratory kebab barbecue attended by all his local friends, who turned out to be a bunch of hard-drinking skiers in cowboy hats and boots.

At the party I ate heartily, and I discovered I had one thing in common with these skiing cowboys—unlike Souren, we all drank some form of hard liquor. Through some devilish impulse I quickly planned my revenge on Souren for the hashish and opium I had been obliged to smoke all winter. In town I had bought a bottle of Serbian plum brandy, sliwowitz, but it had lain dormant ever since I had discovered my host's antipathy to alcohol. Now, at the party, before the inevitable reefers came out, I knew I must strike.

As we were stuffing ourselves with kebabs, I climbed down the basement stairs bringing with me my bottle of sliwowitz. I found the Armenian surrounded by his kebab-laden cowboys who had all been swilling whiskey, bourbon, and gin. As I hoped, Souren's decanter remained empty, affording me an opportunity to fill it to the brim with plum brandy. I raised my glass in a toast to Souren, our friend, my host and patron. Souren turned his head quickly as he saw all the young and old cowboys raise their glasses. "To Souren!" "Souren!" We all drank quickly. I could not have touched the other drinks at the party, but kosher sliwowitz had been a staple of our home—my father and I had drunk it at holidays and special occasions. Now I would have to drink more than I was used to, but I told myself it was for a worthy cause.

I refilled Souren's nearly empty glass and raised mine: "To the Erevan!" "The Erevan!" roared the cowboy chorus. Now I gave him a break, let him chat and eat more kebabs for an hour. Then I approached swiftly and silently, filled his glass with sliwowitz and declaimed: "To Victoria!" "Victoria!" Souren looked around suspiciously, then drank up. I clapped my arm on his shoulder in friendship; I was beginning to reel and slowly I walked upstairs to rest. Forty-five minutes later Souren was embracing several of his friends. Now, I thought. I refilled his glass, and raising mine, I cried: "To our beautiful dancers!" A roar went around the room as every cowboy's throat registered their warm appreciation for those fleshy sights that had sent fires through their loins. Souren smiled bashfully under Victoria's watchful gaze and emptied his fourth decanter of yellow, sweet, one hundred-proof sliwowitz. I retired to the pillow-bolstered couch and watched my host slowly fade, shrink, and eventually slink upstairs for the rest of the night.

By the next morning Souren had recovered, and all was forgiven. He and Victoria drove me the short distance to the Aspen airport where the frightening little plane would scrape the mountain tops as it delivered me, exhausted, to Denver. Looking out the window on the flight back to New York, the world seemed to be bright, glittering with desire.

PART IV

THE JOURNEY TO KLEZMER

Chapter 11

⫼

Antranik Aroustamian

From Kharkiv to East Harlem

ONE YEAR PRIOR to my adventures at the Erevan nightclub, I made the acquaintance of the finest Armenian musician I had ever seen or heard. Antranik Aroustamian was certainly the greatest musician with whom I had worked and from whom I had learned in my early youth. Antranik was also a contrast with the other local kemanchist, Zebulon. For the latter, growing up as a penniless orphan in Derbent in Dagestan—music was just one of several crafts that he had learned in order to survive. Zebulon once said about his friendly rival: "Antranik know only music, what else can do?" As a man so deeply immersed in and achieving such success with his music, indeed what else would he want to do? Like Zebulon, Antranik had no local community and so he was essentially on his own in New York. He had grown up in Russia and Ukraine, but his family had originated in Iran. As an Armenian with a high musical education and an active career in the Soviet Union, he had little in common with the musicians from among the descendants of the Anatolian Armenian immigrants from the First World War era.

Antranik incorporated a unique mixture of musical styles, ranging from the West, to Armenia, to the South Caucasus, to Iran, and to the *klezmorim* of his native Ukraine. He had attended the Kharkiv Conservatory. He had studied the Western violin, and he was able to elicit extraordinary sounds on the traditional *kemanche*. It was only through Antranik that I could hear the full sonorous depths of this ancient spike fiddle. Thus, Antranik affirmed the possibility that a great musician could organically embody the East and the West.

My Introduction to Antranik

The beginning of my trail to Antranik takes me back to the art history section of the library at New York's City College in the late 1960s. On a sunny spring afternoon, I ordered an art book which was brought to me by the librarian, a suave and handsome Iranian gentleman, sporting a square black moustache. Somehow it came out that I was a Turkish speaker and the Iranian mentioned that he also understood that language. When I asked if he spoke Azerbaijani Turkish, he only smiled and said that, although he was educated in Switzerland, a rather older form of this language was the parole of his family in Tehran. This piqued my curiosity. In response to a further question, he replied that the families of Qajar princes into which he had been born, preserved their old imperial Turkic language, in addition to Persian. This utterly unexpected piece of family history seemed to break the ice between us, and he introduced himself as Amir Jahanbani. When he asked me about my education, my study in a Jewish yeshiva prompted his remark that he was equally skeptical about "the Bible and his grandson the Qur'an." We both laughed.

After my graduation from City College in 1970, and a couple of years after my entry into the graduate program at Columbia University, I was leaning against a pillar outside the entrance to Kent Hall. Amir—now a lecturer in Persian at NYU—chanced to enter the lobby. He smiled and said he was pleased to see me "leaning against the walls of academia." He also mentioned a performance that week at NYU by a great musician from Azerbaijan—Antranik Aroustamian—a performer of the bowed kemanche. Although at that time the NYU campus was rather unfamiliar territory for me, I took the information and thought I might attend.

At the concert later that week I could see two figures on stage—an older man playing a spike fiddle, a kemanche, and a younger, evidently Iranian man playing the wooden Persian *dombak* or *zarb*. I was charmed by the sweetness and inventiveness of the kemanche playing. Afterward Amir brought me up to the performer and introduced me in our common language—Azerbaijani Turkish. I filed away this information.

I continued to see Amir occasionally. He and his wife Ferishteh—an excellent cook—had opened up an Iranian take-out business in the Village. At one such meeting at their home he mentioned the Armenian kemanche player I had seen at NYU. Sometime later, probably in early

1974, I received a call from an elderly voice. The foreign-sounding voice greeted me over the telephone, using a string of polite phrases whose exact meaning might not have been entirely clear to the speaker. Gradually our conversation switched to a mélange of Caucasian and Istanbul Turkish. My interlocutor was none other than Antranik Aroustamian. Now he was seeking a percussionist to accompany him on several public performances, including one for the sister of the current Shah, at the Iranian Embassy in Washington, D.C. As Antranik explained, the young Iranian drummer I had seen on stage with him was unable to follow precise instructions for accompaniment. He hoped that I would be interested in learning his own arrangements of the traditional Azerbaijani and Armenian melodies. I was intrigued. Although he had performed both for Stalin and Reza Shah of Iran, at this point he shared a kind of rooming house with South Indian immigrants in East Harlem. Soon I found myself journeying further uptown to Harlem, where middle-class white youths like myself rarely ventured.

Although Antranik and I almost shared a common language (Azerbaijani and Istanbul Turkish), we spoke but little. Perhaps in part because of his artistic greatness he was extremely reticent. I remember him mainly through memories of his performances and our rehearsing together, and I have but few mementos of him. I do possess a rather poor-quality private recording of the concert he gave (with my accompaniment) at the Asia Society in New York on October 31st of 1976, and a rather better-quality recording of our rehearsal for that concert, held four days earlier in his tiny bedroom/living room. A more public memento is his solo recording from the 8th Festival des Arts Traditionnels held at Rennes in 1982, under the title: *The Art of the Armenian Kamancha: Antranik Aroustamian.* Among the facts noted in the minuscule bio on the CD case, are that he was born in Kislovodsk Russia in 1918, did his musical training in Kharkiv Ukraine on the Western violin, spent the War years in Iran "where his family originated," but later returned to the Soviet Union. He rose to direct the Armenian Philharmonic Orchestra in Yerevan, then became a soloist in the Baku Philharmonic of Azerbaijan, and finally joined the Oriental Music section of the Moiseyev Ensemble in Moscow. "He then left for the United States." According to the website recently put up by his later student, Homayoon Beigi, Antranik passed away in 1993.

Armenians

Although our common language was a kind of Turkish, I was aware that Antranik's nationality was Armenian. Ten years had passed since I had first set foot in Harout's magical club near Waverly Place. But it had become clear that most of the evenings' musical fare was Turkish popular music—indeed I had made some of my first steps in the Turkish language by memorizing a couple of songs that the Aleppan singer had dictated to me. For the musicians there and for most of their audience, Armenian music was not of so much interest. As the clarinetist Steve Bogosian explained to me: "Armenian music is naïve, but Turkish music is sexy." I did not meet anyone there comparable to my friend Christopher, the Greek American icon painter, who would have been able to guide me somewhat in the liturgical music of the Armenian church, as Chris had done for the Byzantine church and its music.

By 1971, I had been able to visit the Turkish city of Erzurum, on the site of Karin in historical Armenia. I carried with me a written recommendation from a hotel owner in Istanbul who was of Erzurumlu origin, and so I was privileged to study the magnificent *bar* dances—even the word was of Armenian origin—including the hair-raising *hançer bar*, or "dagger dance." But of Armenians I saw not a one—after the World War I genocide, there were apparently none left in the city. For the next couple of years, I had arranged larger and smaller workshops where I taught such bar and *halay* dances. One of these was in Boston, where one of my students was a young Armenian woman. Her father, an elegant gentleman who had been born in the ancient city of Van was now the editor of an Armenian newspaper in Watertown, MA. He invited me to a dance class given by a young dancer from Yerevan. Some of these dances were familiar while others were entirely new to me. I had also acquired a number of recordings originally issued in the Soviet Armenian Republic. Here and there I caught similarities with the dance repertoire I recalled from Harout's, and some from the playing of Zebulon. But mostly the musical repertoire and style was something quite distinct.

At times, my ear caught melodic phrases reminiscent of Ashkenazic music of various types. These in turn recalled an incident long before when my father was still alive. We were riding in a taxi, probably coming from the train station, after visiting relatives in Montreal. Inexplicably the driver was tuned to a radio channel that was playing songs in Greek, Turkish, and Armenian. My father enjoyed all of it, but he remarked on one of the Armenian songs, which he described as purely Hasidic in style. When I came to hear more examples of both repertoires I could only agree. But why? How? This was completely inexplicable. At that point in my life, I would have been unable even to formulate the question more precisely. But a creative musician like Antranik who lived his whole life between several related cultures, not infrequently sensed certain musical connections which did not remain abstract for him, but which he could build on artistically.

From Lincoln Center to the Asia Society: Antranik and Zebulon

Less than two years after his arrival in New York, Antranik—possibly with the help of Amir Jahanbani—booked Alice Tully Hall at Lincoln Center for his American debut. His accompanists were a curvaceous, doe-eyed Armenian pianist from Beirut and myself on *daf* and dombak. As we had little time to rehearse, I appeared only in a couple of pieces.

Zebulon came to the concert with his students. There was a tearful reunion backstage as he and Antranik embraced after more than forty years. Zebulon remarked several times how grey Antranik had become, and the Armenian kept repeating :"What I went through in Russia, what I went through!"

After intermission, Antranik came out to a partly darkened stage and began to glower at his kemanche, then at the audience, then again at the kemanche. When everyone, especially the kemanche, was sufficiently intimidated, he launched into his fantasy which was somehow connected with one of the best-known Armenian airs in which a lonely exile asks for news of his homeland and family from a crane flying overhead. "The Crane," in Armenian "Grunk," has been a favorite in the Caucasus for over a century. This was followed by a strangely similar-sounding piece entitled "Prayer of Israel" learned by Antranik from Jewish klezmorim in his native Ukraine.

When I visited Zebulon that weekend, he was thoughtful concerning Antranik's concert. Speaking to his students and me he commiserated with Antranik's problems in earning a living in America, despite his former economic security in the Soviet Union. Then he laid the blame partly on the Armenians: "Look at Armenish; in all America one kemanchist have, but no give job!" I knew this to be true; but Antranik would never cooperate with the local musicians, of Anatolian origin, whom he regarded as totally ignorant of Armenian music. Zebulon also considered that Antranik himself might also be at fault: "See how Antranik play Grunk? That no Grunk, that fantasia. But who come concert?—Armenish grandfather, grandmother. They no want hear fantasia, want hear Grunk. But where Grunk?" Unaware of Zebulon's critique, the *New York Times* picked up on this concert and ran a short but respectful review.

Antranik and Zebulon shared a repertoire of Caucasian dances of Azerbaijani, Armenian, and other origins. But whereas Antranik played most of them in the fast virtuosic style of the mugham interludes and finales, Zebulon evidently had long experience in using the melodies for actual dancing. In the 1960s the talented New York Armenian oud player John Berberian had recorded an intriguing tune that he named "Sevan 5/4," whose melody was spread unevenly over the asymmetrical rhythmic cycle. But when I played it on the santur for Zebulon, he was skeptical:

"This Russian-Armenian tune, not from the old days. Armenians had some special songs, but the dances were all the same, like the rest of the Kavkaz. But now the Russians want everyone should have own nation-tunes—must be special for Turks, special for Armenians, special for Tat, for Lezghi, for Georgians. But in Derbent, in Baku, in Tabriz, no one played this tune."

Antranik knew exactly who had created this tune—an Armenian composer of his generation, and Antranik had conducted it with the Orchestra of Armenian Folk Instruments in Yerevan. It was new Armenian folk music, and he liked it very much. Still, he would not include it in his concert suite of Armenian dances—it sounded too innovative, too modern. But since Zebulon had left the Caucasus in the 1920s, all this history was known to him only a general way.

The adoption of violinistic positions on the kemanche, such as Antranik had done, was an anathema to Zebulon. Antranik epitomized much of what Zebulon rejected. Aside from the mugham, which he played rarely in this country, Antranik's repertoire was rich in rubato melodies of Armenian and other origin that became the raw material for his own "fantasies" on the kemanche.

In order to fulfill my obligations as an accompanist properly we conducted several rehearsals, mostly in Antranik's tiny room in East Harlem, and occasionally in my almost equally tiny studio on Riverside Drive, down the hill from Zabar's. After what I imagine had been far more satisfactory accommodations in Baku and Moscow, somehow Antranik appeared cheerful enough in his little room, with his Caucasian *tar* stuffed under his bed. Whenever I walked into the kitchen for a glass of water I usually bumped into one or more of the quiet and polite South Indian men with whom he shared the flat.

Our best common language was a kind of Turkish patois, more Azeri on his side and more Istanbul on mine, with his occasional word or phrase in English—a language he never really mastered. Fortunately, I recorded one such rehearsal on my cassette machine. Listening to it again after so many years I can understand why he appreciated my accompaniment. I had heard some rather good Iranian dombak playing—technically more agile than mine—but there was never a need for such precise coordination as Antranik demanded, coming from his Soviet stage, folkloric, and concert background. Almost every tremolo on the frame drum daf or the Persian dombak was prearranged. Antranik was particularly demanding with my accompaniment for his semi-improvised cadenzas to his Caucasian or Persian dance melodies. He practiced these at a variety of dynamic levels, and I can only marvel at his control of the bow, which allowed him to barely scratch the strings of his kemanche. My snapping or brushing on the drum had to maintain a clearly perceptible rhythm, although never interfering with the delicate filigree of his bowing. Some of these cadenzas had to be repeated two or three times until he said "OK." Using the Azeri word for rehearsal, he would often repeat "tamrin," and "there is no harm" (*ayb yokh*), meaning we will rehearse it until it is really right, and he was comfortable with the arrangement.

In the breaks from these rehearsals Antranik offered only very few glimpses of his previous life in the Soviet Union, and keeping to my adopted Turkish manners, I never asked him direct questions. In fact, I never understood what his native language might have been. He was clearly fluent in Russian, Azerbaijan Turkish, and in Persian. I never heard him speak Armenian, that I can recall, but he must have to be able to conduct the Armenian Philharmonic in Yerevan in that language.

Once Antranik explained something of his musical background, and even showed me a photograph of his first teacher on the kemanche. To my surprise, this teacher Sasha Oganashvili (1889–1932) was a Christian Georgian. As Antranik explained, he was both a master of the performance of the classical mugham music on the kemanche and a scholar who could "sit and discuss with the Russian musicologists." Comparing this information with what I had learned from Zebulon about his teacher Vartan Mangasarian—an Armenian master of the tar from Derbent—it was clear that the mugham performance and theory was really the transnational music of the cities of the South Caucasus. This was true whether the peasants in the region spoke Armenian, Georgian, Lak, Lezghi, or another Dagestani language, Tati or Azeri Turkish. This latter language had been in fact the lingua franca of all the urban centers such as Derbent, Shemakha, Yerevan, or Tbilisi. In the eighteenth century the great Armenian kemanchist and poet Sayat Nova (1712–1795) had performed for the King of Georgia in both Georgian and Azerbaijani Turkish, as well as composing songs in Armenian.

Thus, as an urbanite, Antranik regarded the Azeri mugham as his own music, much as the Istanbul Armenians regarded the Ottoman *makam* as their music. But due to his considerable professional experience in Yerevan, and to the Soviet policy of allowing, indeed insisting, that most acknowledged and official nationalities should teach and perform their own national music, Antranik was more knowledgeable in the secular Armenian musical tradition than his place of birth and education in Russia and Ukraine would suggest. The Tsars had ruled the South Caucasus since the early nineteenth century, and there was a considerable native Christian presence, who were their natural allies. Russian rule had arrived rather later in Central Asia, where there were no native Christians, and so the harsh Soviet policy toward the *maqom* music as "feudal" and socially backward was only mitigated in the 1960s, with the help of Uzbek musicians from within the Communist Party. In contrast, even under the Soviets the feudal Azeri mugham music was allowed to retain much of its traditional place among Muslims, Christians, and Jews in all of the major Caucasian cities.

This information about his teacher Sasha Oganashvili was one of the few bits of biographical data that Antranik ever offered me. As far as I could tell he had never married, and he did not mention any children. My friend Steve Wolownik—the Ukrainian multi-instrumentalist through whom I had met Zebulon—did inform me that Antranik had a brother who played the tar in Northern California. He had apparently immigrated somewhat earlier, and apparently Ashot Aroustamian had lived to the age of 114! But Antranik never mentioned him. As for romantic engagements, I know of only two. One was with a much younger Jewish girl in the Soviet Union, whose picture he kept in his wallet. And that spring, Antranik visited me with his new friend, a dark Russian Jewish woman his own age. Masha was tall and buxom, with an open and intelligent face. I appreciated that they were willing to sit on my Anatolian *kilim*, amid the bolsters on the floor, while I offered them tea—truly as bohemian a form of student hospitality as could be imagined. I cannot recall what language we all spoke. Some months later he told me the news that Masha was seriously ill and would need an operation. She later recovered, but I did not meet her again.

Somewhat before the appearance of Masha, Amir had arranged for us to play at a private concert of rather wealthy Iranians in Manhattan. As I recall there was much good food, but only a little music. One older Jewish American woman seemed particularly moved by the music and pointed out—with much bathos—the similarity in destiny of the Jews and the Armenians, a point with which Antranik agreed.

Thanks once again to Amir's guidance, Antranik finally got the opportunity to perform something like a complete program, with the accompaniment that he wanted, at New York's Asia Society. A laudatory review in the

New York Times followed. There was no official recording of the concert, so it was fortunate that one of Zebulon's students was in attendance, and secretly recorded it. Afterward he gave me a copy of his rather muffled recording. This was apparently Antranik's more "public" program—for an ethnically mixed audience—featuring mainly abbreviated versions of Azerbaijani mugham and its incidental dance tunes as well as the corresponding Iranian melodies of the same type. One of the latter was his own composition, named "Ferishte" or "angel," which was also the name of Amir's wife.

The Iranian Embassy and Princess Ashraf ol-Molouk

With all that has passed since 1979 and the creation of the Islamic Republic of Iran, it may seem peculiar that Mohammad Reza Shah Pahlavi (1919–1980) was not very popular among many in the United States. Several Iranians I knew in the 1970s, including the santur player Nasser Rastegar-Nejad (1939–2018), came to this country partly out of opposition to his rule. Nevertheless, it now surprises me that in 1976, when Antranik announced to me by phone that our next gig would be at the Iranian Embassy in Washington, D.C. to celebrate the visit of the Shah's twin sister Princess Ashraf ol-Molouk (1919–2016), I was less than enthusiastic. Even though it was springtime, I fell ill with the flu a week prior to our appearance. Antranik even suspected me of malingering!

The two of us had an uneventful flight, and we were taken by cab to our hotel. We were to perform that evening, along with a separate appearance by a younger Iranian santurist, living in the States. I do not think that we conversed very much, but Antranik did mention that he had performed once for the current Shah's father, Reza Shah Pahlavi (1878–1944). Antranik had somehow used his family's Iranian origins to slip across the border, before the Nazi invasion of Ukraine, where he was then still studying in Kharkiv. I am sure that he did not swim across the Aras River like Zebulon had back in 1926! Apparently, someone—perhaps Amir—had suggested that now that Antranik was a resident of the United States, it might add a certain luster to the Princess's visit to be attended by this famous musician who had once entertained her father in Tehran.

Looking at the rather impressive photos of Princess Ashraf ol-Molouk, I try to conjure up a beautiful and charming lady. But in my memories from the Iranian Embassy, she did not exude any particular charisma. She paid scant attention to any of the music, although she did come over to Antranik and offer a few polite words in Persian. I was not introduced to anyone, and so I remained more or less invisible. The overwhelming impression that I had from the Iranian Embassy experience could be summed up in three words—paranoia, suspicion, and arrogance. Everyone, except perhaps the Princess, seemed to look around in every direction before expressing even the mildest opinion. The young santurist—who did show some interest in me—stood with his back to the wall, looked straight ahead, and only asked me a few questions out of the corner of his mouth. I did not get the impression of an ancient court, where each gesture had been preordained and could be accomplished with grace and delicacy.

Perhaps the most notable event of the evening came during the intermission following the performance by the young santurist. The current ambassador, a tall and dark man, rose to say a few words of introduction about Antranik. He had a tall, alcoholic, mixed drink in his hand. As he strode to the center of the room he deposited the tall glass on the nearest available surface, which happened to be the strings on the face of the santur! The young musician could not stifle the look of pain that suddenly overcame his face. Antranik shot me an ironic glance but said nothing. Our performance lasted about twenty minutes and consisted of a few of his Persian and Persianesque pieces. There was no gracious dinner. After our performance we were hustled back to our hotel. Over our minimal repast, Antranik said nothing about the Princess, but seemed astonished by the behavior of the Iranian ambassador. He kept repeating, "For shame. His father would never have done such a thing!"

When I met him in his hotel room the next morning, Antranik was somehow inspired to rehearse a number of the pieces that we had played the previous night. He also seemed to have thought of a few new details for one of his pieces. I pulled up a chair and enjoyed listening to him. But when his playing began to exceed half an hour, I had to remind him that we had to depart for the airport rather soon, so he would need to pack up and gather his things. He paid no attention. He played for another twenty minutes perhaps and showed no sign of stopping. Against my wishes I felt compelled to remind him that we were not unlikely to miss our flight back to New York. At long last he consented, and hastily gathered up his things. A cab was found for us, and soon we were on our way to the airport. But, as I had feared, by the time we arrived our flight was closing. As we both rushed to enter the line, he turned to me and said urgently: "Why are they not holding the plane for us?" This sentence suggested a world of elite privilege that Antranik must have enjoyed in his Soviet past.

Klezmorim and Tatars

By the following year, Antranik began to play a much smaller role in my life. It was now high time that I actually started to write my doctoral dissertation! Turkey was sliding into a near civil war—so I did not visit there—but even from a distance I maintained my study of the Ottoman Sufi mystical musics.

Amir Jahanbani, who was beginning to develop his own teaching career at The New School in New York City, did not have the time to seek many performance opportunities for Antranik. Having arrived prior to the major post-Soviet immigration, unable to utilize his Russian language or musical contacts, Antranik seemed basically dependent on outside help and guidance. Unfortunately, he seems not to have met the brilliant Armenian American composer Alan Hovhaness (1911–2000), who had moved to Seattle around the same time that Antranik arrived in New York. The dream of the brilliant musicologist Gomidas Vartabed (1869–1935) to uncover the roots of Armenian folk and liturgical music on both sides of the Ottoman/Russian border could not come to fruition in America. Indeed, a musician like Antranik could have played a role in such a revival.

One of the last performances I engaged in with Antranik actually led indirectly to the music of the European klezmer, in a way that I could never have predicted. Antranik phoned me to ask if I could accompany him, not at a concert, but at a party. This time he was invited by Armenians from Romania, and there would also be an Armenian accordionist from that country. This sounded intriguing enough, so soon I made my way up to his small room in Harlem.

There, in addition to a lighter version of our usual program, Antranik showed me a couple of Crimean Tatar melodies he knew, and which he imagined his Romanian countrymen might also be familiar with. Then he said something, the significance of which I only came to understand some years later. He played me a Crimean dance tune in duple time—actually one that I had heard from the Bessarabian Martin Kalisky on his mandolin a few years before. Then he played an unknown, but somehow not unfamiliar melody. He added: "This is a Jewish dance. Is it not very similar?"

"For sure," I answered. "But where did you learn this?"

"In Kiev. There was a Jewish ensemble there before the War."

"What kind of ensemble?" I asked.

"It was a kind of folk dance theater, some of it almost a kind of comic theater. It had some very good violinists. I learned this piece from them. Some of their tunes resembled the Tatar melodies."

Years later this exchange replayed itself in my mind. There can be no doubt that Antranik was referring to the State Ensemble for Jewish Folk Music and Song of the Ukrainian SSR, led by the violinist M. I. Rabinovitch. The preeminent Soviet Jewish ethnomusicologist of the time, Moyshe Beregovski (1892–1961)—whose own dissertation from the Moscow State Conservatory would be on the theme of klezmer music—was then working as an academician in Kiev and was involved in this ensemble.

Only a year later I would read Beregovski's seminal 1937 Yiddish article on "Jewish Instrumental Folk Music"—then available from the YIVO Institute. But his other essays and some small parts of his music collection were only published by Mark Slobin in 1982. So, back in 1976 I could only take in the tidbit of information, without having any way to assess its wider meaning. Nor was I in the position to follow up with further questions, some of which Antranik certainly could have answered. But the vibrant sound of his kemanche playing *freylekhs* and *khosidls* never left my ears!

The Tatar side of the equation would prove to be even more elusive. Sometime in the following decade I would meet a Crimean Tatar singer from Turkey named Selma Ağat/Akbikei, who had completed an MA thesis on Tatar instrumental music. Somehow, she was told to contact me. She was a beautiful, light-haired young woman, about my age. She met me at Columbia University, and gave me a copy of her MA thesis, plus a cassette with copies of a unique collection of Crimean instrumental recordings, as well as a cassette of her own vocal performance from Turkey. She explained to me that these old recordings had been made in Germany during World War II. This was part of a propaganda initiative by the Nazi government to win over the Tatar population of the Crimea to their cause. The ultimate results were well-known—Stalin deported the entire Tatar civilian population from the Crimea to Central Asia. Her family was among the fortunate ones who had fled to Turkey long before the War. By this time, she had heard something about what was being called "klezmer music," and she learned that I was involved in it. So, I agreed to prepare a cassette for her with a number of instrumental pieces to listen to. In the interim I read through her Turkish thesis, listened to the band recordings, and the recording of her vocal performance.

A couple of weeks later we met once again at a restaurant on Broadway. Her thesis had a number of highly interesting sources and photographs. As usual for Turkey at that time, there was almost no analysis of any kind. But the old recordings were a revelation! The band was almost exactly the same as a klezmer string and wind ensemble of that era, except that the violin was given more prominent solos than I was used to from the klezmer band recordings. The other major difference was the percussion—this was clearly coming from a Turko-Tatar tradition, with several mysterious rhythms, and also a very clear seven-eighths rhythm. As Antranik had pointed out, several of the melodies were strikingly Ashkenazic, and the performance style was highly heterophonic—the violin, clarinet, and trumpet played variations on the same melody simultaneously. This was much like a klezmer ensemble of the time, but perhaps even more so.

For her part, she said she was deeply impressed with the clarinet of the Galician klezmer Naftule Brandwein (1884–1963).

"How so?" I asked.

"He sounds like a Tatar clarinetist coming from a distant village, beyond the mountains. More or less the same music, but with an exotic intonation."

Neither of us could explain any of this. I told her that a few years ago I had interviewed an Ashkenazic musician named Jacques Press (1903–1985), born in Tbilisi, who had attended the concert we arranged for Dave Tarras in 1978. After the concert he gave me his card and invited me to call. When I went over to his place on Riverside Drive, he revealed that his father had been a klezmer fiddler from the Crimea. Along with his Jewish work, he had played with a Tatar band. Mr. Press still recalled some of the Tatar tunes and played them for me on the piano. Later on, his father had moved to Tbilisi and joined the Philharmonic Orchestra there, finally immigrating to California. Mr. Press had grown up in LA and made his career as a musical arranger for Hollywood. Later I reflected, was this Ashkenaz/Tatar symbiosis a product of the period of Russian rule in the nineteenth century? Or, like the Armenian connection, was it of much older historical provenance? In later years I also learned that the last generations of Tatar musicians had also played a number of Moldavian dance melodies, in addition to the items that they shared with klezmer musicians. Since the Khans of the Crimea had also ruled Bessarabia for several centuries as the clients of the Ottoman Turks, it is not unlikely that something of the klezmer and Moldavian Gypsy musical symbiosis had also reached the Crimea, perhaps as early as the eighteenth century.

Meanwhile, Antranik and I still had a Romanian party to play. I remember it as a humorous if rather chaotic affair. Unlike the Iranian party of a couple of years back, we presented no concert music, only dance tunes, to the mainly middle-aged company. The only musical moment I can remember is our attempt to play the well-known Crimean dance *qaytarma*. This is the universal dance of the northern Black Sea region, whose cognate in Romania is *geamparele*. What Antranik knew, however, was the version known in the South Caucasus as "Baku Qaytarması," which Zebulon also played. The crucial difference is the rhythm—seven-eighths rhythm in the Crimea and in Romania, six-eighths rhythm in Azerbaijan. As the percussionist, it was my task to try to level the difference between the two. But since no one was dancing, this musical disagreement led to no serious consequences, and the audience took it in with good cheer.

That Romanian party was my public performance swan song with Antranik. The writing of my dissertation caused me to withdraw from any performing for over a year.

Around this period, I was invited to come into a recording studio with Antranik. We went through all of our usual pieces. But somehow his solo items proved problematic. As much as he concentrated and glowered at his kemanche, somehow he could not achieve the result he desired. I do not know who was paying for the recording, but in the end he canceled it. In 1982 he was invited to the Festival de Musique Traditionnelles in Rennes. The very elegant solo recording—with no accompaniment—came out posthumously. From this time until his death a decade later, Antranik Aroustamian began to receive more recognition in New York, France, and Switzerland. By then, I was teaching at Princeton and later at the University of Pennsylvania and was not performing at all. Around this time, the Iranian American scientist Homayoon Beigi became Antranik's kemanche student, and he followed Antranik's later career in America. I regret not having seen Antranik when he was somewhat more acknowledged as a musician in the United States. When he finally passed away in 1993, Beigi and Masha arranged for Antranik's burial in a Russian church cemetery in Rockland County, New York. Beigi later played at his memorial service held at Columbia University.

I will always be grateful for the musical lessons and experiences that I owe to Antranik. His unique background, combining the musics of Iran, Azerbaijan, Armenia and even some exposure to the music of the Crimean Tatars and the klezmorim of the Ukraine helped to guide me into the next phase of my musical life. May his memory be a blessing!

Chapter 12

###

Andy Statman

From Bluegrass to Greek to Klezmer

ONE YEAR AFTER Antranik Aroustamian made his presence known to me, another outstanding musician entered my life. But he did not speak broken English along with his native language or languages; nor was he my senior. Andy Statman emerged from that other segment of my musical world, populated by American-born contemporaries who were mostly natives of either the Bronx, Brooklyn, or Queens. But for all that, his musical genius illuminated my life for years.

As I perfected my skill on the Persian *santur* I discovered that its resonant timbre also suited a branch of folk music coming from Ireland and Scotland. It was a kind of hammer-dulcimer that had been played there. By the early 1970s, I found myself playing santur and banjo duets with a former classmate of mine from Music and Art High School. Alan Feldman (from the Galician Feldmans) was a master of the old-timey banjo. He also developed a passion for Irish fiddle tunes. For a time, we both had Irish or Irish American personal involvements in Boston, and we discovered that Boston was an Irish city, perhaps to the extent that New York was a Jewish one. Our Irish and Scottish-tinged melodies and improvisations were much appreciated in Boston. Apart from playing in clubs, our street performances in Cambridge turned into major public events, sometimes with audiences of well over forty people staying for an hour.

As a child of the 1960s, I was aware of the larger movement toward both American and British Isles folk music. Some of the most competent local practitioners were natives of my own neck of the West Bronx, such as Andy

May and Kenny Koszek; the latter remains a leading figure in bluegrass music today. I had enjoyed musical sessions and parties with these friends. Once, after a concert by the bluegrass group The Wretched Refuse in the West Village, Alan introduced me to the mandolinist I had just enjoyed on stage. This mandolinist had heard that I was involved with a number of immigrant musicians from Greece, Turkey, and the Caucasus. He wondered whether I would be willing to share any of these contacts with him. I answered in a friendly but reserved manner. This kind of interest coming from the American-oriented musical quarters was entirely new to me. Over the past decade I had found such openness almost exclusively among the children of Greek, Ukrainian, or other East European immigrants. I had grown accustomed to keeping this part of my life separate from my friends in my educational or artistic environments. The one major exception was Christopher, the Greek icon painter from the High School of Music and Art. But now the versatile Andy Statman made his appearance.

Soon we would meet, and we developed a little repertoire of British Isles, Balkan, and Caucasian melodies. Occasionally I sang a folk song in Turkish. Andy was a Queens native, and several of these masters resided in that borough, or in Brooklyn. While of Volhynian-Jewish origin, Andy's parents were American-born, and so their household was English-speaking. Yet the absence of Russian and Yiddish, let alone Turkish—all of which aided my work with some of these musicians—was no barrier for Andy. Either their English was more or less adequate, or if not, Andy's intuitive musicality and charming personality led the way to high-level musical communication.

Three years passed, and at last I was reaching some degree of proficiency on my village *cimbalom*. Andy had begun to study the Epirote clarinet with Perikles Halkias. It was time for Andy to learn the Smyrnaic style and so Limberis became the source. One Sunday afternoon my visit to Limberis coincided with the end of Andy's lesson. I was delighted to see his handsome face concentrating over his mandolin while he picked out the Ayvaliatiko *zeimbekiko*, soon to be a part of our growing repertoire. Andy's candor and musicality reached out even to dour Mrs. Limberis who seemed to genuinely enjoy his lessons with her husband.

Very soon I introduced Andy to most of my teachers, including Antranik Aroustamian. On his own, Andy contacted the Bessarabian mandolinist Martin Kalisky. As a mandolinist, Andy was mainly a performer of bluegrass. Even without having traveled to the British Isles he intuited the Scottish background of many of the tunes and genres and was able to demonstrate his impressions to me. Since the mid-1970s I had been traveling to Ireland—initially with our mutual friend the banjo-playing Alan Feldman, and then on my own. At that time Ireland was a revelation to me; a West European country whose people had little property and seemed to care most about witty conversation, good music, and good beer. As an Istanbul carpet dealer had expressed it to me—"The Irish are not like other Europeans; they have souls!"

I became acquainted with some of the leading revival players residing in Dublin. I spent many sessions at local pubs, listening to and chatting with singers of the level of Paul Brady. At one point, I was invited by him to the Dublin singers' pub where I had the temerity to perform a few songs in Yiddish, Romanian, and Turkish to the assembled singers. Then I was invited to perform some of these at the Dublin Folk Festival. On the strength of that appearance, Andy and I were invited to be the opening act for Brady's performance at New York's Town Hall venue in 1977.

Local music was still very much part of Irish culture while I was there in the 1970s. But, due mainly to heavy immigration either to England or to North America, Irish folk music was not in the healthiest state. Many tunes and whole repertoires were being forgotten with no documentation. And so, in my own generation a number of urban-born musicians and singers went to the Irish villages to learn older instrumental tunes and vocal styles, both in English and in Gaelic. It was not a coincidence that the Irish became one model on which I could base my later research into klezmer music. And it was in this period that I married my first wife—Siobhan Gibbons—a native of County Roscommon, a region rich in flute playing. Near her village stood the magnificent grave of Turlough O'Carolan (1670–1738), the famous Irish harper and composer. Through my research there into Irish music I even discovered what may be the last reference to the now extinct Turkish harp, the *çeng*. In the memoirs of the harper Arthur O'Neill (1734–1796), he praised the construction of an Ottoman çeng that had been purchased in Belgrade and brought to Cork. He was even able to tune it and to play Irish airs upon it with great success!

Another part of the musical equation with Andy were the Greeks. During the same month Andy was studying independently with the Epirote clarinet virtuoso Halkias and with my Dodacanese cimbalom teacher Pavlos Limberis. Back in undergraduate school I had known the Greek American musicians and some of their families, eventually performing with the group Leventiko Pende in the Catskills. The guitarist in the group, George Vikos, now approached me to play santuri/*cimbal* with a new *rembetiko* ensemble, Paleoparea, being put together by Thanassis Galanopoulos. Thanassis was a charming and beautiful singer who had grown up with the songs of the *rembetis* in the port city of Piraeus. He was now the superintendent of a building on West 10th Street, where we would rehearse the songs of Vamvakaris and the more sophisticated songs of Hadjidakis and Theodorakis. Even now when I traverse through the West Village, I recall those dynamic rehearsals! Someone in the group must have seen me with Andy Statman, and now they suggested inviting him. Of course, his mandolin playing fit well with the group. I still have a flyer for our concert together with Paleoparea at CAMI Hall, near Carnegie Hall, in the summer of 1977. It was gratifying for me to spot my old friend Christopher—the icon painter—enjoying the music from the audience!

That very year, Paleoparea's performance with Andy and me would take a turn toward klezmer. That autumn, once the semester began, Thanassis's group was going to perform at McMillan Hall at Columbia University for a Greek students' society. Andy was already an avid discophile, and frequented flea markets in Brooklyn that sometimes sold old 78 RPM records. A few weeks before this concert he informed me that he had found some nice old Jewish recordings there that we might want to learn. He dubbed a couple of the dance tunes onto a cassette and brought me a copy. One of the old New York klezmer orchestras from the 1920s was playing a *bulgar* tune, which was recognizably Jewish but with some phrases that we felt the Greeks would relate to. At the McMillan Hall concert, Thanassis had suggested that Andy and I do one mandolin/cimbalom duet. We chose that piece, one our partners in Paleoparea had not yet heard. At the concert, while Andy and I played, pandemonium broke loose among the packed audience of mainly male Greek students! Somehow this profound and yet celebratory music struck a chord deep in their psyches and collective memories; we were almost mobbed on stage. Afterward, during intermission, Thanassis came up to us and asked us to please play more such tunes at our next concert! It was no coincidence that this encouragement came not from any American Jew, but from a Greek musician. Andy and I would soon take Thanassis's words to heart and attempt to find a living source for this old Jewish music.

13

Dave Tarras Plays Again

Dave Tarras and the Klezmer 'Revival'

ANDY AND I were working on a Macedonian duet of alto-saxophone and *davul* drum at a rehearsal and dance space on West 96th Street. It was then rented by the Balkan Arts Center, which was based in the very building in which I was living on 110th Street. During a break from our Macedonian Gypsy-style playing, Andy put a question to me. He had been studying with superb musical teachers, such as Limberis, Antranik, and the Bessarabian mandolinist Kalisky, all of whom played some Jewish dance and listening tunes. These were the kinds of things that my father would have associated with a klezmer musician back home. But these tunes were peripheral to their larger repertoires. Andy asked me: Did I know anyone who played such tunes as the central part of their musical performances? I thought for a moment. Then I mentioned the clarinetist, Dave Tarras. He had recorded numerous records, old and new. I had not met him, but my parents had; they had heard him playing in the Catskills a few years ago. Andy took it from there on his own. He looked Tarras up in the local musicians' union directory and located him among the clarinetists. He telephoned Tarras and was soon invited to meet him at his apartment in Brooklyn.

Dave Tarras (1897–1989) was no one's "discovery." He had been a dominant force in American klezmer music for forty years. The influence of his style and repertoire spread also through his performances and recordings with Yiddish theater singers. All of us who have heard those little clarinet sighs and glottal catches behind a throaty Yiddish singer have imbibed Tarras's conception of Jewish music. During the 1950s and 1960s I heard his recordings on WEVD, and I bought several of his 78 RPM and LP record-ings.* Tarras was also a known figure to the North Bessarabian Edinetser and Britshaner *landsmanshaft* societies. Fleeing from Ukraine during the Russian civil war with its terrible pogroms, Tarras had spent some time in my father's *shtetl* Edinets, which was then under Romanian rule. There he imbibed the local, mixed Jewish/Gypsy klezmer repertoire, which he then developed on his own in America.

When Tarras was in semiretirement in the 1960s my parents had no-ticed his name displayed on a billboard in a "bungalow" colony near their own summer colony in the vicinity of Monticello in the Catskills. Seeing his name, they decided to spend the weekend there to listen to and dance to his music. But when Saturday evening came Tarras was seen strolling about the colony grounds with no apparent intention of setting up for his performance in the casino. Alarmed, my mother went up to him and asked what time he was going on stage. She was shocked to hear him reply that he was vacationing in the colony and had not intended to play at all. He was hard put to explain to my mother why his name was written large on the bungalow colony billboard. Either due to my mother's persuasive charm (later on he used to tell me she was "a smart lady"), or to his embar-rassment at the owner's evident manipulation of his name and reputation, Tarras did perform that night. My mother felt she had won a victory that was well worth the price of the weekend.

After meeting Tarras, Andy took up the clarinet and quickly learned the new fingering. This also enabled him to pursue his interest in Greek clari-net music with the old Epirote musician Perikles Halkias. After six months of lessons Tarras sold Andy one of his old clarinets. This vintage but still bright-sounding instrument added to Andy's enthusiasm for klezmer mu-sic. From time to time, I would ask Andy for his impressions of Tarras, and his most characteristic reply was that Tarras was "like an old watchmaker," precise and cautious in all of his dealings. I felt that it was important that I not meet Tarras until Andy had established a firm relationship, which would be based on his study of the clarinet. I was confident that Tarras would recognize Andy's extraordinary talent, and he did.

After a year of study, Andy's work suffered a setback when Tarras's wife Shifra died suddenly. Theirs had been a very long and happy marriage.

---

* Parts of this chapter were first published as, "Klezmer Revived: Dave Tarras Plays Again," in Ilana Abramovitch and Sean Galvin, eds., *Jews of Brooklyn* (Waltham, MA: Brandeis University Press, 2000), 186–89. The current version has been expanded considerably.

The two of them had fled through Ukraine together and come to America as immigrants. Tarras was disconsolate and for several months he was unable to teach. He moved out of the house he had shared with Shifra, even tearing up some of his sheet music and throwing out some of his 78 RPM recordings.

After leaving Aspen, for most of 1975, I traveled through the Western United States and then on to Europe and Turkey. I kept up with Andy's studies through his occasional letters. At one point he was working simultaneously with Tarras, Halkias, and the two Caucasian fiddlers, Zebulon and Antranik.

Paris and Ha-Neros Ha-Luli

That summer I found myself in Paris, during the hot month of August when most Parisians took their vacations. Staying in Le Marais district, I was not without Jewish contacts. One of them was a middle-aged woman painter named Gurevitch—like my mother's Belarussian *mishpokhe*—but born in Cork on the western coast of Ireland. I also bumped into Orhan, a young Turkish folk dancer, whom I had visited earlier in Ankara. He was about to leave his studies in the United States and start a job working for a Turkish oil company.

Despite my very active socializing I had plenty of time to stroll through the beautiful if overheated streets of Paris. On one of these long daytime walks my senses were overcome by the memory of one of the recordings that Andy had found that year in a Brooklyn flea market. It was the very oldest klezmer recording I had yet heard, recorded before the First World War in Lemberg—Lviv, which I believed must have been in the eastern part of the Austrian Empire. The label was written in Hebrew, Latinized according to the Galician dialect—"Ha-Neros Ha-Luli," or as the Sephardim would say "Ha-Neirot Ha-Lalu"; "These Candles." This was the beginning of one of the prayers for Hanukkah, normally one of the gayest of Jewish festivals. But rather than a celebratory brass band, this old 78 RPM recording featured a single violin—played by "H. Steiner"—accompanied by an unnamed player of the *cimbalom* or *cimbal*, the klezmer hammer-dulcimer. The violin performed a rubato melody utilizing a penitential synagogue mode. His performance was of breathtaking sadness.

In the America of my postwar generation, the klezmer violin had become a myth, something akin to Marc Chagall's paintings of fiddlers on the roof. But now for the first time I was exposed to what this music had actually sounded like. Nothing I had yet heard could compare with the tragic dignity of this violin/cimbalom duet. I recall having played it for a poetically articulate Scottish American professor at Berkeley, and she had described it in a note to me as "the most painfully beautiful fiddle music on record." Some years later, my other friend at Berkeley, Professor Martin Schwartz, had found a copy and issued it on his memorable LP *Klezmer Music: The First Recordings*. Through that medium it had been picked up by the Hungarian string band Muzsikas in their fieldwork on the former Jewish music in Transylvania during the early 1990s. They had used it to play to their elderly Gypsy musician informants in order to identify the kind of music they were seeking. One of them, on hearing the recording answered, "I am one hundred percent, one thousand percent certain that this is Jewish music!" But during that summer of 1975 this ancient recording was apparently known to exactly two living people in the world—Andy Statman and me. As much as I loved and enjoyed the inventive and gay dance tunes that Tarras played on the clarinet, I might never have mustered the determination to explore klezmer music were it not for the improbable survival of this rare document of klezmer violin music in Europe. I wanted to learn where this music had come from. It was almost twenty-five years later, in 1998, that I would finally meet in New York, Yermye Hescheles (1910–2010), a Galician Yiddish poet and journalist from the region of Lemberg/Lviv, who had played the violin with klezmer fiddlers very much like Steiner. But in 1975, I could not have imagined that this quest of mine would become a lifelong journey.

Meeting Dave Tarras

When I returned to the States half a year later, I purchased a Greek *santouri* which was tuned like a cimbal. I was ready to learn the melodies Andy had studied with Tarras. My spacious new apartment at 110th Street and Broadway resounded with a few Tarras favorites, such as the "Bessarabian sîrba," or the "Hebrew Dance," as well as older *freylekhs* and *zhoks*. Two years after he had started to take lessons with him, Andy and I decided that it was time for me to meet Dave Tarras.

Tarras had remarried recently, to Adele—the owner of the bungalow colony in the Catskills—who had cleverly used his name as bait to lure my parents. He had moved into her Coney Island apartment in which she had been living alone since the death of her first husband.

I remember meeting Andy on the IND subway. We rode to Coney Island together, getting off at the final stop. It was springtime and the weather was pleasant and sunny. We walked under the elevated tracks past the new "gastronoms" of the recent Jewish immigrants from Odessa. Dave and Adele were living in a large, modern apartment complex, which resembled structures in the Long Island City section of Queens rather than the older brick buildings of this Brooklyn neighborhood. The complex was located in a square somewhat recessed from the rest of the city and rather quieter. We rang the buzzer, entered, and went up to the tenth floor.

At first glance the apartment we entered, and the elderly couple who greeted us, were so unexceptional I almost felt that we must have come to the wrong place. Looking around I could have been visiting one of my father's *landslayt* in the Bronx of thirty years ago. Every visible object might have been chosen by a Feldman family decorator. The only somewhat unusual point was the extreme cleanliness and order that was evident in every corner of the living room. Adele was a very short woman with faded blonde hair, large, thick eyeglasses and a meek, pleasant smile. I recognized Dave Tarras's face from one of his LP record jackets, but I was not prepared for his height and the intimidating forcefulness of his movements. Tarras was standing as Adele opened the door. His posture and expression as he greeted us told me that he viewed Andy as a special person in his life, and that I might partake of some of that specialness. Tarras spoke English about as well or as badly as my father had. His intonation was similar—a broad, southern Yiddish accent that few in America would recognize as Jewish. They were of about the same height, but Tarras had blond hair and blue eyes instead of my father's black curls and dark eyes. Tarras's speech was slow and deliberate, due partly to his discomfort with English grammar, but also due to his habit of carefully weighing every word.

Andy made the introductions, and Tarras offered me a seat on the couch while Adele rushed to serve the tea and cookies. I was still a graduate student, and I had some trouble explaining what I was supposed to be writing about. Andy told them that I played the cimbal. Then Tarras mentioned his late friend Josef Moscovici (1879–1954), who had been an outstanding performer of Romanian and Jewish music on the large concert cimbalom. He asked me about my parents. When I answered that my father—who had passed away seven years earlier—had been a Bessarabian from Edinets, he warmed up visibly, praising the country, its music, and its wine. He had even spent some months in Edinets. Tarras described it as "a lively Jewish town." It was only when I was able to visit and do research in Edinets over thirty years later that I came to understand what a delightful place it is even today.

This introduction opened the way for my weekly or biweekly visits to

Tarras's apartment over the next two years. I also made frequent visits to the home of his accompanist, the accordionist Sam Beckerman, who was the nephew of the great klezmer clarinetist Shloimke Beckerman (1884–1974) and the cousin of the contemporary klezmer Sid Beckerman (1919–2007). I became used to carrying my cimbal, wrapped in its woolen and canvas cases, on the IND subway line from Manhattan to Brooklyn. On some occasions I brought my tape recorder as well. Meanwhile Ethel Raim and I had written a grant proposal to the National Endowment for the Arts (NEA), requesting a year's funding for a new project in what we called "Jewish instrumental folk music," as "klezmer" was still an obscure term of the Yiddish lexicon. The concert of November 1978 was one result of this project, which had been funded through her organization, then called the Balkan Arts Association, and later the Center for Traditional Music and Dance. In a short time Tarras shifted his perspective on life from that of a successful, but now retired musician to that of an active performer. He was an authority on a music which was gradually coming back into demand, that obscure object of desire to be known henceforth as "klezmer music."

Dave Tarras Plays Again

This was the final sound check before the crowd would come pouring in. The turnout for this concert of "Jewish Klezmer Music," featuring "The Dave Tarras Orchestra" in November of 1978 was much greater than anyone had expected. Fifteen hundred elderly Jewish people were forming a line outside, and several hundred more had to be turned away. The hall where the concert was being held, now rented by a Spanish landsmanshaft, and called the "Casa Galicia," was familiar to many of the people as Webster Hall. There, klezmer bands led by such stars as Naftule Brandwein and the young Dave Tarras had played for their frequent dance parties back in the 1920s when they were all young and newly arrived from their poor and pogrom-ridden homelands in Russia, Ukraine, Poland, and Romania. My Bessarabian father had told me, "We never danced so much at home as we danced in America." Eventually, most of them found a place for themselves somewhere in the growing American middle class, many at its lower end, a few toward the top. Their children usually entered the professions and businesses of their families, but the music to which their parents or grandparents had danced as young immigrants was no longer a major part of their lives. Several families I knew still owned a few old 78 RPM discs. More owned the newer, LP records on which they could hear the clarinet, trumpet, and saxophone playing the klezmer dances which had been popular in the New York of forty or fifty years ago—the frey-lekhs, the *sher*, the zhok, and especially the *bulgar*.

The musician they had now come to hear was no longer leading an "orchestra," but merely a trio of clarinet, accordion, and snare drums. Tarras could no longer even count on the violin and piano with which he had worked thirty years earlier, much less the twelve piece brass, wind, and string orchestras to which these immigrants had danced in this very hall in the 1920s and 1930s. Besides, he had lost touch with most of the tunes he used to play back then, even though he composed many of them himself. He had retired from professional playing ten years earlier, and for fifteen years prior to that, his clients' tastes had changed so much he had little need to play most of these klezmer tunes. They were also more difficult technically than the current "hits," and the last thing he wanted as a professional was to make any mistakes on stage.

An hour before the doors opened, a tall, slightly overweight but solidly built man in his late seventies began to step slowly and carefully across the wires which crisscrossed the low-lit stage. His stride expressed both confidence and caution, great willpower tempered by a precise knowledge of his current physical limitations. When he reached the center of the stage the lights revealed a handsome, almost boyishly fleshy face, with remnants of reddish-blond hair still not entirely white, while his blue eyes shone behind thick eyeglasses. While the lights were being adjusted, he went over an old tune on the clarinet. Standing in the wings I watched his fingers fly up and down the keys. I recognized an old bulgar which was the first recording that Tarras had made in this country. This scene was to be repeated at each concert he would give during the following two years. Prior to each one, he invariably warmed up his fingers with the same bulgar, which, however, he never performed on stage. By now his repertoire consisted exclusively of the old Yiddish theater songs which were more familiar to this audience than the dance tunes of their distant youth. I felt the poignancy in Tarras's persistent, indeed unshakable, habit of checking the clarinet and loosening his fingers with the same tune which had helped to bring him recognition and success as a young immigrant klezmer.

Before Tarras went out on stage, his students, Andy Statman, and I played a few very old klezmer tunes from Europe; most of them not part of the American klezmer repertoire in living memory. Our instrumentation was also exotic—I accompanied the familiar clarinet with the klezmer cimbal dulcimer. Andy's tone on the clarinet was sweet and remarkably mature. The audience reacted enthusiastically even to this exotic material. When Tarras emerged he and his accompanists gave them something of the faded post-klezmer repertoire of twenty years ago, but with a warm and subtle style that retained much of the appeal of his music since the 1920s. Perhaps only his improvised *doina* suggested something of his earlier klezmer repertoire. The audience, my mother included, was literally entranced. By the end of the program, pandemonium was breaking loose. During one of the encores, a middle-aged man wearing a yarmulke leapt up from his seat and danced spontaneously; the entire audience was seized with something approaching frenzy. I thought of the biblical tale of the Golden Calf, and how we ought to have prepared one to place in the center of the dance floor! Soon the floor was cleared of chairs, and many people danced whatever they could. Tarras played a few of the klezmer tunes still in his active repertoire; I led a line of the bulgar. I leaned back and allowed my shoulders to bounce lightly as my father had done while dancing. When I stopped dancing, I observed that the audience was more diverse than I had initially thought—a variety of American-born Jewish types were there dancing in addition to the immigrants in their seventies and eighties. If the "klezmer revival" had a beginning, I would give this date in November 1978 when "Dave Tarras played again."

The public reception of Tarras's first and subsequent concerts was surprisingly strong. Shortly after the first concert, Nat Hentoff published an article in *Jewish Living* entitled "King Klezmer and His Dynasty," describing Tarras as "a stately, broad-shouldered man, [who] played with that total authority which requires no extraneous dramatics." Hentoff also recognized a link between Tarras and us, his students: "Dave Tarras' musical lineage spans three generations, and he needn't look far for an heir." Two years later, after a second concert, Harold Steinblatt's lengthy review in *Jewish World* was entitled "Klezmer Music is Alive and Well and Playing in New York."

The next stage of our NEA klezmer project involved bringing Tarras and his group to the senior centers of the Jewish Association for Services for the Aged (JASA) located in Brooklyn. These were always festive events, during which the incredulous residents seemed to be greeting a part of their past, miraculously returned to life. Miriam Berliant, the director of the Williamsburg Center of the JASA wrote to us: "As the director of the Center, I was overwhelmed with joy to see my people sing and dance and clap with such enthusiasm. . . . It was a cold snowy day outside, but in our center it was 'fraylach' and warm." For these people, the resonance of Tarras's music and personality was immediate—they had heard him long ago, and they required no mediation to discover his significance. But what surprised me was the broader recognition of the value of Tarras's music, even among Jews who might have heard him only on records or on the radio, and only in their childhood.

As I had mentioned, Tarras himself was no longer playing Tarras's repertoire. He left that to Andy and me. Our first solo concerts were not only received enthusiastically, some of them were stampedes! At one concert held on the Upper East Side, I had to rush out before the performance to be sure that Nica Constandache, my elderly Romanian aristocratic friend—now totally blind—would not be hurt by the crowds. The tones of Andy's clarinet seemed to awaken some distant memory, some dream of childlike happiness that this music had once symbolized in the Jewish collective consciousness in America.

Dave Tarras Plays Again Part II

While leading a line of bulgar at the wild party immediately following Dave Tarras's concert in Casa Galicia in November 1978, I could sense the catharsis and liberation that the audience was feeling. I was also aware that the only Jewish dance that some people were able to follow was the bulgar. This was a transnational dance of the old Istanbul butchers' guild, known as *kasap* and *hora in* Turkish, and *sîrba or hasapiko serviko* in Greek. That is what Tarras and his band were playing, along with various current Israeli and neo-Hasidic "hits." At the concert he had not even been playing that, but what I had described as a "faded post-klezmer repertoire." Still, the entire program—beginning with the Yiddish songs by Feygele Yudin and Ethel Raim, and the short program by Andy Statman and myself—had contributed to this overwhelming catharsis. I saw the film of the concert soon afterward, but I did not have the opportunity to view the video of the dance party until almost thirty years later! There I saw several young people who later became friends and colleagues in the klezmer/Yiddish revival. I could see that the improvised dancing was mainly a mixture of Israeli and ad hoc Ukrainian patterns—Ashkenazic dance, per se, was almost nowhere to be seen. But I also observed the posture of the dancers—even with the almost total loss of gesture, steps, and figures. Both young and old still displayed the dignified erect bearing of Yiddish dance.

Andy and I had been working with Tarras for some years, and the importance of that concert did not make itself felt to us immediately. We had more urgent tasks—first to organize the recording of Tarras and his trio for the LP *Music of the Traditional Jewish Wedding*. To our delight Tarras took to this with gusto, researching some of his previous repertoire, and even a couple of items from much earlier, possibly familial klezmer tunes.

Incidentally, although I was still a graduate student, Tarras was in the habit of calling me "The Professor." Once, while we were all seated at his dining room table, Tarras had raised one hand and proclaimed: "The Professor should write about me!" Indeed, my first article devoted to klezmer music, "Bulgareasca/Bulgarish/Bulgar: The Transformation of a Klezmer Dance Genre," which came out in the journal *Ethnomusicology* in 1994, mentions his repertoire in several places. Nevertheless, it was over twenty years later that I had accumulated enough material to write about all this in my monograph *Klezmer: Music, History and Memory* (Oxford University Press, 2016), in chapter 5: "The Old World Jewish Wedding."

But in 1979 I was not aware that Tarras had not had the occasion to play for such a wedding for well over fifty years. He himself never spoke about it, but dutifully set about practicing the nondance items still in his repertoire that might have been appropriate as Old World wedding ritual music, i.e., "Opshpiel far di Makhetonim" (track 2); "Kaleh-Bazetsn" (track 4); "Fun der Khupeh" (track 5); and "Opfirhren di Makhetonim" (track 12), as well as wedding table music "Doina" (track 6); "Ba dem Zeiden's Tish" (track 7); "A Pastukhl's Kholem" (track 8), and the Yiddish songs idiosyncratically titled "Kishinev" (track 9). The remaining items—sîrba, *honga*, zhok—are all dance tunes emanating from the Moldavian transitional klezmer repertoire. When the Canadian collector Ruth Rubin had interviewed the New York Galician fiddler Berish Katz (1879–1964), close to the end of his life, he was able to recall a variety of Old World melodies for the *kale-bazetsn* ceremony. It is striking however that Tarras's "Kale-Bazetsn" is also an Old World melody of apparently Moldavian Jewish lineage.

I also took this opportunity to visit Tarras and ask him about the dance forms he had chosen. This usually led to his getting up to dance, and sometimes to his leading me around the room in a zhok or a honga.

For Andy and me the real pleasure was listening to Tarras's clarinet and Sam Beckerman's accordion, recreating sounds that had not been heard from them for decades! Several times Andy and I stood up and cheered in the recording booth when we heard a particularly striking tone wafting in from the studio. Soon afterward there were the small local concerts that we had arranged at various Jewish centers and old-age homes in Brooklyn and New Jersey, where Tarras was a very familiar name. It was in those months during the following winter and spring—much more than at the first concert—that we began to sense almost a sea change in the attitude of the public toward this music.

"Jewish Klezmer Music"

We began to rehearse for our own LP, to be entitled *Zev Feldman and Andy Statman: Jewish Klezmer Music*. In the title I reused the name I had come up with for Tarras's concert. I had chosen "klezmer music" as the best English translation for "klezmerishe muzik" or "klezmerishe folksmuzik," used by Moyshe Beregovski in his seminal Yiddish-language article on the subject from 1937. The great Ukrainian-born musicologist knew that Yiddish possessed a venerable word for the Jewish musical guild member, the "klezmer," which had originated as far back as the middle of the sixteenth century. But there was no general term for the Jewish repertoire played by the klezmer that had included both dance music and wedding ritual melodies. This music became the topic of Beregovski's own dissertation from Moscow in 1944. The Ukrainian/Israeli musician Joachim Stutshewsky had Hebraicized it as "muzika klezmerit" in 1959. Here I added the word "Jewish" since I could be sure that almost no one in America would have much of a clue as to the meaning of "klezmer music."

As it turned out, we did not need to search for a label. Dan Collins of the Irish American Shanachie Entertainment company approached us, as both Andy and I were known by younger musicians in Ireland. This led to an intense period of choosing repertoire—which mostly fell to me—and then rehearsing either at my place in Manhattan or at Andy's in Brooklyn. Unlike all other then-available Jewish LPs, ours featured only an Old World repertoire. We made a point of utilizing several rare scientific transcriptions—originating both in Bessarabia and in Belarus—as well as several old 78 RPM recordings.

As the clarinetist, of course Andy led in most of the selections, which were generally based on the classic 1920s recordings of the great immigrant klezmer clarinetists, Shloimke Beckerman (Sam's uncle), and Naftule Brandwein. Neither of us had been trained in musical transcription, so we learned these pieces entirely by ear. Andy's rendition of Naftule's "Kallarash," "Doina," and "Fihren di Makhetonim Aheim" ("Escorting the In-laws Home") have become classics in their own right. "Fihren di Makhetonim" was a rare example of the introverted wedding ritual klezmer melodies to have been recorded in New York among the immigrant generation. It was a challenge to do justice to this wonderful piece, and we both put our souls into the endeavor!

From my graduate school research—usually in the Russian language—I was already quite familiar with the Slavic and East European Collections of

The New York Public Library. I still possess the hardcovered notebook in which I copied out Ivan Lipaev's groundbreaking article from 1904, "The Jewish Orchestras," which I discuss at some length in *Klezmer: Music, History and Memory*. For repertoire and the Jewish tuning of the cimbalom, I located Nikolai Findeisen's Russian article, "The Jewish Cimbalom and the Lepianski Family of Cimbalists," from 1926. Since the original journals were so old and fragile, I was not initially allowed to photocopy them. Hence, I painstakingly copied them out (musical notations and all) with pencil. I was not allowed to use a pen, which might damage the original pages. I owe both of my cimbal solos on our recording to Findeisen's transcriptions. I wrote of the Kaleh-Bazetsn: "In Belorussia this solemn music accompanied the ritual seating of the bride." Of course, Findeisen added no suggestions as to tempo or general performance style. Later I understood that the melody draws on the famous "Avinu Malkenu" hymn composed by the second Rebbe of Lyubavitch almost two hundred years ago. I brought it down to Sam Beckerman in Brooklyn, and together we reconstructed a performance style. Amazingly, forty years later, when the Russians reissued a recording of the Lepianski's performing this piece, I understood that my tempo and phrasing were very close to theirs.

At the same time, I came across the unique documentation of the mixed klezmer and *lautar* ensemble of the central Bessarabian town Orhei. This had been collected in the 1920s and only published in 1964 by the cantor Moshe Bik, long after he had immigrated to Israel. Written in Hebrew, it is a priceless musical and sociological document. I continued to consult it for repertoire up until the mid-2000s. But in 1979, Andy and I decided to perform only a ritual waltz for the Jewish bride. It had been composed by the "Judaized" Gypsy lautar fiddler Petru Tsigeuner. Although called a "waltz," musically it combines Ashkenazic with Crimean Tatar musical movements. Our instrumentation of mandolin and cimbal gave free reign to both of our musical fantasies.

Despite the "foreignness" of both the instrumentation and most of our repertoire, I was somehow confident that our music would resonate more widely. Thus, on the album jacket I could write:

We consider it a pleasure to be able to express ourselves in a style which we find basically natural. We feel that we will have succeeded if people of whatever origin will sense something of the joy and vitality, the strength and endurance that went into the creation of this music and will see its relevance to their own lives.

Much later, in 1996, when Michal Shapiro published her Ellipsis Arts CD *Klezmer Music: A Marriage of Heaven and Earth*, she would write:

> When I started to work on this project, I owned one klezmer music record. It was by Andy Statman and Zev Feldman . . . I played Andy and Zev's album with some regularity. . . . The music had a dignity and lack of sentimentality that appealed to me.

Thus, my words turned out to be much truer than I could ever have imagined.

Back in 1979, on occasion we brought our rehearsals to Tarras's place in Coney Island, to get his input for one of his own pieces. After the recording was finished, this led to very enlightening sessions between Tarras and me, as he explained through his solo dancing how our versions could be improved and made more expressive. Tarras was a superb dancer, whose every movement held musical meaning.

Only one piece on the album—the "Ternovka Sher"—came directly from Tarras, but most had been in his repertoire at one time. We conducted our final rehearsals for the recording in Tarras's living room in Brooklyn. We were pleased that he had no criticism to make of our version of "Ternovka Sher," even though we chose a slightly faster tempo than his early recording. And for me, the best moment came when we played him our "freylekhs fun der khupe." When I switched from doubling the melody to playing a strong rhythm on the lower strings of the cimbal, Tarras lay back in his easy chair and let out a *krekhts*, a groan of delight. That was his highest praise.

Andy and I were usually hired to play at weddings by families who already were somewhat familiar with this older music and their dances. Rarely was this knowledge very precise or detailed, but the feeling and the posture were there. I can recall one summer night at a wedding in Long Island, where our hosts requested us to play the "Lekhu Neranena" finale from Brandwein's "Kallarash," and they proceeded to dance with sprightly steps for what seemed like half an hour! At another wedding in Manhattan, I had the delight of playing for groups of young women of Yiddishist background, all dancing the sher contra dance in couples together!

One of our most memorable weddings took place in the synagogue in the elegant Gramercy Park area of Manhattan. The *khupa* was set up in the synagogue, and after the brief ceremony we played an elaborate *freylekhs fun der khupe*, originally from Ukraine. After the other guests had filed into the dining hall, where we would shortly join them, one man turned and walked toward us. He was perhaps in his late sixties, short, and rather stocky with almost no neck visible at all. He spoke English with a thick Southern Yiddish accent. After the passage of thirty-five years, I can still see the energy that he emanated. He fixed us with his gaze and exclaimed: "Freylekhs! What freylekhs! I haven't heard such freylekhs since I came to this country. In the war we were hiding in the forest, waiting to ambush the Germans. We would sneak up to their barracks, then throw our hand grenades. When the Germans ran outside, we would shoot them. We killed every one! Then we would run back to the forest. And . . . we would dance," he proclaimed, raising his arms to the skies. "We would dance freylekhs!"

Hearing this tale my own catharsis and liberation were complete!

Postlude

I WAS NOW on my way to reaching the fabled Klezmer Island. Although my journey there had been begun with my partner Andy Statman, within a few years there were many other younger musicians making their pilgrimages. It must be observed, though, that many of these would-be pilgrims became caught on the shore, as it were. They were enmeshed in the kind of American-Jewish, "Yinglish," nostalgia that Andy and I had sought to avoid. The klezmer music that Andy and I were performing represented the antithesis of this American style and repertoire. This mild self-mockery of the Jews had infiltrated itself musically so that it took some effort to reimagine a musical expression of the Jews while they were still in Eastern Europe, or in the early years after emigration. Initially we were presenting this music simply out of love, admiration, and respect for our elders and teachers. We learned this Jewish music in the same way that we had learned Greek and Armenian music, from a combination of living masters, old recordings, and a few old notations. It took us very much by surprise that the Jewish klezmer music would reach a large audience with astonishing rapidity. But it was almost a decade later, with the reunification of Germany, that the klezmer revitalization became truly international. Germany became the most attractive and sophisticated market for klezmer music, and several of the most creative American-born practitioners immigrated there, to Austria, or to Hungary.

Initially I was somewhat removed from all this, as by 1981—only three years after recording my klezmer album with Andy—I had begun my first teaching position at Princeton University. I was teaching Ottoman Turkish language and culture. I had visited Turkey before, but now I could receive grants to do research in more depth. Back in 1975, I had been introduced to the dervishes of the Halveti Order in Istanbul. Soon after, I also met some people connected with the Mevlevi Sufi Order. Later in that decade I was invited to accompany these Halveti dervishes as a percussionist on their tour throughout the United States. The sponsors of these tours also invited a few of the leading Ottoman musicians from Istanbul. I was thus able to meet and to accompany musicians of the caliber of the bowed *kemençe* player Ihsan Özgen (1942–2021) and the *ney* players (flautists) Niyazi Sayın and Kudsi Erguner. In New York I had been exposed mainly to the folk songs and popular dance music from that part of the world. Now I could seek out the more artistic and transcendental performances and compositions. This new potential was so overwhelming that my memories of loosely related musical styles among the klezmorim of Europe had to await a more favorable period of my life.

After I left Princeton in 1984, I began immediately to work on a National Endowment for the Humanities grant to translate the Ottoman musical treatise and notations of the Moldavian prince and classical *tanbur* player Demetrius Cantemir (d. 1723). Shortly after Dave Tarras's demise in 1989, I was approached to contribute something dealing with the Romanian component in the klezmer repertoire. This resulted in my 1994 article in the journal *Ethnomusicology*, "Bulgareasca/Bulgarish/Bulgar: the Transformation of a Klezmer Dance Genre." But the continuing early Ottoman music project demanded my attention, until it resulted in my first monograph, *Music of the Ottoman Court*, published in Berlin in 1996.

While describing my experiences at the Balkan Phonograph shop in the mid-1960s (see Chapters 4 and 8), I had recalled the proprietor Aydın Aslan presenting to me an early recording of Tanburi (Djemil) Cemil Bey (1863–1916) on the lute tanbur:

> On the reverse side the performer switched to a resonant lute-like instrument. . . . Its sounds seemed not to be produced by the mere contact of plectrum and string; rather they were drawn down from another, unearthly realm. . . . I could hear the sound of metallic strings and an ethereal aura surrounding the entire instrument.

The tanbur had been the central instrument of Ottoman court music, but by the 1970s it was also on the decline and had rather few players in Turkey. At that time, the tanbur had no players in the New York area. In 1980 I was privileged to attend a concert at Cathedral of Saint John the Divine, featuring the *neyzen* Niyazi Sayın and Tanburi Necdet Yaşar (1930–2017), the leading tanbur player of Turkey. He had been the student of Mesut Cemil Bey (1902–1963), the son of Tanburi Cemil Bey. Suddenly Ottoman music in all of its dignity and glory appeared before me! Three years later in Istanbul I was able to meet Necdet Bey. He had taught previously for the ethnomusicologist Robert Garfias at the University of Washington. Now, thanks to a letter from Philip Schuyler, a former student of Garfias—whom I had known while he was teaching at Columbia and who had arranged his earlier concert at St. John the Divine's—Necdet was encouraged to stride up to me at a concert of the State Turkish Music Chorus in Istanbul, and offer me his help. I was then beginning to study the courtly vocal repertoire with a member of this chorus—Fatih Salgar— who later would become its director. Necdet Bey became my teacher and friend for the remainder of his long life. Within a few years I was also able to invite both him and Ihsan Özgen to perform in New York and in Philadelphia, with my accompaniment on percussion. The *New York Times* review, by Peter Watrous, of our small concert in 1988, pointed out some of the most transcendental aspects of this music:

> The two musicians exhibited astonishing, but gentle, virtuosity. . . .
> The music was refined, pared down to its essentials. . . . With its delicacy and lightness, the music seemed as if it were overheard in a dream.

But it was only ten years later—after I had finished writing *Music of the Ottoman Court*—that I could focus once again on the deeply meditative side of the older klezmer music. As we saw in chapter 13, it was Andy Statman's discovery of a single 78 RPM recording from pre–World War I Galicia that set me on the path to reach the Klezmer Island:

> This old '78 featured a single violin . . . accompanied by an unnamed player of the *cimbalom*. . . . The violin performed a rubato melody utilizing a penitential synagogue mode, and his performance was of breathtaking sadness.

Back in 1940 Montreal, Israel Rabinovitch had described this kind of playing as remembered by his father from older Jewish weddings in Belarus. But his Yiddish tale—entitled "Unzer Heimisher Klezmer in Djazzland"—points to the incongruity of this introspective Old World klezmer music with his current immigrant and Canadian-born audience. In Old World klezmer playing—as in Old World Jewish dance—these moments of introversion and transcendence were quite prominent. In my concerts with Andy, I would always include one or two of these solo pieces, sometimes learned from some of the rare pre-Holocaust notations from Belarus, Ukraine, or Moldova. These also came to include transcriptions made by the great researcher in Kiev, Moyshe Beregovski, that had been published in America in 1982 by Mark Slobin. My last klezmer performance from 1985—a solo *cimbal* concert presented at a Jewish cultural center in Long Island —featured almost only such "display" compositions.

The great Yiddish dancer Nathan Vizonsky (1898–1967) in Chicago, as well as the extraordinary Yiddish set designer Boris Aronson (1898–1980) originally from Kiev, both writing in the interwar era, stressed this transcendental aspect of Jewish solo dance as well. But by the time I was reaching maturity, this kind of Jewish dance barely existed. Hankus Netsky (2015) writes about how marginalized this type of dancing had become in his native Philadelphia even prior to World War II. There it was called simply the "Dance for the Old Men."

Among the next group of klezmer revivalists, related sounds were occasionally created by the violinist Deborah Strauss (following the senior violinist Leon Schwartz, 1901–1989), and Deborah's mentor Kurt Bjorling in Chicago. But in general, the next stage of the revival was not about that. Other than a single recording by Kurt's Chicago Klezmer Ensemble (1985), the entire klezmer wedding ritual and listening repertoire remained untouched. Much as I admired Dave Tarras's clarinet playing and compositions, at most he still could perform and occasionally compose the more elaborate processional wedding tunes. These had a quasi-choreographic function within a dignified formal wedding procession, or for a Hasidic *rebbe*. In his last recording—which Andy and I had produced in 1979—*Music for the Traditional Jewish Wedding*, Tarras reached back into his memory and his archives for what he could salvage of the wedding klezmer music that by then had almost no currency in America for perhaps fifty years.

Almost twenty years later in New York, in 1998, I was introduced to the Galician Yiddish poet and former klezmer Yermye Hescheles (1910–2010). The year that I spent interviewing Hescheles transformed my entire understanding of klezmer music. At last, here was someone who had played that older style of music that was preserved on those ancient klezmer recordings from his native Austrian Galicia! I introduced him both to the violinists Alicia Svigals and Steven Greenman, with whom I was then playing. With Hescheles's encouragement I formed the klezmer ensemble Khevrisa, dedicated to this Old World repertoire.

Even with some of the Greeks, there were moments of introspective lament, as in the Epirote moirologia playing that my father had so much appreciated. But these occupied but a small part of the repertoires performed by either Greek or Armenian musicians in the United States. The only musician whom I knew in New York who actually developed some of these introspective ideas was Antranik Aroustamian. For this purpose, he utilized a variety of Armenian rubato songs, at times influenced by the related klezmer violin playing. Here his *kemanche* was able to sing into the heavenly spheres! While recording my LP with Andy Statman in 1979, perhaps unconsciously I followed Antranik's model in my solo rendition of the Yiddish wedding song "Alineynem," as a fully rubato piece.

My early exposure both to the *davenen* prayer of my father's little synagogue in the Bronx and to the Byzantine chant of St. Spyridon's Greek Orthodox Church in Washington Heights had presented me with the key to unlock the deepest mysteries of both klezmer music and the music of the Ottoman Court and the dervishes. Over the course of many decades this indeed became a journey from the Bronx to the Bosphorus, and to Bessarabia and back. During these past forty-odd years I have usually conveyed the results of my musical explorations through the medium of scholarly writing, teaching, and the organization of concerts. My physical sphere of activity focused mainly on Istanbul. Toward the end of the Soviet system these explorations reached into Uzbekistan and among the Bukharan immigrant musicians in Queens, especially the composer and poet Ilyas Mallayev (1936–2008), as well as the *sozanda* women dancers and poetic declaimers, led by Tofakhon Pinkhasova (1928–2010).

Later opportunities permitted me to return to my father's region of Moldova, and to the newer Moldovan musician diasporas in Germany, Israel, the United States, and Canada. Apart from scholarly research, these many human and musical interactions would demand a much fuller written presentation. But in this book the reader will find some record of how a much younger writer reflected on the life experiences of an earlier group of musical diasporas, who had all met within the city of New York.

ACKNOWLEDGMENTS

Unlike my academic books where several chapters were read and critiqued by colleagues, the process here was quite different. Over many years I had shared a story or two with various friends and sometimes with musicological colleagues. But I can thank two readers for having a formative influence on the book. First of all, the poet Robin Magowan has shown an unflagging interest in these tales for over two decades. Why this is so I can perhaps attribute to his early travels in Greece and deep love for Greek dance and music, and later for klezmer music. Add to this his lifelong experience with New York. Robin took the trouble to read almost every chapter and to make very concrete suggestions about rhetoric and vocabulary choices. I cannot thank him enough!

More recently, my friend and Upper West Side neighbor, the writer Jane Mushabac (Shalach Manot)—part of whose Turkish family had lived in the very same Bronx neighborhood as mine—had read several of the early chapters and made very concrete suggestions. I owe much to her unflagging interest and enthusiasm!

GLOSSARY

ashoog Performer of oral poetry in Azerbaijan. Same as Turkish *ashik*.

Azerbaijan Territory in the Eastern Caucasus, formerly known as "Shirvan." Ceded by Qajar Iran to Tsarist Russia in 1828, it was renamed Azerbaijan after the neighboring Iranian province. Following WWI, it became a Soviet Republic and then an independent Republic. Its leading city is Baku.

baaltfile Precentor; prayer leader in a smaller Ashkenazi synagogue.

Bessarabia Portion of the Principality of Moldova, east of the Prut River, annexed by Tsarist Russia in 1812 from the Ottoman Empire. Today's Republic of Moldova.

bouzoukee Twentieth-century urban Greek, fretted, long-necked lute, based on the Turkish bozuk.

bulgar Jewish line dance based on the Moldavian bulgareasca, in turn a development of the Istanbul butchers' guild, the kasap, butchers' dance.

chifte-telli (T. Çifte-telli) Improvised erotic couple dance.

cimbal (tsimbl) Klezmer hammer-dulcimer.

cimbalom Hungarian large dulcimer with legs and dampers.

daf Wooden frame drum ("tambourine").

Dagestan Multiethnic territory in the Eastern Caucasus, its major city is Derbent. Ceded by Qajar Iran to Tsarist Russia in 1813. It remains a part of the Russian Federation.

darabukka "Hourglass drum," classically made from ceramic. Also known as "dumbek."

dastan Epical tale among nomadic Uzbeks.

davenen   Form of improvised musical prayer among East Ashkenazim.

freylekhs   Common Jewish circle dance in the Jewish South (Ukraine, Galicia, Moldova).

halay   Complex line dance among Kurds and Armenians.

hassapiko   Greek urban dance, based on the dancing of the Istanbul butchers' guild, the kasap, butchers' dance.

hazzan   (Yid. khazn) Cantor in the Sephardic and Ashkenazic synagogues.

kanun   A type of large zither with a thin trapezoidal soundboard.

kemanche   Skin-faced, bowed fiddle in Iran and the Caucasus.

kheyder   Jewish elementary school in Eastern Europe.

klezmer   Member of the Jewish musicians' guild, originating in sixteenth-century Prague and diffused throughout Jewish Eastern Europe.

landsmanshaft   Fraternal organization of regional Jewish immigrants in America.

lautar   Professional musician in Moldo-Wallachia, usually of partly Roma and partly other origin. They generally term themselves "Tsigane" (Gypsy) rather than "Roma."

makam   Ottoman modal system.

mekhitsa   Barrier separating the women's rows in a synagogue.

mugham   Azerbaijanian modal system and performance repertoire.

Qajar   Iranian royal dynasty, of West Turkic origin; ruled 1789–1925.

oud   A short-necked, pear- shaped, fretless lute in Turkey and the Arab countries.

peshrev   The leading genre of Ottoman instrumental music. Since the 16th century it became the opening part of the Ottoman concert.

reimbetiko   Repertoire of urban music of working-class Athens, developed following the population exchange with Turkey in 1923.

santouri   Greek version of the klezmer cimbal, with identical tuning.

santur   Iranian hammer-dulcimer.

sher   West European contra-dance (German "scher"), apparently entered East European Jewish folklore from Germany during the eighteenth century. By the following century it became musically "Judaized."

shtibl   Small Ashkenazic synagogue.

shtetl   Small town in Eastern Europe, often on the private land of the nobility, and frequently with a majority Jewish population.

Simkhes Toyre   (Seph. "Simhat Torah") Festival of "Rejoicing in the Torah."

sîrba   One of the basic line dances in Romanian culture; one precursor of the bulgareasca/bulgar.

taksim   Turkish makam improvisation in flowing rhythm.

tar   A long-necked, skin-faced, waisted lute family instrument, used in slightly different forms in Iran, Azerbaijan, Armenia, and Georgia.

tsamiko   Mainland Greek men's line dance with a martial spirit, in a three-quarter rhythm.

zeimbekiko Greek popular dance and musical genre, developed out of the *zey-bek* culture, and flourishing in Greece following the Greco-Turkish population exchange of 1923.

zeybek 1) social bandit organizations within southwest Anatolia, from the later eighteenth to the nineteenth centuries; 2) dance culture of the *zeybek* bandits.

READINGS

Beigi, Homayoon, "In Memory of Andranik Aroustamian," Artists 4 Peace Website, 2024.

Beregovski, Moyshe. "Jewish Instrumental Folk Music" (Yidishe instrumentale folks-muzik). In *Old Jewish Folk Music: The Collections and Writings of Moshe Beregovski*. Edited and translated by Mark Slobin, 530–48. Philadelphia: University of Pennsylvania Press, 1937, 1982.

———. *Jewish Instrumental Folk Music: The Collections and Writings of Moshe Beregovski.* Second Edition (2014). Revised by Kurt Bjorling. Evanston, IL: Kurt Bjorling, 2015.

Bucavalas, Tina, ed. *Greek Music in America.* Jackson: University of Mississippi Press, 2019.

Feldman, Walter Zev. "Bulgareasca, Bulgarish, Bulgar: The Transformation of a Klezmer Dance Genre." *Ethnomusicology* 38, no. 1 (1994): 1–35.

———. "Remembrance of Things Past: Klezmer Musicians of Galicia, 1870–1940." *Polin: Studies in Polish Jewry*, 16 (2003). Oxford: Littman Library of Jewish Civilization.

———. *Klezmer: Music, History and Memory.* New York and Oxford: Oxford University Press, 2016.

Frigyesi, Judit Niran. *Writing on Water: the Sounds of Jewish Prayer.* Budapest: Central European University Press, 2018.

Holst, Gail. *The Road to Rembetika: Music of a Greek Sub-Culture, Songs of Love, Sorrow and Hashish.* Athens: Anglo-Hellenic Publishing, 1975.

King, Christopher C., *Lament from Epirus: an Odyssey into Europe's Oldest Surviving Folk Music.* New York: WW. Norton Press, 2018.

Kostakowsky, Wolff. *The Ultimate Klezmer.* Arranged and Edited by Joshua Horowitz. Owings Mill, MD: Tara Publications, 2001 (original, 1916).

Loeffler, James. *The Most Musical Nation: Jews and Culture in the Late Russian Empire.* New Haven, CT: Yale University Press, 2010.

Netsky, Hankus. *Klezmer: Music and Community in Twentieth-Century Jewish Philadelphia.* Philadelphia: Temple University Press, 2015.

Rabinovitch, Israel. "A Village Klezmer in Jazzland." In *Of Jewish Music, Ancient and Modern.* Translated by A. M. Klein. Montreal: Eagle Press, 1950.

Radulescu, Speranta. *Chats About Gypsy Music* ("Taifasuri Despre Muzica Tiganeasca"). Bucharest: Paidea, 2004.

Stutschewsky, Joachim. *The Klezmorim: Their History, Way of Life and Creations* (Hebrew). Jerusalem: Mosad Bialik, 1959.

Wilson, Serena. *The Legacy of Little Egypt: A History of the Belly Dance in America.* New York: Serena Studios, 1994.

DISCOGRAPHY

Andranik Aroustamian. *L'Art du Kamantcha d'Arménie*. Arion ARN 60443, 1982.

Dave Tarras. *Music for the Traditional Jewish Wedding*. Center for Traditional Music and Dance Ethnic Heritage Recording Series, EFACA8902, 2007 (original recording produced by Zev Feldman and Andy Statman, 1978).

Zev Feldman and Andy Statman. *Jewish Klezmer Music*. Shanachie, 2000 (original 1979).

Khevrisa: European Klezmer Music. Smithsonian Folkways, 40486, 2000.

Tanburi Cemil Bey. *Traditional Crossroads*. CD 4264, 1994.

Walter Zev Feldman is a leading researcher in Ottoman Turkish and Jewish music, instrumental in the 1970s Klezmer Revival. His notable works include *Klezmer: Music, History, and Memory* (2016) and *Music of the Ottoman Court: Makam, Composition and the Early Ottoman Instrumental Repertoire* (1996; 2024, revised edition). Feldman has extensively studied the instrumental traditions of Moldova's klezmer and lautar communities. He is the Academic Director of the Klezmer Institute.

Andrew Feffer, *Bad Faith: Teachers, Liberalism, and the Origins of McCarthyism*

Colin Davey with Thomas A. Lesser, *The American Museum of Natural History and How It Got That Way*. Forewords by Neil deGrasse Tyson and Kermit Roosevelt III

Wendy Jean Katz, *Humbug: The Politics of Art Criticism in New York City's Penny Press*

Angel Garcia, *The Kingdom Began in Puerto Rico: Neil Connolly's Priesthood in the South Bronx*

Jim Mackin, *Notable New Yorkers of Manhattan's Upper West Side: Bloomingdale–Morningside Heights*

Matthew Spady, *The Neighborhood Manhattan Forgot: Audubon Park and the Families Who Shaped It*

Robert O. Binnewies, *Palisades: 100,000 Acres in 100 Years*

Marilyn S. Greenwald and Yun Li, *Eunice Hunton Carter: A Lifelong Fight for Social Justice*

Elizabeth Macaulay-Lewis, *Antiquity in Gotham: The Ancient Architecture of New York City*

Jean Arrington with Cynthia S. LaValle, *From Factories to Palaces: Architect Charles B. J. Snyder and the New York City Public Schools*. Foreword by Peg Breen

Boukary Sawadogo, *Africans in Harlem: An Untold New York Story*

Stephanie Azzarone, *Heaven on the Hudson: Mansions, Monuments, and Marvels of Riverside Park*

Mark Bulik, *Ambush at Central Park: When the IRA Came to New York*

Raj Tawney, *Colorful Palate: Savored Stories from a Mixed Life*

Joseph Heathcott, *Global Queens: An Urban Mosaic*

Francis R. Kowsky with Lucille Gordon, *Hell on Color, Sweet on Song: Jacob Wrey Mould and the Artful Beauty of Central Park*

Jill Jonnes, *South Bronx Rising: The Rise, Fall, and Resurrection of an American City*, Third Edition

Barbara G. Mensch, *A Falling-Off Place: The Transformation of Lower Manhattan*

Felipe Luciano, *Flesh and Spirit: Confessions of a Young Lord*

Maximo G. Martinez, *Sojourners in the Capital of the World: Garifuna Immigrants*

Jennifer Baum, *Just City: Growing Up on the Upper West Side When Housing Was a Human Righ*

Davida Siwisa James, *Hamilton Heights and Sugar Hill: Alexander Hamilton's Old Harlem Neighborhood Through the Centuries*

Annik LaFarge, *On the High Line: The Definitive Guide*, Third Edition. Foreword by Rick Dark

Marie Carter, *Mortimer and the Witches: A History of Nineteenth-Century Fortune Tellers*

Alice Sparberg Alexiou, *Devil's Mile: The Rich, Gritty History of the Bowery*. Foreword by Peter Quinn

Carey Kasten and Brenna Moore, *Mutuality in El Barrio: Stories of the Little Sisters of the Assumption Family Health Service*. Foreword by Norma Benítez Sánchez

Kimberly A. Orcutt, *The American Art-Union: Utopia and Skepticism in the Antebellum Era*

Jonathan Butler, *Join the Conspiracy: How a Brooklyn Eccentric Got Lost on the Right, Infiltrated the Left, and Brought Down the Biggest Bombing Network in New York*

Nicole Gelinas, *Movement: New York's Long War to Take Back Its Streets from the Car*

Jack Hodgson, *Young Reds in the Big Apple: The New York Young Pioneers of America, 1923–1934*

Lynn Ellsworth, *Wonder City: How to Reclaim Human-Scale Urban Life*

Larry Racioppo, *Here Down on Dark Earth: Loss and Remembrance in New York City*

Bonnie Yochelson, *Too Good to Get Married: The Life and Photographs of Miss Alice Austen*

For a complete list, visit www.fordhampress.com/empire-state-editions.